ROMANS 1-8

VERSE BY VERSE

Michael Pearl

No Greater Joy
1000 Pearl Road
Pleasantville, TN 37033

Published and distributed by:

No Greater Joy
1000 Pearl Road
Pleasantville, TN 37033

Printed in the United States of America

ISBN 1-892112-08-6

All Bible quotations are taken from the Authorized Version.

Visit our web site: **http://NoGreaterJoy.org**

Request our free bimonthly magazine – *No Greater Joy*

ROMANS 1-8
VERSE BY VERSE

1-17 Introductory remarks

1:1 Paul, a servant of Jesus Christ, called *to be* an apostle, separated unto the gospel of God,

The book of Romans is written by **Paul,** who calls himself **a servant of Jesus Christ.** Jesus said he would not call us servants, but friends (John 15:15). Yet Paul, as did other apostles and ministers, chose to refer to himself as the "*servant of Jesus Christ*." It was the *act* of serving that led him to designate himself as a servant. *Servant* is an activity, not a relationship. He was a son who served. One cannot call himself a servant unless he is in the service of God.

He was **called to be an apostle**. Paul did not choose a career, he was chosen by a blinding light, and *called* by a voice like thunder (Acts 9:3). He was **separated unto the gospel of God** by Divine choice before he was born. *"But when it pleased God, who separated me from my mother's womb, and called me by his grace, To reveal his Son in me, that I might preach him among the heathen; immediately I conferred not with flesh and blood: (Galatians 1:15-16)."* It is called the **gospel of God** to establish its divine authorship and to link it to the old covenant ministry of God to the Jews.

1:2 (Which he had promised afore by his prophets in the holy scriptures,)

The gospel is not a new religion. It is the fulfillment of what God was doing in the Law and the Prophets. The gospel was clearly predicted by many passages in the Old Testament. There has never been another religious document that has so substantiated itself through fulfilled prophecy. Over 340 prophecies concerning the earthly life of Jesus Christ were recorded in the Old Testament.

...in the holy scriptures.... Different from the modern "scholarly" viewpoint, Paul believed that the copies of the Bible available in His day

1

were *holy* scriptures. To him, inspiration was not limited to the original autographs.

1:3 Concerning his Son Jesus Christ our Lord, which was made of the seed of David according to the flesh;

The prophecies are **concerning** his Son Jesus Christ our Lord. So we see the gospel is not a belief system; it is a person.

This fourfold name (**Son, Jesus, Christ,** and **Lord**) is a full and complete description of His person and His ministry.

- He relates to the Father as **Son**. Many Old Testament passages speak directly of God's Son: Psalms 2:7-12; Proverbs 30:4; Isaiah 9:6; Zechariah 12:10.

- His name is **Jesus**: *"And she shall bring forth a son, and thou shalt call his name JESUS: for he shall save his people from their sins (Matthew 1:21)."*

- His office is **Christ**, the anointed, Messiah: *"And Simon Peter answered and said, Thou art the Christ, the Son of the living God (Matthew 16:16)."*

- In authority, He is **our Lord**. *"Ye call me Master and Lord: and ye say well; for so I am (John 13:13)."*

...which was made of the seed of David according to the flesh. He did not begin in the womb, as do other men. According to the Spirit, he was the pre-existent Son of God; **according to the flesh,** he was **made** (by birth) to be the son of David. All Jews understood the prophecies which stated that Messiah would be of the **seed of David,** descended from King David (Jeremiah 23:5; Matthew 21:9; 22:42).

...according to the flesh is defining that which came by natural descent from David. It was only the human nature contained in a body of flesh that the eternal Son of God received from David. He who was before David was **made** to be of the seed of David only in the realm of **flesh**. We have a similar statement in John 1:14: *"The Word was made flesh...."* See also: 1 Timothy 3:16; Philippians 2:8.

1:4 And declared *to be* the Son of God with power, according to the spirit of holiness, by the resurrection from the dead:

Again, Paul is emphasizing that in contrast to there being a point in time at which Jesus was *made* to be the son of David, He did not become the Son of God at his birth. He was simply **declared to be** that which he always had been—**the Son of God**. That God had a son was already revealed in Old Testament scriptures: Psalms 2:7,12; 110:1,4 with Luke 20:41-44; Proverbs 30:4; Isaiah 9:6; Ezekiel 21:9-10; Zechariah 12:10.

...according to the spirit of holiness is understood when we view it as a parallel to *"according to the flesh."* On the human side, he was *made to be the son of David according to the flesh*. On the Divine side (the pre-existent soul), He was **declared** to be what He always had been in spirit, **the Son of God**. He was <u>made</u> to be the Son of **David**, but simply <u>declared</u> to be the **Son of God**. It was the *flesh* that was made to be of the seed of David. It was that pre-existent *spirit of holiness* that was declared to be the Son of God. That which did not previously exist was *made*. That which previously existed was simply *declared*.

You will note, by the lack of capitalization, that the King James translators were aware that this *spirit of holiness* was not a reference to the Holy Spirit, but to the personal spirit of the Son of God.

This blending of the two natures, the human *(flesh)* and the Divine *(spirit of holiness)* was revealed with **power, by the resurrection from the dead**. The unprecedented resurrection proved Christ's deity beyond any doubt (2 Peter 1:3; John 10:18).

1:5 By whom we have received grace and apostleship, for obedience to the faith among all nations, for his name:

By whom, not from whom. He is not viewing Christ as the *channel* of grace, but as the *source* of grace.

...we have received grace.... *"For the law was given by Moses, but grace and truth came by Jesus Christ (John 1:17)."* Grace is not God's feelings toward us, it is His provision to us. Paul has already informed us in verse 1 that he was *separated unto the gospel of God. "But when it pleased God, who separated me from my mother's womb, and called me by his grace, To reveal his Son in me, that I might preach him among the heathen; immediately I conferred not with flesh and blood (Galatians 1:15-16)."*

In linking **grace and apostleship**, it seems that Paul is further reiterating his unique calling. He was *called to be an apostle* at the same time that he **received** the **grace** of God in salvation. (Acts 9:15). That same grace further sustains him in service. *"But by the grace of God I am what I am: and his grace which was bestowed upon me was not in vain; but I labored more abundantly than they all: yet not I, but the grace of God which was with me (1 Corinthians 15:10)."*

Paul received grace and was given the office of an apostle that he might bring about **obedience to the faith among all nations.** The emphasis is on **all nations**, as opposed to only Jews. **Obedience** to the faith is not obedience to laws. It is to obey by believing (1 John 3:23).

The *grace and apostleship* leading to *faith among all nations* finds its ultimate purpose **for his name**—that the name of Jesus should be exalted.

1:6 Among whom are ye also the called of Jesus Christ:

Paul is recognizing the believers in Rome to be among those who have responded to the call to believe. This is significant in that he, as a leading Jew, is going on record as recognizing gentile participation in the calling—something many Jewish Christians were loath to do.

3

1:7 To all that be in Rome, beloved of God, called *to be* saints: Grace to you and peace from God our Father, and the Lord Jesus Christ.

To all, emphasizing that it is gentiles as well as the Jewish Romans. Men do not become **saints** by their good works. They are **called,** as to an appointed office. It is a title given to one that responds to the call to believe the gospel. The word *saint* (Gk., *hagios*) is the same word translated *Holy* in the proper name Holy Spirit. A saint is *declared* to be holy.

Grace here is not God's attitude toward us, but His provision in Christ. The **peace from God** is not inner peace, not subjective; it is objective peace, as when two parties cease warring and establish peace. This peace is with the **Father** and the **Lord Jesus Christ.** Again he has stated the threefold name of the Son.

1:8 First, I thank my God through Jesus Christ for you all, that your faith is spoken of throughout the whole world.

Since "all roads lead to Rome," the whole world would hear of the strange events occurring when many Romans became Christians. Paul was actively thanking God for their faith.

1:9 For God is my witness, whom I serve with my spirit in the gospel of his Son, that without ceasing I make mention of you always in my prayers;

"For God is my witness" is near to being an oath. Paul is assuring the Romans that he is not lightly speaking when he says that he has been praying for them. He again is careful to state the relationship of God and **his Son**. He further reinforces the fact that the gospel concerns the person of God's Son.

Paul served God, not in the letter of the Law, but with his **spirit**. *"But now we are delivered from the law, that being dead wherein we were held; that we should serve in newness of spirit, and not in the oldness of the letter (Romans 7:6)."* See comments under 7:6. Paul had not ceased to pray for the Romans at those times when he prayed.

1:10 Making request, if by any means now at length I might have a prosperous journey by the will of God to come unto you.

When Paul prayed for the Romans, he put in a request **that by any means** (God providing the way) **now at length** (sometime in the future) he **might have a prosperous journey by the will of God** (his coming was contingent upon the will of God) **to come unto** the Romans.

1:11 For I long to see you, that I may impart unto you some spiritual gift, to the end ye may be established;

He had a deep desire to come to Rome and use his power as an apostle to impart some spiritual gift that would help them become more grounded in the faith. Romans 11:29, 12:6-8; 1 Corinthians 1:5-7, 7:7, 12:4-11, 13:2; Ephesians 4:7, 8; 1 Timothy 6:17; James 1:17; 1 Peter 4:10; 2 Peter 1:3.

1:12 That is, that I may be comforted together with you by the mutual faith both of you and me.

If they were established in the faith, it would result in the Roman Christians being able to in turn comfort Paul. He wanted to minister to them that they might minister to him.

1:13 Now I would not have you ignorant, brethren, that oftentimes I purposed to come unto you, (but was let hitherto,) that I might have some fruit among you also, even as among other gentiles.

He wants them to be aware of the fact that on many occasions he sought to come to Rome, but was hindered from doing so. He desired to have spiritual fruit (souls brought to Christ and built up in the faith) among them just as he did among other gentiles.

1:14 I am debtor both to the Greeks, and to the Barbarians; both to the wise, and to the unwise.

Paul felt an obligation to the **wise**, educated **Greeks** and to the **unwise**, ignorant heathen, the **Barbarians**. He didn't leave anyone out because of ethnic origin, culture, or education.

1:15 So, as much as in me is, I am ready to preach the gospel to you that are at Rome also.

He assures them of his willingness and desire to come to them at Rome.

1:16 For I am not ashamed of the gospel of Christ: for it is the power of God unto salvation to every one that believeth; to the Jew first, and also to the Greek.

Paul was **not ashamed** to have his gospel tested by those in the political and cultural centers of the world. His good news was more than words to tickle the ears or platitudes to inspire. When men's philosophies and religions are put to the test, they often fail to perform as promised, shaming the proponent. But the gospel had repeatedly proven itself to be the **power of God** to effect real **salvation**. It did not 'impart' power; the message itself was the power of God in action. Men didn't have to apply it; it applied itself to the men who heard it. It carried its own power to save all that believed.

Paul does not state that the gospel included the power to "cause" men to believe, as Calvinism teaches; rather, belief was a precondition, wholly the responsibility of the sinner, which belief then released the power of God to effect salvation.

This power of the gospel extended to **everyone** that believeth. To

5

offer the gospel to everyone was uniquely different from the tribal religions and national gods of his time. The Jew felt that Jehovah was their
exclusive God—to know Him, you must become a Jew.

...to everyone that believeth, both Jew and Greek. He was never
ashamed, not only because his gospel was effectual, but because its sole
requirement, *believe*, was a condition everyone could meet.

He was not ashamed to offer it as a sure hope to the **unwise** heathen
and to the **wise** Greek. It was not based upon, nor did it depend upon,
wisdom; yet it proved to be wiser that the wisdom of men. Nor was it
hindered from working just as effectually when received by the **unwise**
and the **Barbarian**.

...to the Jew first, and also to the Greek. The Jew was first in or-
der because they had first received the oracles of the Law (Romans 3:2).
The Jew was first in opportunity because Paul found it strategically ad-
vantageous to offer the gospel to the **Jews** before going to the **Greeks**.
Through their knowledge of the old covenant types and sacrifices, the
Jews were prepared to understand and believe. Romans 1:17

1:17 For therein is the righteousness of God revealed from faith to faith: as it is written, The just shall live by faith.

For therein (in the events and message of this gospel, which he is
not ashamed to preach to the Romans) **is the righteousness of God revealed.** As seen in parallel passages, this righteousness is: without Law
(Romans 3:21), not to be our own (10:3), to be from God (Philippians 3:
9), and a gift of God (5:17). See 3:21-22.

Paul, like all devout Jews, was jealous on behalf of the **righteous-
ness of God.** Other religions lowered their standards for fellowship with
God. They did not satisfy the legal demands of a justly offended Deity.
The very suggestion that a sinner could be admitted into fellowship with
God on any basis other than righteousness was unthinkable to a religious
Jew. It would degrade God's holiness to suggest that He would accept
less.

In light of the Jew's concern to guard the righteousness of God, Paul
is not ashamed of the gospel, for it is even more effective than Mt. Sinai
in revealing the *righteousness of God*. The gospel Paul is about to declare in the book of Romans does not lower the Law's standards, rather it
raises the standards so high that only one man can meet them. The gospel
demonstrates how God was able to remain righteous while remitting the
sins of the old covenant believer. See 3:25-26.

The gospel is the declaration that the righteousness God requires has
been provided as a gift to the believer.

The gospel further manifests righteousness by enabling the one who
has had righteousness imputed to him to actually do the righteousness
that was heretofore unattainable under the Law. See 8:3-4.

In the preaching of the gospel, the righteousness of God **is revealed**

from faith to faith—old covenant faith to new covenant faith, Jewish faith to gentile faith, imparting faith to imputing faith. *"Seeing it is one God, which shall justify the circumcision by faith, and uncircumcision through faith (Romans 3:30)."* The righteousness of God is manifested in the salvation of old covenant Jews, as well as in the salvation of church-age gentiles. Under the old covenant, faith was only a small bud not yet fully opened. In Christ, faith blossoms into a full flower. Though it is the same flower planted in a Jewish garden, it is now visible to the whole world.

Paul is about to show that the same righteousness of faith remains an essential part of salvation. He is assuring the Jew that he is not inventing some new form of salvation that is alien to Scripture. It was by faith then; it is by faith now. He is going to add a new dimension to faith and righteousness, but the elements remain the same. The difference is that the old covenant Jew was justified as his faith worked to *produce* the righteousness of God, whereas under the new covenant, the sinner is justified as his faith becomes the *channel* through which God imputes righteousness. The believing Jew was given grace to experience a measure of righteousness. The new covenant believer has righteousness imputed to his account. This one *righteousness of God* is revealed from the <u>appropriating faith</u> of the old covenant believer to the <u>imputing faith</u> of the new covenant believer.

Though works of righteousness were necessary to their salvation, it had to be more than a mere external obedience to the Law. *"For thou desirest not sacrifice; else would I give it: thou delightest not in burnt offering. The sacrifices of God are a broken spirit: a broken and a contrite heart, O God, thou wilt not despise (Psalms 51:16-17)."* They were to enter into and abide in a humble life of faith and worship. Out of that faith would flow obedience to the righteousness of God in daily experience. God could look at their heart of faith and life of obedience and graciously count them as righteous, though legally they must still be viewed as sinners. Though they did not understand it, their salvation was conditioned on future atonement based on something more worthy than animal blood. More will be said of this under 3:25-26.

Under the old covenant, their faith would issue in a righteousness that was beyond that produced by unaided mortals. It was truly the *righteousness of God* being revealed through their faith and obedience. *The just* were living by their faith. Their faith was a working faith, an appropriating faith, an obedient faith. It was a living faith that allowed God to work through them to obey the Law of Moses.

Certainly the old covenant believer never produced perfect obedience to the Law of God, but God chose to be gracious and forgiving, accounting those obedient believers acceptable in His sight. No one was saved by his works. That is, no one attained to a level of righteousness that rendered him acceptable by his own goodness. Yet God required that the faith of the sinner should issue in obedience to the Law of Moses. If one was not obedient, he was damned. This is most vividly seen in Deuteronomy 30:15-20, Ezekiel 3:20, and Ezekiel 33:12-18. Today this old covenant salvation is still taught as gospel by the majority of Christianity.

...as it is written, The just shall live by faith. This is a quotation from Habakkuk 2:4, also quoted in Galatians 3:11 and Hebrews 10:38. Paul quotes this passage from the Old Testament to reinforce the concept that faith is a key element in a man's relationship to God. He is saying to the legalists, "After all, faith was the manner in which a man found life under the old covenant, so there is nothing new or strange about it being the key element in the gospel I preach."

1:18-32 God known through nature

1:18 For the wrath of God is revealed from heaven against all ungodliness and unrighteousness of men, who hold the truth in unrighteousness;

This is a continuation of the thought begun in verse 16, that the gospel is for Jew and gentile alike. His argument will be that since the wrath of God comes on all without distinction, is it not likewise reasonable that all have equal opportunity to come under the covenant of faith?

Paul is about to embark upon a chronicle of the universal degeneracy of man (Jew and gentile alike). He is showing why there must be a way of salvation that will provide a righteousness acceptable to God, and that the benefits should extend to both Jew and gentile alike.

The **wrath of God** is more than anger. It is more than the natural consequences of sin, which is death. God's wrath is the necessary response of the Chief Judicial toward elements that are incompatible with His moral government. It is the duty of the Eternal Governor of the universe to rise up against rebellion and wickedness. It is at this point that all philosophies and most religions draw the line and go no further. "What kind of father would be wrathful with his children? What have we done to deserve our Creator's eternal wrath?"

The following verses describe the willful degeneration of men and explain why they are universally under the wrath of God.

The wrath comes **from heaven**, the very seat of universal moral government, denoting the seriousness of the offense.

That God is wrathful implies that men are to blame. Why are men blameworthy? Personal **ungodliness and unrighteousness**.

Ungodliness is a self-imposed condition, the wrong moral choice. Having been created in the image of God, man has the potential to be godly. Ungodliness is man's fault, not his misfortune. Man is *ungodly* in areas where he could and therefore should be godly.

The wrath of God is revealed against men **who hold the truth in unrighteousness.** Paul will prove that the human condition is a blameworthy state by showing that all men are made responsible by holding truth. If men were devoid of the truth of God they would never feel guilt. A sense of personal guilt is irrefutable testimony that one has willfully violated his own sense of right and wrong. If a man were ignorant of having broken an unknown law, he would not and could not blame himself. Nor could God blame him. To blame is to accuse of irresponsible conduct, to find fault. A man could not be faulted for not obeying an unknown and unknowable law.

What does it mean to hold truth?

...hold.... To *hold the truth* is to know God (Note v. 21, *"...when they knew God"*). They did not know God intimately, but with sufficient understanding to render them responsible.

Paul, like a prosecuting attorney, is going to prove that all are under sin (3:9). To do so he must establish guilt beyond any reasonable shadow of a doubt. Guilt is self-blame, and self-blame comes when one cannot excuse the self. If a man had no knowledge of his responsibility, of the truth, he would not blame himself.

Some commentators do not understand the foundation of Paul's argument. They think men are guilty for not knowing the truth. So they attempt to give a novel definition to the Greek word **katecho** *(hold)*. Even many Greek lexicons have followed this spurious approach and have translated **katecho** as *suppress* or *resist*. A man cannot resist the truth unless he first *holds* it.

The Greek word for *hold* (**katecho**) is found 19 times in the New Testament. It is translated *hold* 3 times, *hold fast* 3 times, *withholdeth* 1 time, *keep* 2 times, *possess* 2 times, *stay* 1 time, *take* 1 time, *have* 1 time, *make* 1 time, *seize* 1 time, *letteth* 1 time, *retained* 1 time, *delivered* 1 time. In all uses, both the translation and the context consistently carry the meaning of *holding or possessing tightly*. The context of **katecho** never carries the meaning of resisting.

With absolutely no basis in the original languages, in this passage alone the NIV translates *katecho* as *suppress*. In all other 18 uses the NIV follows the King James Version in translating **katecho** as *hold firmly, hold unswervingly, keep, hold him back,* or something similar to the KJV. This singular departure, which should be embarrassing to a Greek scholar, is apparently due to their failure to understand what Paul is saying.

To **hold the truth** is to intellectually embrace it and assent to its jurisdiction. It is to concur that *the law is good* (7:16).

Once a man becomes aware of the truth, he can never become unaware of it. He can choose *not to retain God in his knowledge* (1:28), calling himself an atheist, but verbally rejecting the truth will never blot out the responsibility awakened by knowledge of that truth. Man can *change* the rightful image of God, which he holds, into an image of an idol (fall down and sacrifice to that idol), but it will never render him ignorant of the truth of God. He will always be held responsible for the truth he has willfully pushed back into the recesses of his mind.

Theoretically, if a man should hold the truth *in righteousness*, that is if he should be righteous in regard to the truth he understands, he would be without blame, for he would be obedient to all the truth as he knew it (John 3:21).

Paul is going to show that all men have violated their own sense of truth by selfishly departing from the path they know to be right. It is on this basis (failure to obey the truth that is held) that all men have placed themselves under the wrath of God.

This passage is a key to understanding the first two chapters of Romans. He has given us a principle that will be the basis of all his conclusions. The principle simply stated is: <u>The wrath of God is directed toward and restricted to those that know right from wrong, yet choose to do wrong.</u> From the following verses we can conclude that the wrath of God is not directed toward those who do not know right from wrong. He will conclude further, as forthcoming passages will declare, that the wrath of God is poured out in <u>proportion</u> to the truth one holds yet violates. In other words, the more you know, the more responsible you are. The more you know and the less you obey, the greater the wrath. The greater the gap between the truth one holds and one's obedience, the greater the damnation.

Theoretically, if one did not know the truth, there would be no responsibility and therefore no wrath—as would be the case with an infant or one born with diminished mental faculties. If one held a little truth with a corresponding amount of obedience, then again there would be no transgression, no guilt, and no blame.

Starting point

Paul is establishing these exceptionally fair ground rules as a starting point for eventually proving that all are under sin. His presentation of the principle that a man is judged according to the truth he holds is not intended to exonerate some, but to condemn all. Granted, according to this principle of judgment, if a man who knew little obeyed the little he knew he would be blameless, but Paul has not supposed it probable that one would indeed obey all the truth he holds. In the course of his argument he will prove that all have come short.

Paul is systematically maneuvering his readers to an intended conclusion. Men argue that it is not just for God to judge a man who is helpless and ignorant, that a man who does his best with what little he knows should not come under condemnation. If Paul held to the contemporary position, that men are born damned because Adam sinned and his children inherited a kind of genetic guilt, then he would totally destroy the basis of his own argument. It is a most unsatisfactory argument that men

are damned for their inherent state. To argue that position is more conso-
nant with arguing fault in God than fault in man.

He is not content to hand the sinner a sentence of condemnation
without first demonstrating that it is a fair and just sentence. If, in the
end, the sinner should offer a defense of unfairness, Paul will simply say,
"All that was asked of you was that you live according to your own conscience, your understanding of right and wrong. If you had done that, you
would be accepted by God." And who could gainsay such an argument?
Accountability in exact proportion to responsibility, and responsibility in
exact proportion to understanding—a truly just and eminently fair position.

If Paul will induce guilt in his readers, he must do so on the ground
of their own presuppositions. No one will accept responsibility for failing
to do what was outside his power or knowledge. No man can force himself to feel duty-bound to do that which was withheld from him through
no fault of his own. The degree to which a man has an inner sense of responsibility, but due to some selfishness or negligence fails to respond as
he knows he ought, is the degree to which he blames himself, and it is the
degree to which other intelligent beings would blame him. So, the wrath
of God is only directed toward those who *hold truth* in an unrighteous
way. Paul will go on to prove that this includes the entire adult population of the human race.

A sinner cannot be convinced that the creator and sustainer of the
universe is indeed a God of judgment and wrath unless it can be shown
to his reason and conscience that he, the sinner, does indeed deserve the
wrath of God. If a man is inwardly convinced that he has lived in a way
that is blameworthy, that he is at fault, that he could have done differently, but through selfishness let the opportunity slip by, then, even if it
were not revealed to him, he would indeed create his own concept of
Hell to correspond to his guilty conscience.

A man cannot be persuaded to repent unless he is convinced that he
has made inappropriate moral choices. To choose differently is to repent.
To reverse the focus of one's entire being is to repent to God. If repentance and faith were merely external conformity brought on by fear of
judgment, one could be induced to capitulate to a higher, threatening
power, but the heart of a man cannot be threatened into a sweet spirit of
surrender. For the heart and soul to desire a change, the mind and spirit
must be convinced of the utter rightness and inherent goodness of making this complete reversal.

In these first two chapters of Romans, Paul's entire argument is
based on the assumption that if a man did indeed live up to his own understanding of truth, he would in fact be without sin. This would be the
case with a heathen, say an American Indian, who never heard the Bible
but obeyed all truth as he understood it. For example, if an Apache Indian always followed his own perception of truth, never acting contrary

to how he felt he should act, he would be a man without guilt or shame. He would never feel the need to appease the gods or to offer sacrifice. If there existed some areas of duty outside the scope of his knowledge, he could not be held responsible. He would not be a transgressor, and as such would be blameless. God would not blame a dog for not flying, nor a fish for muddying the water. Would God or any intelligent creature blame a man born lame for not walking? So no intelligent being, neither man nor God, would blame a man for failure to do that which was beyond his intellectual grasp. This is a principle universally held, and for good reason. Therefore Paul uses it to his advantage in convincing all men that they are voluntarily under sin.

Alternate salvation?

Many, not being familiar with Paul's teachings, will fear that this opens up an alternate way of salvation by works—"Do the best you can and you will be all right." But if you follow his argument, you will discover that admitting to the principle is not the same as admitting to its practicality. We know it to be a foregone conclusion that all men have violated their own understanding of right and wrong and are hopelessly lost without God, which is the conclusion to which Paul will eventually arrive in chapter 3. But Paul is not addressing his argument to those who are already receptive to the truth. He is preparing the most philosophical and contentious sinner for his eventual conclusion, *"For all have sinned and come short of the glory of God (3:23)."*

1:19 Because that which may be known of God is manifest in them; for God hath shewed *it* unto them.

The wrath of God is revealed from heaven against men that *hold* truth in an unrighteous way, **Because**... and following is a description of how they hold truth unrighteously.

That which may be known of God will vary from person to person. It will vary with culture and religion. There are as many different degrees of the knowledge of God as there are people. It is **in them**— intuitive knowledge. No man with all his mental facilities is without some knowledge of God.

...for God hath shewed *it* unto them. John said of Jesus, *"That was the true Light which lighteth every man that cometh into the world (John 1:9)."* The Spirit of God is active revealing to every man all that he is capable of understanding. This knowledge of God is not external, that is, it does not come though reading the Bible or through scientific investigation. It is an inner witness based on an outward revelation seen in nature.

1:20 For the invisible things of him from the creation of the world are clearly seen, being understood by the things that are made, *even* his eternal power and Godhead; so that they

are without excuse:

Paul tells his readers how it is that the heathen *know God*. He explains how God has *shewed it unto them*. He defines the *external* means God uses to impart the *internal* knowledge of Himself. God is not known as objects are known. Any knowledge we have of Him must come as He reveals Himself. The things we know are said to be **invisible**. He names three invisible things:

- God is **eternal.** That which is eternal must be the cause of all causes. All men intuitively know that God is The Eternal, without beginning or ending.

- Creation confirms our innate knowledge that God is eternal **power.** The cause of all power must be equal to or greater than the sum total of all power—thus God is omnipotent.

- Natural creation is so stamped with the marks of the Creator that it reveals the **Godhead** to us. By this personal, divine revelation seen in nature we know that there is one God over all. Other invisible things revealed in creation are, God's goodness, love, justice, judgment, wrath, etc.

These things are readily visible through viewing **the creation of the world**. They are not vague truths drawn out by sages and prophets. These truths are so prominent that Paul says they are **clearly seen.** This act of seeing God through nature is not a visual or mental process that depends on our discovery or reasoning. God's Spirit speaks daily to each individual heart through the visual aid of nature.

This revelation seen in nature eliminates all claim's of ignorance. The degree of knowledge gained through nature will not come close to the knowledge available through Scripture, but it is sufficient to make a man responsible. According to the truth he has seen and yet disobeyed, he is **without excuse.** Where he is unaware of truth, he would feel no compulsion to offer an excuse, nor would anyone blame him. That truth of which each man is personally consciousness is a sufficient weight of responsibility.

1:21 Because that, when they knew God, they glorified *him* not as God, neither were thankful; but became vain in their imaginations, and their foolish heart was darkened.

They are *without excuse* **Because that, when they knew God....** Here is confirmation that natural revelation, received by all men, causes all men to *know* God. Man unavoidably knows God. This is not to know him in forgiveness or in an intimate way, but simply to know of His attributes and of the glory and righteousness of His person. They responded to this knowledge by making a choice to disregard the truth *"clearly seen,"* and so...

...they glorified him not as God. The very first sin listed is not murder, idolatry, or sexual impurity; it is failure to *glorify God.* They did not do what one ought to do in regard to One so high and holy. When common people come into the presence of the king they all bow in recognition. To glory in the glorious need not be written law to be universal duty. To fail to glory in the glorious is to rebel against that which is of supreme value, and it is to elevate the less glorious to the place of the supreme. To not glorify God is the greatest of sins. It is the beginning of rebellion against His authority. It is a statement that our values are not in agreement with what is inherently valuable.

Man is naturally endowed with an inclination to glory in the glorious, as when he stands before beauty and grandeur. It is predictable that when one first views Niagara Falls, he will, as it were, worship. If a man turned his back on the falls, making it a point to show no appreciation of its gradure, then it is clear that he came to the experience with a prior attitude, an agenda that found expression it demonstrating his lack of appreciation for that which others find glorious. When a man knows God, as all men do, and yet glorifies Him not, then he has a conflicting agenda, which agenda is willful and unworthy. He is at fault in his choice to glorify some things but not glorify God. He has shown his preference, and the preference demonstrates a fault in his character. The preference renders him unworthy of and unfit for God's presence. To not glorify God is the root of all sin.

...neither were thankful.... Paul, in proving that all men are sinners, lists unthankfulness as the second distinctive mark deserving of the wrath of God. A man that sees the work of the Creator, understands his very breath to be the gift of God, yet neglects to be thankful, is proud and self-willed. A man may think that he has received a raw deal and therefore cannot be thankful, but he has not excused his unthankfulness, he has confirmed it and thereby rendered himself *"without excuse."*

...became vain in their imagination.... God endowed us with some of the abilities of a creator. We can imagine a thing as we would have it be and then apply ourselves to bring it to pass. Thus we are architects, gardeners, artists, writers, scientists, and inventors of many things. We have control of our imaginations and can determine what directions they will take. Therefore, if we imagine the impossible or the ridiculous, it is a *vain imagination.*

Men, uncomfortable with an eternal God of infinite power and authority, imagined Him to be something less. The concept of an all-knowing, completely righteous God that judges all sin is a hindrance to comfortable, personal indulgence. So men "rethought" God.

...and their foolish heart was darkened. In the Bible, the word *heart* is used to describe that center of the human soul wherein resides moral intentions, affections, and motives. God had illuminated the heart of every one born into the world (John 1:9), but that light had dimmed in the advent of imagination over the light of truth.

1:22 Professing themselves to be wise, they became fools.

In their imaginations, observing the creations of their own minds, they thought themselves wise. They recorded their musings, established universities, and praised their mutual knowledge. They called it Philosophy, Science, and Comparative Religion. They gave degrees to these professors and called themselves "Doctor of psychiatry" or "Doctor of Divinity." Men called them enlightened. God calls them **fools**.

1:23 And changed the glory of the uncorruptible God into an image made like to corruptible man, and to birds, and four-footed beasts, and creeping things.

They **changed,** indicating that they well perceived and understood the **glory** of God. It was a conscious act involving rejection of held truth, not ignorance of truth. The self-deceived *"fools"* imagined the **uncorruptible God** to be in the image of a **corruptible man.** When they tired of bowing down to a human statue of wood and gold, they further imagined God to be in the image of **birds,** then **beasts,** and finally **creeping things**. The world's religions can be traced by going to the museums and viewing the images of men, women, birds, animals, and creeping snakes and insects. These people were not "unenlightened, misguided victims of their time." They were *fools* remaking God into an *image* more compatible with their lusts.

Other than Judaism and Biblical Christianity, there is no religion that demands so high and holy a life as does just plain natural revelation. Men will willfully turn away from glorifying the eternal God of righteousness to foolishly serve an imagined god that permits them to selfishly indulge their flesh without fear of judgment to come.

When men accept a distorted image of God, they lose the only reference by which they can identify themselves. If we glorify God as God, then we can know man as man; otherwise we become philosophers who ask questions while resenting answers that imply responsibility.

1:24 Wherefore God also gave them up to uncleanness through the lusts of their own hearts, to dishonour their own bodies between themselves:

Wherefore, because of the former, willful actions of man, **God gave them up to uncleanness.** The underlying motive for rejecting the revealed God is always indulgence of the flesh. Nearly all of the ancient religions even sanctified prostitution and immorality, directing indulgence as part of their worship. God responded by releasing the hand that pulled away. He *gave them up* **to uncleanness**, the object of their pursuits. The means by which God gave them up was **through** their own **lusts**. They had given Him up <u>for</u> lust, so He gave them up <u>to</u> lusts. They had become preoccupied with their own bodies. Instead of reaching out as sons of God, distributing love and good will, they turned inward and found pleasure in their own bodies. Like maggots they fed upon the flesh until they worshipped the creature. They took their tabernacles of flesh, which the Creator had given as vessels for the human spirit, and **dishonored their bodies between themselves**. By mutual consent, they made an industry of provoking, stimulating, and gratifying one another. What they did with and to their bodies was a dishonor to the Creator of the body as well as to the body itself. Our present generation is reinventing body dishonor. *"But every man is tempted, when he is drawn away of his own lust, and enticed. Then when lust hath conceived, it bringeth forth sin: and sin, when it is finished, bringeth forth death (James 1:14-15)."*

1:25 Who changed the truth of God into a lie, and worshipped and served the creature more than the Creator, who is blessed for ever. Amen.

They **changed** the **truth of God,** of which they were all aware (they held the truth, verse 18), into a **lie** conceived in their imaginations. Their lusts suggested to them that the body alone was the object of devotion, so they **worshipped and served the creature**. Some of them attempted to maintain devotion and worship of God while indulging in the flesh, but the result was that they worshipped and served each other's bodies **more than the Creator.**

Paul found their rejection so appalling that he felt the need to set the record straight, so having declared the Creator to be **blessed forever,** he says **Amen** to his own praise.

1:26 For this cause God gave them up unto vile affections: for even their women did change the natural use into that which is against nature:

God shines the light of truth on every soul that comes into the world (John 1:9). They took what they understood of the truth of His nature and changed it into a corruptible image around which they practiced immorality. He honored their choices and gave them up to their uncleanness. Their uncleanness drew them further into lusts until they worshipped their very bodies. **For this cause God gave them up unto vile affections.** They had no **affection** for things lovely. They loved the obscene and the vile. They pulled away, and He gave them up to their choices. Just because it feels like love, it is not thereby necessarily holy. Affection can be **vile** if it is unduly placed.

For some reason, we expect men to be base and vile, but not women, not our mothers and daughters. But, **even their women did change the natural use into that which is against nature.** God designed a **natural use** of the female body. The male body is the counterpart, like the positive and negative of the magnetic field. God placed within each of us natural drives toward the opposite sex. Such drives are wholesome within themselves. But women **changed** what God had made into something **against nature.** Lesbian acts were and are <u>contrary to nature</u>. Such drives are not natural. They must be cultivated, invented in each new generation. No one is born a Sodomite. The fall of Adam did not alter the nature of male and female, turning all into queer beings. If one commits sodomy, one does so **against** one's own **nature.**

Note: this sin was not a result of the nature they received from Adam. This sin was **against nature**, as all sin is, not a product of it. Paul's teaching stands in conflict with most religious philosophies.

1:27 And likewise also the men, leaving the natural use of the woman, burned in their lust one toward another; men with men working that which is unseemly, and receiving in themselves that recompence of their error which was meet.

...leaving the natural use indicates they were endowed with *natural* tendencies, and through a conscious, responsible act they left that former, *natural* state for the lower, base, perverted imaginations of their own lusts. Again, the sin was a perversion of the *natural* design of body and soul.

Thrills can be created where none actually exist by daring to throw off the natural in exchange for the perverted. All human appetites can be cultured and conditioned to enjoy a diet that is otherwise naturally repugnant. With a life dedicated to *uncleanness* (v. 24), a god in their own *image* (v.25), and surrender to *vile affections* it was a short step to release their lusts on their own sex. Eroticism between same sex partners is a perversion of nature and will be entirely eradicated in eternity.

...burned in their lust one toward another; men with men. The source of their drives was self-induced lust, not natural tendencies, for they *burned in their lust.* Lust focused on the unnatural does not have natural gratification. In truth, there is no satiation for sinful lust. Lust is the end of lust. It escalates until it is an uncontrolled burning. Having scratched a spot that doesn't itch until it does itch, one can then offer what seems an acceptable excuse for further scratching. An alcoholic can plead inability because of the hold alcohol has on his will. He would excuse his habit, but we know him to be initially at fault. As proven by the experience of many, the heroin addict can and should break his addiction. The sexually perverted can and should break their addiction. If they do not, they compound their guilt and publish their blameworthiness. The burning power of lust, far from being an excuse, is incriminating testimony to the constant supply of mental fuel feeding the consuming fires.

They were **working** that which is unseemly, bringing to pass through their own initiative, causing to occur that which is unseemly. The sins of the flesh are **unseemly,** not fit to be seen, unwholesome. They should never be viewed on the screen or be described in books. *"For it is a shame even to speak of those things which are done of them in secret (Ephesians 5:12)."*

...and receiving in themselves that recompence of their error which was meet. They received *in themselves* the just and equivalent reward for their wrongdoing. That is, something occurred within their own persons that was retribution for their sins. Is not the addiction itself the present worse punishment for substance abuse? Sodomites are never "gay." They are unfulfilled and unhappy people who have lost touch with all that is good and wholesome. How can they be fulfilled? Unnatural lust can only have unnatural fulfillment. Their own misery and loneliness is a present *just recompense.* And yet there is something more: if they continue in their sin, the inner scaring on their souls will eventually lead to reprobate minds.

The **recompense,** return on their sin, was **meet.** That is, it was most appropriate and suitable to the sin itself. In some way the nature of the recompense exactly fits the nature of the sin. The judgment was not the result of God responding to their sin. Inherent within the sin itself was the immediate and initial penalty. The consequences are certainly psychological, mental, emotional, but also physical. According to this, we would expect the physical aspect of sodomizing to produce a deadly illness that causes putrefaction of the contact area. But if such a disease occurred, people would deny that it was a judgment for sin.

1:28 And even as they did not like to retain God in *their* knowledge, God gave them over to a reprobate mind, to do those things which are not convenient;

It is inevitable that one who violates the laws of nature should eventually deny the God of all nature.

...they did not like to retain God in their knowledge. They *did not like* [It was a decision springing from their affections and intellect] *to retain* [implying that they once knew God, or at least were exposed to that knowledge] *God in their knowledge.* It was a choice they made to banish God from their *knowledge.* Has not America officially outlawed knowledge of God in its educational institutions? Men that do not take into account God in all matters of life *do not like to retain God in their knowledge.* So we see that atheism and agnosticism are not natural.

God gave them over to a reprobate mind. The **reprobate mind** was not the cause of sin but the result. This is the third and final time that God has responded to their sin by *giving them up.* As they pulled away, He first gave them up to *uncleanness* (v.24), then to *vile affections* (v.26), and now to a *reprobate mind.* The first two conditions were recoverable because the mind was still intact. This latter release is into an altered mental state.

To be **reprobate** is to be set aside as unfit and unusable. As they received *in themselves* the *just recompense,* their *minds* began to lose touch with reality. For a thrill or for convenience, their minds imagined reality as they would like it to be. They were given up to the lust that followed, until they came to believe their own lies. Convincing themselves that there is no God to whom we must give an account, they not only cut all the wires, but destroyed the telephone as well.

They are comfortable now. There is not even any need for arrogance or boast of knowledge. The struggle has ceased. They await the blackness of eternity, convinced that it all stops at the decorated box, the coffin.

...to do those things which are not convenient. The sins of sexual perversion are indeed *not convenient*, as defined in Webster's Dictionary: not suited, adapted, fitted, proper. That which is not adapted and suited to the original design is inconvenient—queer. Can you think of anything more inconvenient than two of the same sex.........? Unfortunately, this superior translation (**not convenient**) has been lost in the modern, commercial bibles.

1:29 Being filled with all unrighteousness, fornication, wickedness, covetousness, maliciousness; full of envy, murder, debate, deceit, malignity; whisperers,

1:30 Backbiters, haters of God, despiteful, proud, boasters, inventors of evil things, disobedient to parents,

1:31 Without understanding, covenantbreakers, without natural affection, implacable, unmerciful:

All of us can find ourselves somewhere in this list of sins. These sins are randomly common to all men, but the reprobate mind is comfortably **filled** with them.

Unrighteousness sums up the entire list. It breaks down into:

- **Fornication.** All sexual impurity comes under the heading of fornication. It includes adultery, bestiality, and sodomy.
- **Wickedness** is just what it is commonly understood to be, evil in principle and practice.
- **Covetousness** is a violation of the tenth commandment (Ex. 20:17). To covet is to deeply desire or long for that which belongs to another.
- **Maliciousness** is a disposition to cause or see another person injured or hurt in some way.
- **Envy** is a feeling of rivalry or competition toward others, so as to desire their gifts, abilities or stations in life.
- **Murder** is the act or desire of an individual acting outside of due process to end the life of another.
- **Debate** is that state of verbal contention that leads to quarrelsome argument.
- **Deceit** is the act of intentionally, for purpose of selfish gain or malicious intent, misleading or causing another to believe that which is not true.

- **Malignity** is virulent, dangerous to life. Morally, it is to have evil intent toward, maliciousness.

He has defined the sins, now he describes the person:

- **Whisperers** are those that slander secretly.
- **Backbiters** are those who speak evil of others in their absence.
- **Haters of God** are those who have feelings toward God that would be the opposite of love. There are more people in this condition than we imagine. Most of the world is angry with God for not "running the universe the way He should." Poverty, sickness, war, a dead child, or sick loved one, and God is despised for not caring. Those who refuse to worship God because they have negative feelings about the way He has managed their affairs are *haters of God*.
- **Despiteful** is the state of looking down upon a person with a desire to hurt.
- **Proud** is the condition of having inordinate self-esteem, possessing an unreasonably high conception of one's excellence of body or mind. Pride is evil not because it elevates the proud one, but because it does so at the expense of others.
- **Boasters** are those who speak of their personal worth, whether of person or accomplishments. It is evil because it is always done with a desire to be valued above others.
- **Inventors of evil things**. Speaking of technology, just because we can make it, doesn't make it right. God endowed us with limited creative powers. It seems that man has found unlimited ways to create evil things. Things are evil when they are designed or used to hurt others or ourselves. Things are evil when they are an aid to indulging the flesh or when they degrade morality, honesty, and family.
- **Disobedient to parents.** In a list with fornication and idolatry is *disobedience to parents*. For a child to rebel against his parents, he must rebel against authority in general.
- **Without understanding.** The average person thinks that to plead lack of understanding is to exempt one's self from responsibility. But when the eyes cannot see because they are willfully closed, failing to see is not excusable. When God has endowed every mature adult with the capacity to understand the truth and then shined the truth in his heart, to not understand is an irresponsible act of rejection. A child who is lazy will claim he didn't understand. Maybe he didn't understand, but he would have if he had paid attention. His lack of attention came from a heart of rebellion.
- **Covenantbreakers** are those who enter into mutual agreement and then fail to keep their end of the contract. Men promise God that if He will do a certain thing they will reciprocate with some act of sur-

render or service. After the baby gets well or they recover from their disease they forget their promise—their covenant.

- **Without natural affection**. Men and women defend their Sodomite conduct by pointing out their "love." They are simply indicting themselves further by verifying that they are indeed *without natural affection.*

    Another area where lack of natural affection is prevalent is toward family, neighbors, friends, elderly people, those in need, the poor, and especially children. Where this love is not prevalent, something unnatural is occurring.

    The sin of Adam did not render us all in a state of hating what we should love and loving what we should hate. God assumes that we are capable of *natural affection*, and holds us responsible to express the same.

- **Implacable** is to be unappeasable, cannot be placated. Nothing will satisfy, irreconcilable.

- **Unmerciful** is that condition of being without mercy. It is common to man to err. If we would function in society, there is continual need for showing mercy. Mercy gives others a second chance. Mercy leads to forgiveness. Jesus said that if we do not forgive others, he will not forgive us (Matthew 6:15).

1:32 Who knowing the judgment of God, that they which commit such things are worthy of death, not only do the same, but have pleasure in them that do them.

For a sinner to know the judgment of God and yet sin is sure testimony that he is worthy of death. In this process of degeneration and depravity, the sinner never completely forgets that God is a God of judgment. He learned this as God revealed it to him through nature. In quiet moments his conscience whispers warnings. If he listened long enough to understand the thoughts of his heart, he would tremble with the knowledge **that they which commit such things are worthy of death.**

And yet a greater sin than all those listed above is to **not only do the same** sin as listed above, but to **have pleasure in them that do** those same sins. That is to say, the lowest state of degeneracy is not in committing acts of indecency, immorality, and murder, but in taking vicarious pleasure in knowledge of others that sin. A man in a state of passion may commit a great sin of murder. He is guilty, but not as guilty as the man who, without passion, enjoys the murder vicariously. He watches it and approves of it. Or, he reads about it and finds it stimulating. America is digging its way to the bottom of the moral dump as it sits in front of a TV enjoying the sins of others. To take pleasure in adulterers and murderers merits the same death sentence as the one who committed the act. *"For as he thinketh in his heart, so is he. (Proverbs 23:7)." "For out of the*

*heart proceed evil thoughts, murders, adulteries, fornications, thefts,
false witness, blasphemies: These are the things which defile a man:
(Matthew 15:19-20)."*

2:1-16 The religious gentile

**2:1 Therefore thou art inexcusable, O man, whosoever thou
art that judgest: for wherein thou judgest another, thou condemnest thyself; for thou that judgest doest the same things.**

This is not a warning against judging others. It is a statement of a
universal principle. **Therefore**, because of the truths expressed in 1:18-
32, the reader is pronounced **inexcusable**. He just concluded a long list
of sins in chapter 1. The sins started with not glorifying God (1:19) and
went through disgusting sexual sins to a list of 21 universal sins and ending with the sin of simply taking pleasure in the sin of others (1:32).

In giving that list of sins, Paul knew that no one could read them
without feeling revulsion or condemnation toward the sinners. Anyone
with a God-given soul would join in judging at least some of those sins
as worthy of death. Paul is not suddenly changing the subject, telling us
not to judge; he is seizing the opportunity he has created to convict the
whole world of sin. The principle is stated in Matthew: *"Judge not, that
ye be not judged. For with what judgment ye judge, ye shall be judged:
and with what measure ye mete, it shall be measured to you again.
(Matthew 7:1-2)."* We are each judged according to our own consciously
held standard, which standard is manifested in our judgment of others. If
I find fault with you, I make an assumption that you have violated some
standard to which we should all be in subjection. Thereafter, I could
never plead ignorant of that law by which I have judged you. God is then
justified in judging me by the same standard I have used on you. If a
man's understanding of truth leads him to use a three-foot ruler to judge
his brother, God will use the same three-foot ruler on the owner. If a man
gains more understanding of the truth, then his measuring stick grows
accordingly, and so grows the standard by which God will judge him.

Luke expresses the principle in a parable: *"And he saith unto him,
Out of thine own mouth will I judge thee, thou wicked servant. Thou
knewest that I was an austere man, taking up that I laid not down, and
reaping that I did not sow: (Luke 19:22)."* The standard by which the
man was judged was first spoken by him, thus God quotes him when
passing judgment.

Paul refers to this principle when he says: *"If then I do that which I
would not, I consent unto the law that it is good (Romans 7:16)."* By
attempting to act in a certain way, even when he fails, he has demonstrated that he is in agreement with the law that demands the action he
failed to perform. He makes himself a transgressor by understanding a
law enough to try to do it. Theoretically, if he had been truly ignorant of

his obligation (the Law), he would not have sought to do it, would not have failed, and would not have been a transgressor though the law was left undone. The principle is that God judges us according to our judgments, whether of others or ourselves. So *wherein thou judgest another, thou condemnest thyself; for thou that judgest doest the same things.*

2:2 But we are sure that the judgment of God is according to truth against them which commit such things.

He is not wasting paper to assure us that God would not be false in His judgments. He is confirming the principles taught in the former chapter: God's judgments are **according to** (in proportion to) **the truth** that a man holds.

Since each person is judged as he has judged others, no one can claim ignorance of law. God, knowing all, can tailor His judgment to fit each individual's understanding and thus guilt. There can be no higher truth or justice than is expressed in God's custom judgments. So we who judge have risen to join God in condemnation of sinners, thus condemning ourselves.

2:3 And thinkest thou this, O man, that judgest them which do such things, and doest the same, that thou shalt escape the judgment of God?

It is a foregone conclusion that all men have judged others. Therefore, we who do **the same** without fear must think that somehow we will escape the judgment we have placed on others.

If a man cannot escape the judgment of his own conscience, how can he **escape** the judgment of God? If we who are so unrighteous condemn others, how can God not judge us? If we are forced to condemn ourselves, is not God forced to condemn us also? Since the judgment of God is *according to truth*, he is challenging those who judge others and think that they may escape the same judgment. Have we not all committed one or more of the sins listed in chapter one? How then do we think we will escape a judgment that is *according to truth*?

2:4 Or despisest thou the riches of his goodness and forbearance and longsuffering; not knowing that the goodness of God leadeth thee to repentance?

Usually God does not punish evil speedily. In His goodness He **forebears** (carries the debt of sin without immediate punishment) and is **longsuffering.** He allows a long time to lapse in which the sinner should see God's goodness in the matter and be drawn to **repent** toward Him. Often men take God's longsuffering to be indifference and so despise what should be hastening them to repent. Every day of impenitence is a vote for sin and a vote against holiness. It is to love what one should despise and to despise what one should love.

If God were swift to judgment, men would be quicker to fear Him, but they would not have a chance to see His **goodness** and desire fellowship with a merciful God. Those who ignore this reprieve are **despising** His goodness in the matter.

When sin was fresh, guilt was at its peak, and the dreaded damnation did not fall, the sinner lost respect and confidence in the concept of a God of judgment. He took the delay to be indifference and thought himself secure.

Men live comfortably with their sin, occasionally stopping to voice agreement with God's judgment on sinners. They imagine the longsuffering and goodness of God to be His blessings and approval on them, when it is nothing more than a space to repent. Men may be living their last moments before damnation counting blessings, but God is counting neglected opportunities to repent.

...to repentance.... Noting sin, God commands *"all men every where to repent."* God grants repentance, not in some mechanical way, but through the wooing of His goodness. He assumes it is the sinner's duty to repent.

2:5 But after thy hardness and impenitent heart treasurest up unto thyself wrath against the day of wrath and revelation of the righteous judgment of God;

Rather than God's patience bringing him to repentance, it hardened his conviction of invincibility. By delaying repentance, he found that he could survive and even prosper without it. A **hardened heart** is one that has resisted the truth until the heart itself goes through a change, making it less sensitive. An **impenitent heart** is something more than a failure to repent. It is to turn away from the opportunity to repent until the heart itself becomes stubbornly set against repentance.

To **treasure up wrath** is to heap up a larger quantity of wrath. It is to cause the amount of wrath to increase with each delay in repenting. Every day of sin and impenitence adds to the guilt and increases God's condemnation of the sinner. Like a dam weakened by high waters, the **wrath of God** increases with each day's sin and pushes against the dam of His longsuffering. The wrath is in danger of breaking forth upon *the day of wrath*, the day of God's **judgment**. That day of wrath will be a **revelation**, a revealing for all to see, of the fact that God is **righteous** in His **judgments**.

2:6 Who will render to every man according to his deeds:

To **render** is to return, as in payment. On the day of judgment, every man, none excluded, will receive payment **according to his** own **deeds**. The punishment will be tailor-made to the deeds of each individual according to his own sin and guilt.

It is most obvious that the basis of condemnation is not the sin of Adam, nor is one condemned because of some inherent state. Damnation is based solely on one's own personal deeds.

Since our works are the conclusive evidence of our character, the judgment of damnation is based on works (deeds). Men who want justice will receive it on that day. Men who want to approach God in their works will stand before His righteous judgment dressed in their own goodness or lack thereof.

There is no mercy or forgiveness in this passage. It is 100% works. Remember, this is not the gospel. It is the Law which must precede the gospel, revealing the gospel to be an absolute necessity in the quest for reconciliation.

2:7 To them who by patient continuance in well doing seek for glory and honour and immortality, eternal life:

If a man **seeking glory and honour** from God, with a hope of **immortality,** were to **patiently continue** to do **well**, it would result in **eternal life**. For some, this is a difficult passage because it seems to conflict with what we know of grace and salvation. But keep in mind that Paul has not yet begun to introduce Christ in his progression of thought. He is taking us through natural revelation to eventually arrive at Biblical revelation. At this point in his argument, he is still dealing with a man that has no revelation from the Bible and no knowledge of Jesus Christ. You must follow the progression of Paul's logic.

Men charge God with being unjust. God is declaring His righteousness by offering men eternal life through a life of continued good works. Men who are told that there is no *other name under heaven whereby we must be saved* cry, "Injustice! What of those who have never heard? What of other religions? What if a man is sincere and does the best he can?" In answer, for sake of argument, Paul is saying, "OK, you want to approach God in your own works; then have at it; if you continue uninterruptedly in good works, you will have eternal life." This offer is made many other places. Romans 2:13 tells us that those who do the Law will be just before God. In Romans 10:5, Paul quotes Lev. 18:5, saying that a man who obeys the laws would *"live by them."* Paul quotes the same passage again in Galatians 3:12, using it to show that the Law could not save one who has already broken it because it only offered life to those who obeyed it. In Luke 10:25 a man says to Jesus, *"[W]hat shall I do to inherit eternal life?"* He asked what he could *"do."* Jesus answered, *"[T]his do and thou shalt live"* —a reference to the Law. Again in Matthew 19:17, a man asked Jesus what he must do to have eternal life. Jesus answered, *"...if thou wilt enter into life, keep the commandments."* See Matthew 7:21 and Romans 2:25-27. Also see comments under 1:18.

Why would God offer salvation by works when we know from many other passages that no one will ever be saved by works? Because even though no one has ever found life under the principle, yet it remains true. In the course of building a case that will eventually prove all men guilty, one must admit to the principle that goodness is rewarded and evil is punished. If a man cannot be saved by perfect obedience to the Law, then he could not be damned when he failed to keep it. Understand, the Law never offers salvation to those who have already broken it. None of the passages listed above tell us that a man who has already broken the Law can begin to keep it and thereby absolve himself of former guilt.

Today's obedience does not produce any superfluous merit. We owe to each day our full obedience. The Law offers life to those who always keep it, for the simple reason that a man who never breaks the Law does not come under its condemnation. Once the Law is broken, there is no provision in the Law for forgiveness. The Law cannot save law breakers. When Jesus told the man he would enter into life if he would keep the commandments, He knew that the man had already broken them. But the man was not willing to face this fact. Jesus was using the Law to bring the man under condemnation. The man had built a defense against the Law and would not face blame. If he had really accepted Jesus' challenge and applied himself to the Law, it would have been a schoolmaster (Galatians 3:24) to bring him under condemnation and put him in a position not to seek to *do* something, but to seek mercy and forgiveness.

The Law was a real statement of what it took to please God and satisfy one's own conscience. It was *ordained to life* (Romans 7:10). But because of universal disobedience, it universally failed to give life. The fault was not in the Law, nor in the offer of life. The offer was not made invalid by the universal failure to obey the Law. The offer still stands to each new generation. It is there to be tried. Those who fail must then turn elsewhere for forgiveness. *"But we know that the law is good, if a man use it lawfully (1 Timothy 1:8)."* The lawful use of the Law is to allow it to function as law functions, as a statement of the boundaries within which we are free to operate. When any law has been broken, there is nothing within that law that can remove the violation or absolve the violator of his guilt. Attempting to use history, that includes a record of both broken law and obeyed law, as a witness on your behalf is legal suicide.

2:8 But unto them that are contentious, and do not obey the truth, but obey unrighteousness, indignation and wrath....

This is the other side. Verse 7 granted life to those that obeyed, so likewise those that fail to obey incur **indignation and wrath**. This throws the responsibility entirely on the individual. If you are damned, it will come only at your hands. You determine your eternity by the way you live in the here-and-now. Isn't this the position to which men resort when confronted with the message of Christ? Sinners resent being told that their salvation is dependent on something outside of themselves. In the course of argument, Paul grants the sinner his position: "Do good and you live; do evil and you die." This is a frank and straightforward challenge to the sinner who would live independently of God. God will respect true goodness. Bring it forth. The sinner defines the ground on which he should be approved, and Paul grants the truth of his proposition, knowing that it will eventually prove to be good testimony against him.

Failure to **obey** is not the result of ignorance of law, but of being **contentious**. To be contentious is the opposite of being content. It is to strive in disagreement. Men who fault God and contend with Him do not *obey the truth*.

Again, note that **truth** is present. They respond to it by being contentious. Their sin is not a product of ignorance and inability, but of refusing to do what they perceive as truth.

The term **obey** ("not *obey* the truth," do "*obey* unrighteousness") is informing us that their actions were not the preordained, blind stumblings of poor, uninformed victims of Adam's sin. Their sin was not inherited. It was an act of their wills, with full understanding of the truth. They will therefore meet with **indignation and wrath**.

2:9 Tribulation and anguish, upon every soul of man that doeth evil, of the Jew first, and also of the gentile;

The **soul** of **every man** that **doeth evil** is filled with **tribulation** in this life and **anguish** of torment in the next. The Jew that received the greatest revelation, and therefore had the greatest opportunity, will be **first** in line for judgment. But the heathen, untaught Greek, who had only the light revealed in nature, will also receive tribulation and anguish for his **evil.**

2:10 But glory, honour, and peace, to every man that worketh good, to the Jew first, and also to the gentile:

Paul again reveals the justice of God. There is **glory, honour, and peace to every man that worketh good**. He carries through with his theoretical proposition (that one is judged by his works) by holding out the certainty of life for those that never break the Law.

Holding greater knowledge of truth, the **Jew** is **first** in judgment. He is first to be rewarded if he does good, and, as we saw above, first in damnation if he disobeys. Increased truth produces increased responsibility. As our potential is raised, God's expectation of us rises. With increased responsibility comes an increase in accountability. Thus, where the learned Jew is concerned, both the reward and the judgment are on a larger scale.

The **gentile,** with his lesser knowledge of the truth, is also under a mandate to righteousness. The Jew was first in order, if not priority, but, through Paul, the gospel also goes to the gentile. This is one of the major themes of the book of Romans. The wrath is revealed on all, gentile as well as Jew, and the glory, honor, and peace is on all—gentile included.

2:11 For there is no respect of persons with God.

In regard to rewards or judgment, all men are treated equally. The equal treatment involves judging each man individually, according to his own light. Placing the Jew first in reward and judgment is not respecting his person; it is not giving preferential treatment based on his person. It is placing the more responsible, and therefore the more accountable, at the head of the line.

2:12 For as many as have sinned without law shall also perish without law: and as many as have sinned in the law shall be judged by the law;

There is no respect of persons, because God tailors the judgment to personal opportunity. Those who have sinned **without** knowledge of the laws given to the Jews will none the less **perish** because of their failure to keep the truth they perceived in nature. But they will perish **without law.** That is, the Law will not play a part in their judgment. On the other hand, those who have sinned while possessing knowledge of the Law will be **judged by the law** they have willfully violated. Their greater light and greater responsibility will cause greater damnation if they are found in violation. *"Because the law worketh wrath: for where no law is, there is no transgression (Romans 4:15)."*

This would take the wind out of a legalistic Jew. From his perspective, he was advantaged over the ignorant gentile who did not have the Law. But Paul informs him that the gentile will not be judged by that Law, whereas the Jew will receive greater damnation because of his exposure to it, with subsequent failure to keep it. Rather than being a status symbol, it is a responsibility.

Notice the absence of the definite article *the* in the phrase *have sinned without law*. Normally we would say, "without *the* law," as it does in the latter part of the sentence. There is no article the first time around because it is not a reference to THE Law of Moses, rather it is a reference to law in general, which can have many sources—nature, reason, other religions, direct revelation, etc. This is a restatement of the principle first seen in 1:18—wrath falls on those that <u>hold</u> truth unrighteously, even when that truth was gained through observance of nature.

Paul still has in view the Jew and gentile question. He is forming the argument that Jews and gentiles alike must answer for their sins regardless of their relationship to the Law of Moses and regardless of the degree of knowledge held.

2:13 (For not the hearers of the law are just before God, but the doers of the law shall be justified.

Verses 13-15 are bracketed as an explanation of the thoughts expressed in 7-12. The above verses are true because of this principle: **"the doers of the law shall be justified."** Those who are brought up with knowledge of the Law have a tendency to become comfortable with it, assuming that mere knowledge of the Law and assent to it is the same as doing it. Paul's purpose here is not primarily to offer the gentile a theoretical salvation through obedience, but to convince the Jew that obedience is the bottom line. He does this knowing that the Jew has in fact failed to obey. He puts forward the principle, "You must do the works of the Law to be justified by it." A broken law cannot mend a man's guilt. If a gentile that does not have the Law is condemned based on his own works, then a Jew that has the Law but does not do it will certainly be condemned.

He is assuring his readers that those privileged to be brought up under the teaching of Scripture are not preferentially treated, as those who are devoid of the covenant witness are not spurned. The principle is that anyone that does his duty, as he knows it, will be accepted by God.

Again, he is not offering an alternative way of salvation; he is vindicating God's judgments and gaining the ears of his hearers by drawing them into a commitment to seek the glory of God through right doing. If he can get them to admit to the need of righteousness and get them committed to doing it, they will come under the realization of their helplessness and see their need for a Savior.

If this offer of justification through the Law is still not clear to you, reread the commentary under 1:18 and 2:6-13.

2:14 For when the gentiles, which have not the law, do by nature the things contained in the law, these, having not the law, are a law unto themselves:

He is explaining why a gentile that does not have knowledge of Biblical law would still perish in sin. Upon observing tribal people or other cultures devoid of Biblical witness, it is apparent that they are conscious of the same basic truth found in the Mosaic Law. In every culture we see men holding concepts of right and wrong that are in agreement with Biblical Law. When they follow natural revelation, they **do by nature** the same things that Moses taught. Though they don't have Moses' Law, they do have a natural law to which they are accountable. Their own conscience is a revelation of the law of God. They are their own law, **a law unto themselves**. To this inner law they are responsible and held accountable.

2:15 Which shew the work of the law written in their hearts, their conscience also bearing witness, and their thoughts the mean while accusing or else excusing one another;)

This passage closes the bracket, concluding the explanation as to why indignation and wrath is poured out on all men (7-12). The gentiles, who have no Biblical revelation, as do the Jews, nonetheless show the same truth in their hearts. This law of God was not written in their hearts by the pen of a prophet, but by Jesus Christ himself (John 1:9) using nature as His visual aid (1:20) to teach *"that which may be know of God (1:19)."* We know that the law is written on their hearts by the fact that they are conscious of it. This consciousness is demonstrated every time they **accuse** someone of wrong-doing, and every time they **excuse** someone for his actions.

We *accuse* and *excuse* based on our perception of the truth. If I believe a man to be in violation of what he ought to do, I cannot help *accusing* him. If I do not believe he is wrong, I cannot help *excusing* him. Based on my understanding of the truth, I judge others, as well as myself. The very attempt of a man to do the things he ought is testimony to his consent to duty. Any failure is then testimony to his guilt.

Every language is full of words whose origin can only be accounted for by universal appreciation for common law. Such words as bad, sordid, perverted, evil, twisted, and depraved suggest a standard. These words would have no meaning if there were no universal standard common to the consciences of all men. Words that discriminate, place a value on actions, and *accuse or excuse* are consenting to the law.

To summarize:

Paul began in 1:17 and continued to this point proving that God is righteous in His judgments. The righteousness of God is revealed in the way He relates to His creation. He reveals truth to all men through nature and by means of direct revelation. He does not show preference, but judges all men according to, and in proportion to, the truth they hold. The law/Law is given both in the heart and in Scripture as a way of revealing responsibility. Obedience to that understood law/Law is the requirement for life. If one chooses unrighteousness he comes under the wrath of God. No man can excuse himself based on ignorance, for through some means all men have at some point in their experience come to know God. This knowledge is what renders all men accountable and eventually constitutes a just basis for individual condemnation. Paul is proving that all men are under personal sin. He has defined this personal sin in terms of immediate, personal, and willful violation of known law.

To make application:

The Native American who lived and died before contact with the western world will not escape the judgment of God. Each and every mature adult entertained a conception of the truth. No matter what the source of that truth, whether from direct divine revelation, observations of nature, their own religious teaching, or the morays of their culture, all were responsible to the truth they held. If that truth had become corrupted and twisted, they were still responsible to that marred and obscured truth. Whether an Indian or a Rabbinical Jew, when one weighs obedience to the truth against personal indulgence and chooses the indulgence, he is a sinner. He feels guilt and knows himself to be a rebel. He condemns others for the same violation and thus condemns Himself. God would be unjust to ignore the reality of his sin and its just deserts. So in judging the sinner, God demonstrates His righteousness.

2:16 In the day when God shall judge the secrets of men by Jesus Christ according to my gospel.

This takes us back to verse 12. Verses 13-15 were parenthetical, an explanation of the text up through verse 12. To maintain the flow of thought, read verse 16 immediately following verse 12.

Sin is rooted in the thoughts. The essence of sin is corrupt intentions. Those who take pleasure in the sinning of others (1:32) have secret sins. Most sin is secret, since it is a thing of shame. Paul tells us that the events of verse 12 will take place in **that day when God** will **judge** even the **secret** sins.

This is a fact **according to** the **gospel** message Paul preaches. He is not saying that all men will be judged by the gospel of Christ. He is saying that all men will be judged by Christ, and that this truth of judgment is a leading tenant of the gospel he preaches.

Paul has concluded his teaching on the heathen and will now speak to the religious Jew.

2:17-29 The Jew's standing before God

17 Behold, thou art called a Jew, and restest in the law, and makest thy boast of God,

18 And knowest his will, and approvest the things that are more excellent, being instructed out of the law;

19 And art confident that thou thyself art a guide of the blind, a light of them which are in darkness,

20 An instructor of the foolish, a teacher of babes, which hast the form of knowledge and of the truth in the law.

Overview of 2:17-20

These four verses are the beginning of a more advanced step in the systematic development of Paul's revelation of the righteousness of God. Up until this point, he has proven that the heathen are well supplied with enough revelation of God to render them without excuse. Additionally, he has addressed that group of readers who, though not Jews, have developed religion sufficient to find fault with the sins listed in chapter 1. He concludes that these religious gentiles must keep the righteousness of the Law if they are to be justified. He now turns his focus to the devout Jew who preserves and propagates the Law of God.

2:17 Behold, thou art called a Jew.

The name **Jew** had come to mean something more than natural descent from Judah. To them it was a statement of superiority. They liked being called by a name they construed to set them not only apart, but also above other men. To them being a Jew meant **resting in the Law**. They saw the Law, not as a judge of their conduct, but as a symbol of their superior moral convictions, a moral status symbol. The Law became their pillow rather than their personal judge. They had copied it, preserved it, argued it, and defended it until it was their property. They had handled it, dissected it, and interpreted it until they had become comfortable with its threats and warnings. It no longer waked them in the night to produce periods of confession and repentance. They memorized it to quote at convenient moments. They decorated it and carried it at the front of their celebrations, but they did not carry it in their hearts. It was no longer a voice from Mt. Sinai; it was proof of their historical significance— something tangible by which they could make their **boast of God**.

2:18 And knowest his will, and approvest the things that are more excellent, being instructed out of the law;

They boasted that they knew the **will of God**. Had not they received it directly from His hand? Not only did they know the will of God, but they personally **approved the things that were excellent**. Their society, even their waste disposal, was founded upon the revealed will of God. Their society indeed did excel all others, simply because they had been **instructed out of the law**.

2:19 And art confident that thou thyself art a guide of the blind, a light of them which are in darkness,

They were **confident** that as recipients and defenders of the Law they were competent **guides** to the spiritually **blind**. The Scripture had prophesied that Messiah would be a light to those that sat in darkness (Isaiah 42:6-7). But the Jews had set aside the hope of Messiah and rested in their own light. They thought themselves to be the **light of them which are in darkness.**

2:20 An instructor of the foolish, a teacher of babes, which hast the form of knowledge and of the truth in the law.

Then how could one so well informed resist being **an instructor of the foolish, a teacher of babes?** The thing that made their pit so dangerous was the fact that they were indeed morally far in advance of the heathen around them. Mankind was morally needy, and the Jews had much to teach the foolish heathen who worshipped images.

The Jewish nation possessed **the form of knowledge and of the truth in the law.** They started with the Law and added their traditions until they created a national religious system of laws and practices designed for public display. Being a hybrid adapted from the original truth of the Law, it still maintained the framework of truth, but it was molded in their personal **form**. This is an explanation as to how they could be so puffed up as described in the above verses. They did indeed *hold* **the knowledge of truth in the law**. They were not mistaken in regard to the value of that body of **truth** that molded their nation. The truth about God and His relationship to man was given to them in the many laws and ceremonies of temple worship and Sabbaths keeping.

2:21 Thou therefore which teachest another, teachest thou not thyself? thou that preachest a man should not steal, dost thou steal?

Keep in mind Paul's objective. The conclusion to which he is carefully drawing is to prove that all are under sin, both Jew and gentile (Romans 3:9). Having described the Jew's confidence in the Law, he will now show they have broken the same Law by which they judge the gentiles.

Paul asks a rhetorical question: "When you **teach another** man, are you not teaching yourself?" The answer is yes. Whether one responds affirmatively or not, to teach another is to teach one's self. The Jews had become so familiar with the Law that they had lost touch with the reality of it being the Law of the living God. They taught others with no application to themselves. Common burglary or petty theft was not one of the sins of these devout Jews. When they preached that a man **should not steal**, they were plotting to ensure the safety of their own stored up possessions. Their "white collar" theft was concealed in their convenient interpretations of the Law. They *"devour widows' houses, and for a pretense make long prayer (Matt, 23:14)."* They worked the Law so they were able to appropriate the property of a poor widow woman. Then they pretended to care by making a long prayer for her wellbeing. It could be like some so-called priests today, who receive money for praying. Also, in their money changing operations, which were strictly according to civil law, the Jews were thieves (Matthew 21:13).

2:22 Thou that sayest a man should not commit adultery, dost thou commit adultery? thou that abhorrest idols, dost thou commit sacrilege?

Thou **sayest...** *"Out of thine own mouth thou shalt be condemned."* They publicly taught against **adultery**; but he asks a probing question. Could it be that behind their religious garb lurked the heart of an adulterer? Christ had already told them that the adulterous look was also sin. (Matthew 5:28). By condemning others, they had established criterion by which they condemned themselves.

They also made a big profession to abhor **idols**, but he uncovers a corrupt motive. In Deuteronomy 7:25 they were told what to do with the idols found in heathen temples: *"The graven images of their gods shall ye burn with fire: thou shalt not desire the silver or gold that is on them, nor take it unto thee, lest thou be snared therein: for it is an abomina-*

tion to the LORD *thy God.*" But in Acts 19:37 there is a suggestion as to a practice that must have been common among the Jews. A government official at Ephesus observed, as if with surprise, that Paul and his associates were not *"robbers of temples."* To **commit sacrilege** is to desecrate a temple by carrying off its contents. It is probable that the Jews either financed or participated in robbing valuable objects from heathen temples. While professing to be against **idolatry**, their true motive was to enrich themselves through the confiscated valuables.

2:23 Thou that makest thy boast of the law, through breaking the law dishonourest thou God?

They bragged about being guardians of the Law and condemned the gentiles. Was God not equally dishonored by their disobedience? By boasting of the moral authority of the Law and professing to be disciples of it they increased the dishonor of God when they broke the Law they so extolled.

2:24 For the name of God is blasphemed among the gentiles through you, as it is written.

The **gentiles,** who were the objects of Jewish derision, were aware of Jewish hypocrisy. They heard one message in public and saw another life in private. The gentiles participated in crooked deals. Jesus characterized them as *leaving off judgment and mercy (Matthew 23:23).* Gentiles laughed and mocked at the idea that these people were in touch with a God that demanded righteousness. They felt no fear to speak the name of Jehovah in blasphemy.

Paul, himself a Pharisee of the Pharisees, knew the inside of Jewish religious life. He has gone behind the scenes and exposed the dark corners. He is not going to let any of the pompous stand behind a false righteousness.

...as it is written is a reference to passages like 2 Samuel 12:14 & Isaiah 52:5.

2:25 For circumcision verily profiteth, if thou keep the law: but if thou be a breaker of the law, thy circumcision is made uncircumcision.

In proving that Jews are equally under sin as are gentiles, Paul is building a case against their most prominent point of defense—*circumcision.* Jews prided themselves in their external differences from other men, a difference derived from obedience.

Circumcision is of value to a Jew if he also obeys the Law, but if he breaks the Law, then God views him as if he were uncircumcised. Just as today men trust in external rites to gain favor with God, so the Jews had come to believe that the rite of circumcision put them in favor with God. No learned Jew would argue with Paul's observation that circumcision was of no value if one broke the Law, but he goes one step further:

2:26 Therefore if the uncircumcision keep the righteousness of the law, shall not his uncircumcision be counted for circumcision?

In verse 25 Paul delivered a blow to the Jewish pride by showing how their failure to obey would render them as if they were not circumcised. He now hits them with the most scandalous of propositions, that not only would the disobedient Jew be viewed as uncircumcised, but that the obedient gentile would be viewed as if he were circumcised. The argument is that if an uncircumcised gentile does by nature the same works of righteousness that are expected from a Jew under the Law, then God will view the uncircumcised gentile as if he were circumcised.

2:27 And shall not uncircumcision which is by nature, if it fulfil the law, judge thee, who by the letter and circumcision dost transgress the law?

Paul is arguing the reasonableness of his thesis concerning the relevancy of circumcision in light of failure to obey the Law. No one is born circumcised. If the *uncircumcised* person (a totally natural state) were to live the righteousness demanded by the Law—even though he never heard it—would he not then be worthy to stand in judgment of the circumcised Jew who is breaking the Law? Paul is indicating that the natural state of uncircumcision could not be a point of blame. The real blame would be with the better-informed Jew, who, despite his knowledge, broke the Law. He is alluding to Romans 1 when he suggests that the ignorant gentile, who by nature kept the Law, would have the moral high ground so as to be able to sit as judge over the better informed, properly circumcised Jew.

2:28 For he is not a Jew, which is one outwardly; neither is that circumcision, which is outward in the flesh:

The outward marks of being a Jew, blood line, circumcision, knowledge of the Law, etc., do not make you a true Jew in God's sight. True circumcision is something that occurs in the heart, not just in the flesh.

Here is a foreshadowing of an important doctrine Paul will develop in his epistles. Physical circumcision is a type of the true circumcision of the flesh, which occurs in Christ's death for us and our death with Him. See 6:2-3.

2:29 But he is a Jew, which is one inwardly; and circumcision is that of the heart, in the spirit, and not in the letter; whose praise is not of men, but of God.

Being a true Jew is something that occurs in the heart, and true circumcision is also in the heart. It is something that occurs in the spirit of the man, not just compliance to the outward letters written in the Law. The motive of the true Jew is to please God, not men. This conclusion no doubt met with much resistance from the Jews who found solace in outward rite and natural descent.

This is not teaching that God has blurred the distinctions between Jew and gentile. To be a true Jew in heart would take a Jew in bloodline obeying from the heart. A gentile who did the righteousness of the Law would not thereby be Jewish. God would count him as circumcised, but not as a descendent of Jacob. This will be a significant distinction when we get to chapters 9-11.

3:1-2 The Jewish advantage

3:1 What advantage then hath the Jew? or what profit is there of circumcision?

The question would naturally arise: if an uncircumcised gentile can be counted as circumcised, what advantage is there in being a circumcised Jew? It would seem that if the gentile who doesn't have knowledge of the Law can know God through the revelation of nature and *do by nature the things contained in the Law,* and the gentile can be uncircumcised and yet counted as circumcised, then there is no advantage in being a Jew.

3:2 Much every way: chiefly, because that unto them were committed the oracles of God.

The question of verse one is answered: There is much advantage in being a Jew. The main advantage being, that God committed to the Jew the Word of God. We might then ask what advantage is it to have the Word of God? Although the heathen are well informed as to the character and person of God, and although God does not rate a Jew closer to God for just possessing the words of God, yet to have the Bible is a decided advantage when it comes to knowledge of redemption. A heathen can know enough to be held accountable, but he cannot know enough to gain forgiveness.

3:3-23 Sinfulness of Jew and gentile alike

3:3 For what if some did not believe? shall their unbelief make the faith of God without effect?

...the faith of God is not a reference to God exercising faith. As in other like passages, it is a reference to that *body of truth* or that dispensation wherein men approach God by *faith* as opposed to the deeds of the Law. Titus 1:1; Acts 6:7; 13:8; 14:22; 16:5; 24:24; Romans 1:5; 3:22; 4:14; Galatians 1:23; 2:16; 3:22, 23, 25; Ephesians 3:12; Philippians 3:9; 2 Timothy 4:7; James 2:1; Jude 3; Rev. 2:13, 4:12. It is often used in contrast to the Mosaic system as in *Galatians 2:16, "Knowing that a man is not justified by the works of the law, but by the faith of Jesus Christ, even we have believed in Jesus Christ, that we might be justified by the faith of Christ, and not by the works of the law: for by the works of the law shall no flesh be justified."* The *faith of God* is a way of relating to God, and it is in contrast to the *works of the law*. It is <u>faith</u> set over against <u>works</u>, and <u>God</u> set over against <u>Law</u>.

   ...what if some did not believe? Paul is answering the oft given excuse, "Well, if this Jesus is the long awaited Messiah of the Jews, why haven't they believed?" What if some Jews to whom the Law was given did not believe; does their unbelief cause God's offer to be ineffectual? Does their unbelief demonstrate a fault in God's program? If a man leaves the doctor's office and later dies, does that make the doctor ineffective? Not if the man refused to follow the doctor's instructions. Was the old covenant legal system a failure? What of the grace offered in Christ? If some of the Jews did not believe on Jesus Christ, does that make the gospel ineffective and therefore prove the superiority of the Law?

   To this day, the objection Paul is answering is still offered by Jews as a reason for rejecting Messiah. "How could Jesus be the Messiah if those to whom he came rejected him? Doesn't the broad rejection prove that he was not Messiah?" Paul answers:

3:4 God forbid: yea, let God be true, but every man a liar; as it is written, That thou mightest be justified in thy sayings, and mightest overcome when thou art judged.

   Does the integrity of the message of righteousness by faith depend upon the approval and acceptance of those Jews who have previously been in subjection to the Law? Paul answers verse 3 with the strongest negative possible, **God forbid**. If it comes down to a choice in integrity, Paul says, for all he cares, let every man be proven a **liar**, but let God be proven **true**. Jewish unbelief validates nothing but individual sinfulness.

   In defense of their unbelief, men often resort to attacking the authority and integrity of God. The rebel entertains a secret hope that if the majority rejects the faith of God, it will somehow prove that God is at fault in His moral government. It is the mentality of a mob that their large-scale, concerted actions weigh on the side of truth against the "overbearing and oppressive civil authorities." The faith of God is not embarrassed by mass unbelief. When men become so arrogant in their sin as to stand in judgment of the Judge, let God be **justified**, vindicated as beyond reproof, in all His pronouncements against sin and the sinner. Let Him **overcome** when the wisdom of this world stands to pronounce their philosophical judgments against their Creator.

   That thou mightest be justified in thy sayings, and mightest overcome when thou art judged. This is a partial quote from Psalms 51:4. It is given further significance when viewed in its original context. David has been indicted for sin and is making his confession: *"Against thee, thee only, have I sinned, and done this evil in thy sight: that thou mightest be justified when thou speakest, and might be clear when thou judgest."* David's attitude is what Paul is putting before us. David's mo-

tive for confession was not just to restore his own fellowship and blessings. He confessed total fault in his sin in order to absolve God of any
indictment from those who would detract from His moral government.
David was not concerned with the sentence upon himself; he just wanted
the judge to look good. Is there any wonder why God said David was a
man after His own heart?

**3:5 But if our unrighteousness commend the righteousness of
God, what shall we say?** *Is* **God unrighteous who taketh
vengeance? (I speak as a man)**
3:6 God forbid: for then how shall God judge the world?
**3:7 For if the truth of God hath more abounded through my
lie unto his glory; why yet am I also judged as a sinner?**
3:8 And not *rather,* **(as we be slanderously reported, and as
some affirm that we say,) Let us do evil, that good may come?
whose damnation is just.**

Overview 3:5-8

Paul is answering an objection that is common in our day and was
obviously common in his day. It is another attack upon the character of
God. Men have judged God to be unrighteous in taking vengeance on the
sinner. This is not a sincere belief, but it is a common defense employed
by those willingly enslaved to lusty passions. Rather than repent of sin,
they claim that sin is a natural part of God's program, part of His great
plan. This moral dilemma they create is for their own mutual salving of
conscience. Their reasoning is dangerously evangelical, based on an assumption about the sovereignty of God and the moral incapacity of man.
"If God is sovereign and in absolute control, then all that happens is part
of His predetermined plan. If man is constitutionally incapable of obedience, then he cannot be held accountable. Therefore, since the sin of man
is unavoidable, and God is using it to get glory from our sinning, (here is
where they depart most severely) let us not be overly concerned with
ceasing to sin. Go ahead and do that which we are destined to do, and
God will be glorified in it." Paul says of those reasoning thus, **whose
damnation is just**.

The faulty reasoning goes like this: "If the good character of God is
better appreciated as a result of contrasting it to my sin..." Or, to state it
another way, "If our unrighteousness affords God the opportunity to display His mercy and offer the gift of righteousness, is not the sinful condition thereby promoting the righteousness of God?"

Paul is actually accepting the assumption that our unrighteousness
commends the righteousness of God. But he takes exception to their conclusions that God would thereby be *unrighteous* to judge the sinner in a
situation where God may have incidentally benefited in some way. If evil
is set in contrast to the goodness of God, thereby displaying God's good-

ness through the stark contrast, it does not follow that the evil is thereby good or even needful.

(**I speak as a man**) Paul is hasty to let his readers know that he is quoting the slanderer and is not the author of this idea, **Let us do evil, that good may come.** Doubtlessly such an absurd philosophy did not come from a sincere desire to promote the welfare of God, but rather to establish an excuse for a life of indulgence, which they had already determined to live.

He answers the question, "**Is God unrighteous who taketh vengeance?**" **God forbid:** (the strongest form of negative in the Greek language) **for then how shall God judge the world?** If God is unrighteous in taking vengeance, He could not be judge of the world—which is exactly the point his detractors hoped to establish. In their twisted thinking, by making God the author of evil they disqualify Him as judge of their sin.

This is a fascinating passage. Paul is assuming that God is bound by, or has bound Himself to what we might call *common law*. Paul is accepting the presupposition of his detractors that God must morally qualify in order to be a judge of others. If God were unjust or unrighteous, He would not have a basis to judge others. Paul holds as a basic supposition that God does not function out of might, but out of right. It is not God's power that makes Him judge, but His goodness and wisdom.

3:7 For if the truth of God hath more abounded through my lie unto his glory; why yet am I also judged as a sinner?
3:8 And not rather, (as we be slanderously reported, and as some affirm that we say,) Let us do evil, that good may come? whose damnation is just.

Continuing to quote his objectors, Paul restates their slanderous argument. He first states the major premise (which is first introduced in 3:4): If when I **lie**, by contrast God is seen as truthful, and His truth is actually advanced by my having lied, why would God find fault with me? The man that would rest on this philosophy has allowed the sovereignty of God to become a doctrine apart from The Sovereign God. Logic built on partial or faulty supposition is a poor substitute for revealed truth. It is the manifestation of a wicked heart that would continue to sin on such grounds.

Paul has cleared the air by disassociating himself from this popular heresy. He has answered those who hold this view. And he now (3:9) uses it as a means of furthering his objective with his reader.

3:9 What then? are we better than they? No, in no wise: for we have before proved both Jews and gentiles, that they are all under sin;

Keep in mind that Paul is working toward the conclusion that all are unrighteous. He continues his argument to prove the sinfulness of the entire human race. This is the third time he has used this approach: Let us review them.

1.   In chapter one, he gives such an awful list of sins that anyone would find something to condemn. Then in 2:1, he turns his focus to the judgmental reader—a judgment which he has provoked—and says, wherein you judge another you condemn yourself. He induced us to judge, knowing that we would expose ourselves to condemnation.

2.   The second time, in 2:17-20, he summarizes the Jewish perspective on sin and sinners. Then in 2:21-24, he takes the judgment they aim at others and turns it on them, proving their guilt.

3.   The third time, here in 3:5-8, he presents a slanderous heresy that was currently prevalent. It is one that any reader would condemn. They were proposing that man should continue to sin because it benefited God in displaying His grace. Again he has provoked his readers to judge these blasphemous heretics. And then, while our fingers are still pointing and our brows are hardened with accusation, he demands, **"What then? are we better than they?"** We are shocked at this seeming change of subject. Weren't we finding fault with those ridiculous blasphemers? He turns a question on us. Our inclination is to think, "Yes, I am not that low. I don't believe in sinning just to glorify God. When I sin, I'm sorry for it." We will hastily admit that all are judicially sinners, equally condemned, and then dismiss the reference to our not being any better, secretly holding a perception that we are indeed better off than that confused bunch who go on sinning in order to glorify God.

Paul answers his question, "Are we better?" **No, in no wise.** In our minds we create a graded scale for sin, running from the perverse to the commonly tolerable. In our own eyes none of us are perverse, but to the righteous God all sin is intolerable.

Obviously Paul's primary concern in verses 5-8 was not just to answer this outlandish slander. He would not have interrupted his flow of thought to deal with a peripheral issue. Paul wooed his readers into the open, causing them to reveal their convictions about right and wrong. It was a case of entrapment. His readers may have become comfortable in a theology that exposed the hypocrisy of the Jews. Remember 2:17-20, the Jews were resting in the Law. They had become too familiar with it for it to bring conviction. So he got his readers relaxed, talking about this absurd heresy. The readers, feeling confident, jump up to condemn the pious hypocrites, and find themselves as it were before Nathan the prophet, *"Thou art the man."* He is not seeking to excite his readers against a heinous sin, as if he were warning them of its dangers. He is proving that all are under sin.

3:10 As it is written, There is none righteous, no, not one:

This is the conclusion Paul has been coming to since 1:18.

As it is written in Psalm 14:3. Again Paul is depending heavily on the Old Testament Scripture to support his teaching. Since it is written in the very Scripture Jews hold sacred, how can they argue that they are not sinners? It is all inclusive and emphatic, **...no, not one:**

3:11 There is none that understandeth, there is none that seeketh after God.

Psalm 14:2, 53:2. Men will seek understanding of any subject. They will seek spiritual illumination for the sake of power or inner peace. The history of man is the history of a quest to appease offended deities, but apart from the ministry of the Holy Spirit and the Word of God, men do not seek after God as God.

This lack of understanding is not a deficiency of intellect or a lack of information; it is a moral failure, a lack of heart understanding. This understanding is available to all who would know the truth. Psalms 119:104, 130; Isaiah 9:10; John 7:17. *"And ye shall seek me, and find me, when ye shall search for me with all your heart (Jeremiah 29:13)."* The heart that doesn't seek is a heart that doesn't care to find, and will become a heart that doesn't understand. That condition of being *without understanding* is avoidable and therefore a blameworthy condition.

3:12 They are all gone out of the way, they are together become unprofitable; there is none that doeth good, no, not one.

(Taken from Psalms 14:3.)

God had defined **the way** and the prescribed path (Ex. 32:8), but they had turned aside from it. They **are together,** as a group, become unprofitable. Each in his own history has **become** unprofitable. In their entirety there was no profit in them, individually or corporately.

...there is none that doeth good, no, not one. To say that **none doeth good** is contrary to all humanists' doctrine. Jesus also said, *"there is none good but one, that is, God (Matthew 19:17)."* Relatively speaking, the actions of men are *good* or *bad* as they effect others. To say that no man does good, is also to say that those that obey the Law are not doing good. Unless we understand goodness to consist in something more than the mere external act, this declaration would not make sense. It must therefore be the case that goodness consists in the motive and not in the act alone. This brings us to a definition of sin and goodness. Ultimate intention or motive must be the criterion for determining good or bad. If a man does the right thing, but for the wrong motive, from God's perspective he has not done *good*. The recipient of his act would call it goodness because it was beneficial to him, but the intention of the former was to use his "good" deed for some form of personal advancement. God, who knows the heart of all men, has not found a single man or woman that was not motivated by selfishness.

3:13 Their throat is an open sepulchre; with their tongues they have used deceit; the poison of asps is under their lips: (taken from Psalms 5:9)

"Woe unto you, scribes and Pharisees, hypocrites! for ye are like unto whited sepulchers, which indeed appear beautiful outward, but are within full of dead men's bones, and of all uncleanness. Even so ye also outwardly appear righteous unto men, but within ye are full of hypocrisy and iniquity (Matthew 23:27-28)." "But the tongue can no man tame; it is an unruly evil, full of deadly poison (James 3:8)." Those who pride themselves in not lying are at least guilty of using their tongues to deceive others. God characterizes our speech as coming from the mouth of a most deadly snake. Tongues drip with deadly poison, waiting to inflict suffering.

3:14 Whose mouth is full of cursing and bitterness: Taken from Psalms 10:7.

To curse is not just profanity or vulgarity. It can occur without any expletives being involved. It can come forth in the most educated and acceptable language. To curse is to pronounce a curse on someone, to consign that one to damnation, to wish or pronounce suffering and judgment upon him. In the end, God will curse the damned. In fact, all are under the curse right now. When a common mortal assumes the authority to curse another, he has cursed himself (2:1). The sophisticated and morally sensitive learn not to utter curses, but they will be found to occasionally speak with **bitterness** toward the unquestionably deserving. The bitterness comes from the same heart as the cursing, and it deserves the same judgment.

3:15 Their feet are swift to shed blood:

They are hasty in shedding the blood of their fellow men. Sometimes it is the medical doctors who are swift to shed the blood of innocent babies "before the third trimester." At other times it is governments who are swift to send the military to kill the enemy. Historically, it is the way men resolve personal conflicts.

3:16 Destruction and misery are in their ways:

The history of civilization is recorded in the different layers of **destruction**. The passing of a people is marked by the remains of their weapons and broken bones.

On a personal level, sin destroys one's innocence, home, marriage, children, and soul. **Misery** of soul and conscience follows the destruction. The nature of man as given by God is such that we cannot be content and at rest until we are at peace with God. Where God is not loved, feared, and obeyed the soul is marked by misery.

3:17 And the way of peace have they not known: (Isaiah 57:21.)

There is no peace within and no peace without. The price of independence from God is to suffer one's own troublesome company. No matter what a man's accomplishments or his station in life, if he has no peace within, his life is a failure.

3:18 There is no fear of God before their eyes. Proverbs 1:17; Psalms 36:1; Ecclesiastes. 12:13.

"The fear of the LORD *is to hate evil: pride, and arrogancy, and the evil way, and the froward mouth, do I hate (Proverbs 8:13)."* A man that doesn't fear God is arrogantly defying His rule and challenging Him to a contest of supremacy. To be in the company of others of like mind is to deprive oneself of the greatest inducement to repentance—example. Thus, there is no fear of God **before their eyes.** Life is full of warnings that should awaken us to impending judgment, but men blinded by lust and philosophy interpret the warnings in ways that leave them without fear of God.

3:19 Now we know that what things soever the law saith, it saith to them who are under the law: that every mouth may be stopped, and all the world may become guilty before God.

At first glance, it seems he is unnecessarily stating the obvious—the Law can only speak to those under it; it cannot speak to those that never heard it. But, his purpose is to remind the Jew that the former indictments he pulled out of the Law cannot be addressed to anyone but Jews, the recipients of the Law. The Law could not apply to gentiles who never heard it. But Jews read the Law, and rather than see their own sinfulness, they condemned gentiles—those to who the law was not given. That is like a fat man putting his skinny wife on a diet. Paul has taken that same law and turned it back again on the Jews, who in fact are the only ones responsible to keep it. Paul has used it as irrefutable evidence against those who were using it against others. The purpose in the Law was to stop the excuses of their mouths. The indefensibly guilty stand mute before the clear evidence of broken law. Their hands have gone to their mouths to silence their own tongues. They gawk in amazement and shame at seeing their own guilt. They know that all answers would be vain excuses, so they silently stand, waiting their sentences—or at least that was the design of the Law.

3:20 Therefore by the deeds of the law there shall no flesh be justified in his sight: for by the law is the knowledge of sin.

Here is the great conclusion to which Paul has been negotiating his Jewish readers. They trusted in the Law for their salvation—a law they failed to keep.

Therefore, because of the foregoing, that *none doeth good*, and the Law justifies only those that never break it (2:7, 13), it is no longer possible to be **justified** by a broken law. Broken laws cry out for punishment. The Law stops the mouth and makes guilty, but it can never forgive. The Law written in stone is like an x-ray, it can reveal sickness, but it cannot heal. The Law fulfills its purpose well, which was to bring men to **knowledge of sin**. Beyond that, it is powerless. See chapter seven.

He doesn't just say that *no one* will be justified in the sight of God, but that **no flesh** will be justified. He puts his reader in proper perspective. *"That which is born of the flesh is flesh."* Would mortal flesh, corrupted flesh, sinful flesh, rise up to the challenge of righteousness, and please the Almighty?

Note the emphasis: *No flesh will be justified* **in his sight**. Paul understands the human tendency to judge relative to what others think. It is not hard to impress other men with one's goodness. Religion itself is satisfied with far less than God demands. The conscience may rest long before it comes in favor with God. It is not in the sight of our fellow men that we must be justified, but in the sight of God.

3:21 But now the righteousness of God without the law is manifested, being witnessed by the law and the prophets;

The righteousness of God is not a term describing a certain level or standard of righteousness, as in a righteousness on level with God. Neither is it a source of righteousness, as in a righteousness that comes through God's assistance.

When an angel does right, it is the angel's righteousness. If a man should do right, even with God's assistance, it is still the man's righteousness. Likewise when God does right, it is God's righteousness. Romans 3:5 and 2 Corinthians 5:21 confirm this. The term **righteousness of God** can never be used to describe the righteousness of anyone other than God. God is righteous in all His person and work, thus, *the righteousness of God*. Righteousness is not impartable. That is, it cannot be passed to another—imputed yes, but not imparted.

The Law is an expression of God's own righteousness. The Jew came to know what God was like and what He expected through the Law. The **law and the prophets** prophesied of a future manifestation of God's righteousness that would come, not through the Law, but through a person (Genesis 15:6; Jeremiah 23:5, 33:16; Daniel 9:24).

3:22 Even the righteousness of God which is by faith of Jesus Christ unto all and upon all them that believe: for there is no difference:

He is introducing that righteousness spoken of in the Old Testament as something more than obedience to the Law. It is a righteousness that is for everyone, based on faith alone. This **righteousness** prophesied in the Old Testament is not achieved by the Law: it is given by **faith of Jesus Christ.**

The wording, "**by faith of Jesus Christ,**" rather than "by faith _in_ Jesus Christ" seems awkward. But by comparing similar wording other places we can see that it is not an attempt to convey the same meaning as "faith _in_ Christ." Galatians 2:16, 20, 3:22-23; Philippians 1:27, 3:9; Titus 1:1; James 2:1. Unfortunately the modern commercial versions fail to note the difference, due mainly to their hasty and careless productions. They do not contain the scholarship or respect for Scripture seen in the King James Bible.

The "faith **of** Christ" is a reference not to our faith or to Christ's faith, but to faith in Christ as a method to salvation. The faith of Jesus Christ embodies the entire plan of redemption, and the terminology is used to set it in contrast to _the works of the law._

Galatians 3:22-23 well illustrates the meaning of the phrase "**faith of Christ.**" _"But the scripture hath concluded all under sin, that the promise by faith of Jesus Christ might be given to them that believe. But before faith came, we were kept under the law, shut up unto the faith which should afterwards be revealed."_ Since the _faith of Jesus Christ came,_ and in so doing released one from the Law, it is obvious that the _faith of Christ_ is in contrast to _the works of the Law,_ and is a dispensation of relating to God by faith, not by works of the Law.

The faith is a body of revealed truth, and something more: it is the person of Christ and the gift of a dispensation of imputed righteousness.

The fact that this righteousness of God is **unto all** defines it as the thing offered. It is in contrast to the _"righteousness which is of the law (Philippians 3:9)."_

...unto all and upon all them that believe: This gift of imputed righteousness (the faith that came) is **unto all,** emphasizing that provision is made for everyone. The offer is _unto all,_ but the gift actually comes only **upon all** them that believe. A gift **unto** you is made available _to_ you. A gift **upon** you has become personal; you are a partaker.

This righteousness is upon **all that believe.** Here is a statement of what God requires for one to receive this righteousness—**believe.**

3:23 For all have sinned, and come short of the glory of God;

He is not reopening his argument that all are sinners. Having proven that already, he is using it as an explanation as to why the righteousness of faith is available to the gentile as well as the Jew. Is it not reasonable that if all share the sinful condition then the provision would be applicable to all? The righteousness of Christ is for _all that believe_ (v. 22), because **all have sinned** and are therefore in need. All share the need (v. 23), so all share the promise of life (v. 22).

The phrase "**come short of**" acknowledges the sinner's effort, but pronounces it insufficient. One may argue his sincerity or point to his efforts, but when measured by the glory of God, we have all _come short of_ measuring up to the glory of God. Paul said, _"when they knew God,_ *they glorified him not as God (1:21)."* And then in 2:7 he characterizes striving for eternal life as seeking *"for glory."* Men seek to recover the *glory* Adam had when he walked with God. But when all have returned from their wilderness of repentance, when God has searched out the deepest devotion and highest praise, He pronounces that **"all have come short of the glory of God."** The smallest sin dulls the brilliant glory of God until it is only darkness. How can darkness ever become light unless the light from above shines down?

The entire human race stands rejected by its Creator. The darkness descends and the glory of God is confined to the heavens above, far beyond the reach of sinful hands and depraved minds. What despair to which Paul has brought us! How helpless is the human race! Our righteousness will forever be insufficient. We are not only separated from God, but our best efforts at reconciliation have been rejected as sinful. We have been pronounced hopeless.

Then at the darkest moment, when the Law has done its work of death, when there is nothing to look forward to but the suffering of eternal damnation, there comes a most unexpected offer.

3:24-31 Justification by faith

3:24 Being justified freely by his grace through the redemption that is in Christ Jesus:

...**justified freely**, he says! This is unheard of. Nothing like it has ever occurred, neither in the Old Testament, nor in any religion or philosophy. To the guilty and condemned this is astounding news—unprecedented legal maneuverings.

To be **justified** is to be exonerated from all guilt, to be officially declared blameless. It is to say that the evidence has been submitted to the highest court, and the accused is declared to be in conformity to all law. The record of his actions demonstrates him to be beyond reproach. Legally, this is a more desired state than having never been brought to trial, for the justified can never be tried for the same offense again. It is to have the full approval of the highest judicial body, and this after the closest scrutiny of the evidence.

- What is the cost of this legal counsel? Being justified **freely...**
- On what basis would one provide justification for the undeserving? *Being justified freely* by his **grace.**
- Whose grace made this possible? **Christ Jesus.**
- By what means did He satisfy the Law's accusations against the sinner? It was **through the redemption** that is in Christ Jesus. Redemption is the liberation procured by the payment of a ransom. Through the death of Christ, God established a basis by which any and all souls could be redeemed.

The payment was not made to the devil. He has no rights to the human race; only the kingdoms of this world are of His making. God did not pay the Law. It is lifeless and without appeal. God ransomed the sinner from the principles of common justice. He paid the price to Himself, and as a statement to any who would question His justice.

3:25 Whom God hath set forth to be a propitiation through faith in his blood, to declare his righteousness for the remission of sins that are past, through the forbearance of God;

To **set forth** is to lay out before the public for full inspection.

A **propitiation** is an appeasement or atonement. The same Greek word translated *propitiation* is also translated *mercy seat* in Hebrews 9:5. The mercy seat was a propitiation. The sinner is under obligation to offer a propitiation for his own sins. Under the Law, the propitiation was made by the blood of animals sprinkled on the mercy seat. It was always the sinner's duty to select a perfect sacrifice and bring it to the place of offering. This is highly unusual to have **God set forth** the sacrifice. He is the one to whom the sacrifice is made. This is like a bank, on behalf of the debtor, paying itself the loan rather than foreclosing. Instead of the offending sinner seeking restitution through sacrifice, the offended God is offering restitution through the sacrifice of Himself.

The propitiation is **through faith in his blood**. There must be something that would distinguish the one that is propitiated from the one that is not. This is not universalism. This passage has been despised ever since the Holy Spirit first inspired it. The fabricators of many of the commercial bibles have hated it badly enough to sacrifice their names in the book of life to be rid of it (Revelation 22:19).

When the Israelites placed the blood of sacrificial lambs on the door posts and went inside to await the destroyer (Exodus 12:13-23), they had faith in the blood to secure the salvation of their first born. When priests went behind the veil to offer sacrifices for the sins of the people, they had faith in the blood sprinkled on the mercy seat (Leviticus 16:15). Paul is speaking to Jews that had exercised faith in the blood of animals. He tells them that now their faith should be in the blood of Christ. The love and mercy of God could not secure forgiveness without the application of the blood of Christ (Hebrews 9:12).

God *set forth* (publicly displayed) Christ as the payment for sin in order to publicly **declare His righteousness for the remission of sins that are past.** The sins that **are past** are <u>not the past sins of believers</u>. The sin of those who were already dead and in Abraham's bosom were the ones who committed the sins *that are past*. The Old Testament believer repented toward God and participated in the designated sacrifices. But it was *"not possible that the blood of bulls and of goats should take away sins (Hebrews 10:4)."* The sacrifices did not actually provide a just payment for sin. The blood of an animal is not an equal substitute for man. The sacrifices left the offender with a consciousness of sin: *"For the law having a shadow of good things to come, and not the very image of the things, can never with those sacrifices which they offered year by year continually make the comers thereunto perfect. For then would they not have ceased to be offered? because that the worshippers once purged should have had no more conscience of sins (Hebrews 10:1-2)."*

The past sins were remitted **through the forbearance of God.** God carried the penalty of sin as a banker carries a note. In a manner of speaking, the old covenant saint was saved on credit. He was saved on the promise of future payment. The penalty of sin—death—must be exacted. When God saved the old covenant believer, He opened Himself up to the accusation of injustice. Justice demands death. Noah, Abraham, Lot, Moses, and David were all sinners deserving of death. On what legal basis did God set aside the death penalty? God seemed to be playing loose with the Law. Would the human race no longer be subject to law? Could man sin and expect to avoid the penalty?

3:26 To declare, I say, at this time his righteousness: that he might be just, and the justifier of him which believeth in Jesus.

Having provided through Christ's propitiation a just payment for the sins of those whom God had already forgiven under the old covenant, God now declares His righteousness in remitting the sins of those that believe in Jesus.

It is a declaration that God has provided a suitable and more than equal payment for sin. The life of Jesus is of more value than all the sinning souls. His blood was sinless blood. When He bore the sin of the world and took the place of all sinners in death, the justice of God was satisfied. The penalty of sin having been met in Jesus, God can now forgive all whom He will, and He cannot be charged with injustice. He is now declared to be **just,** and at the same time is able to **justify** any and all sinners that believe.

3:27 Where is boasting then? It is excluded. By what law? of works? Nay: but by the law of faith.

This system of salvation excludes any possibility of boasting. The *law of works* (that is a salvation that is merited by obedience to the commandments) would encourage one to boast; but the *law of faith* makes no such allowance. The Law could not exclude boasting—faith does.

The **law of faith** is stated as the antithesis of the **law of works**. See Romans 9:31-32. The law of works is not a written law. It is that rule of action whereby works of obedience merit acceptance with God. Paul has well proven that no one will be justified by the *working principle of law*, but rather by the *working principle of faith*. The law of works is not invalid; it just remains unattained by any but Christ.

See 8:2 for a discussion on the various uses of the word *law*.

3:28 Therefore we conclude that a man is justified by faith without the deeds of the law.

Paul has now arrived at the high point of the gospel: Justification is by faith, and not by the Law. The fact that pride is inherent in a works salvation, but impossible in a grace and faith salvation, becomes a good argument for faith—at least to those who value humility. **Therefore,** because of all the foregoing arguments, plus the fact that boasting is excluded, **we conclude that a man is justified by faith**.

3:29 Is he the God of the Jews only? is he not also of the gentiles? Yes, of the gentiles also:

The gap between Jew and gentile was mostly of Jewish making. The Jews were very ethnic about their God, not believing that He could also be the God of the gentiles. They considered God the exclusive property of their nation. They understood Him to be the creator of all men, and they understood that the whole world had a duty to worship only Jehovah, but they did not think the rest of the world was fit to be in association with their holy God. The covenants had been made with the Jews only. If God wanted gentiles in His family, He could go make a covenant with them as he had with Israel.

Paul makes it clear that this atonement is for the whole world, making Him the God of gentiles as well as Jews (Hosea 2:23).

3:30 Seeing it is one God, which shall justify the circumcision by faith, and uncircumcision through faith.

The Jewish conviction was that this God, justifying sinners that had never even made an attempt to keep the Law, could not be the same God that thundered from Mt. Sinai. But the gospel is that this **one God** will justify Jew and gentile alike, based on faith alone.

...justify.... To be justified is to be vindicated, declared to be without fault or blame, whether by one's own self or by another. The word justify is by no means an exclusively theological term. Here, it is God justifying the sinner from condemnation of the Law. The word *justify* is not always synonymous with being saved, born again, or converted. One may justify himself (James 2:24): You say you have faith, then justify that claim with the works that accompany faith. God justifies man, but man also justifies God—of course, in a different way (Luke 7:29). God also justifies Himself (Romans 3:4). We point out the different usage of the word *justify* so that when you come across one of the passages where it is used differently you will not be surprised or confused.

...by faith/through faith.... Paul makes a difference in *by* and *through*. He uses two different Greek words, as you see accurately translated in the King James Bible. The Jew is justified **by** (Gk. *ek*) faith. The gentile is justified **through** (Gk. *dia*) faith. The basic meaning of *ek* is *by, out of, by means of, emanating from.* It is expressing the means or source. The basic meaning of *dia* is *through*, as in the *channel or means.* The hundreds of Biblical uses of these two words both in Greek and English well demonstrates the differences. If you want to study it in Greek, note the decisive distinction in Romans 11:36 *"For of (by—ek) him, and through (dia) him, and to him, are all things: to whom be glory for ever. Amen."* If *by* and *through (ek & dia)* were synonymous, then this passage would be a foolish redundancy. Paul makes a distinction by declaring that all creation is *by (ek)* Christ, but it is also *through (dia)* Him. He is assuring us that Christ is the initiator and force of Creation, but he is also the means or channel of its institution.

...by faith.... Faith produces, or is the source from which the justification proceeds. Faith is the means or the initiator of justification. Since the circumcision (Jews) were already under the Law and in the system of faith, their justification came not by *(dia* through) the Law, as in a passive channel, but *(ek)* by the *means of* faith. Whereas, concerning the gentiles, who had no faith from which could emanate justification, it was through *(dia,* channel) faith that justification was imparted.

The circumcision (Old Testament Jews) were justified "by" faith, that is faith was the means by which the sinner was able to do the righteousness that saves, whereas the uncircumcision (gentiles) were justified "through" faith, that is, faith is the channel through which God imputes the righteousness that saves. *"By faith"* expresses the means. *"Through faith"* expresses the channel.

So, was there a different kind of salvation for the Jew? No, in our present dispensation, both are saved by faith, without any kind of meritorious works. Then why make a difference by applying different words—*by* or *through*? The Jew considered himself already in the faith of Abraham. He must now direct that faith toward Christ, and it would be the means of his salvation. Whereas the gentile, who was totally devoid of faith, would be brought to faith by the Holy Spirit and thereby faith would be the channel—the gentile being a recipient of faith, not one who directs his faith. *Ek* and *dia* are used interchangeably in other places, but Paul desired to make a distinction here.

3:31 Do we then make void the law through faith? God forbid: yea, we establish the law.

When he says **through faith,** he is not speaking of individual and personal faith, but of that method of salvation called "*the faith which was once delivered unto the saints (Jude 3)."*

Since no man is justified by the Law, and since a gentile, who has never seen or heard of the Law, can know God, and since the uncircumcision can be justified without the Law or circumcision, it would appear that the Law is void of any authority or usefulness. It appears to have been superseded by *the righteousness of faith.* Does the coming of *right-*

eousness by faith make the Law void? Only those who misunderstood the original intent of the Law would think so.

Paul answers the question with the strongest negative possible, **God forbid**. Contrary to appearances, **we establish the law**. The gospel of Christ does not set aside and replace the Law; it fulfills the Law by allowing the Law to convict the sinner and bring him to Christ. The Law typified and prophesied of Christ until Christ came and filled to the full the intent of the Law. Christ said, *"Think not that I am come to destroy the law, or the prophets: I am not come to destroy, but to fulfill (Matthew 5:17)."*

The Law/law (the law revealed in nature and the Law of Moses) must precede the gospel like diagnosis must precede treatment. The Law/law was the first stage of Divine revelation; the gospel completes that revelation. It is not a question of one or the other; it is the one built on the other. Like the framing of a house is then covered with siding, so the Law has disappeared behind the finish of the gospel, but it will forever be the structure on which the gospel is built. Religion, Judaism especially, has attempted to make the Law serve a purpose contrary to its nature. It finds completion and fulfillment only in Christ.

In the book of Galatians, Paul speaks of the Law as our *"schoolmaster to bring us to Christ."* One graduates from grade-school to go on to high-school, not as a rejection of grade-school, but as a graduate of it. High-school is built upon the grade-school and encompasses it. One that is in high-school is no longer under the government of the grade-school, but he is not without government. He is under the government of high-school. To not be under the jurisdiction of the grade-school is not to deny its jurisdiction; it is simply to be under a jurisdiction that encompasses and supersedes the grade-school. Likewise, when one graduates to high-school, much that was required of the immature, grade-school students is not longer a law for the high-school students, who are now expected to be ruled by a more mature sense of responsibility.

So, to the Jew that would object to the gospel of Christ with an argument that Paul is discounting the Law to replace it with something new, he has explained that the purpose of the Law is to prepare men to come to Christ that they might be justified by faith alone; and only in that capacity as forerunner of the gospel does the Law find fulfillment. In Christ, the ceremonies and daily observance of the Law are set aside, but the righteousness which the law required is far better realized in Christ than it could ever be under the Law.

4:1-25 Abraham, example of imputed righteousness

4:1 What shall we say then that Abraham our father, as per-

taining to the flesh, hath found?

Paul is continuing his unfolding of the truth of justification by faith without the deeds of the Law. No argument would be complete without an analysis of Abraham. Since Abraham is the patriarch of patriarchs, the father of all who call themselves Jews, the manner in which he was made acceptable to God is most significant.

Paul has just shocked the Jews by announcing that their circumcision is of no avail in justification (3:30). When confronted by Christ, the Pharisees expressed the Jewish confidence in Abraham: *"They answered and said unto him, Abraham is our father. Jesus saith unto them, If ye were Abraham's children, ye would do the works of Abraham (John 8:39)."*

Paul shows from the Old Testament Scripture itself that this *right-eousness of faith* has been God's plan from the very beginning. By putting Abraham on the witness stand for *"justification by faith,"* rather than through *"circumcision and the Law,"* the Jews have lost their star witness to the other side.

...as pertaining to the flesh is a reference to the circumcision which is in the flesh. After an introduction to his subject, he picks up the argument in 4:10, showing that Abraham did not have the same confidence in the flesh as does his professed followers.

4:2 For if Abraham were justified by works, he hath whereof to glory; but not before God.

Apparently the Jew had gone on record as against pride and boasting. This is the second time Paul has leaned on this argument (3:27). It was strong enough that Paul could assume without proof, as an unquestionable presupposition, that any dealings with God must always be on a ground of humility. To simply suggest that a doctrine afforded opportunity to boast, was to rule it out without further argument. To suggest that Abraham would, or even could, boast of his own contributions to justification was unthinkable.

Apparently, while preaching great swelling words of justification by the grace of a merciful God, they were practicing extreme legalism. Somehow they did not make the connection. They read and quoted the same Scripture that Paul is using to prove justification by faith, but when it filtered down to practical theology, they were all works. In their practical theology they extolled the obedience and works of Abraham. They exhorted their followers to avail themselves of the grace of God that they too might become pleasing to God, as did Father Abraham. Surely they pointed to his tithing and faithfulness to obey God, inwardly believing that he must have gained favor with God through his faithfulness.

Paul reasons that if Abraham did indeed gain justification by his works, then he could actually boast. Why not? If he worked and endured where others did not, what greater right to boasting? But since the Scripture does not represent Abraham in this light, but rather quite the opposite, it cannot be that Abraham, nor anyone else is justified by works. The very thought of Abraham boasting before God sent a shudder through the Jews. They taught that the only ones who could be justified are the humble and contrite. They had made their perception of humility into the greatest work of all.

4:3 For what saith the scripture? Abraham believed God, and it was counted unto him for righteousness.

Paul says, let us go back to the source, **what saith the scripture?** In most circles, it is not as simple today as it was then. If you share the uninformed opinion of many, that all English bibles are Scripture, there is no telling what "scripture" might say. Modern bibles say many things, often contradicting each other. In a rush to make profits, the publishing companies turn out a new English version on the average of one every nine months. The scholarship is somewhere between poor and hostile to the words of God. The deluge of modern versions clashes in thousands of places. But regardless of the confusion, the Scripture is still given by inspiration of God and still speaks clearly to the English speaking populace in the King James Bible.

For what saith the scripture? He follows with a quote from Genesis 15:6. Abraham knew nothing of Jesus Christ. He was not asked to believe anything about personal salvation. Sarah was barren to begin with, but then God waited until she was past childbearing age before informing Abraham that she would have a child. When Abraham believed what God said about the birth of this child, God counted it unto him as righteousness. Abraham had no idea that his belief would mean anything beyond the birth of the child. In fact, his faith was not even a condition for the birth of the child. God made an unconditional promise and Abraham simply believed God.

...and it was counted unto him for righteousness. Abraham was not righteous in all his deeds. He started out his career disobeying God by taking Lot with him. Even his faith was far from perfect. He later came to doubt the promise of a miracle child and sought fleshly means through Hagar of bringing the promise to fulfillment. If uninterrupted faith were a condition for imputed righteousness, Abraham would have been intermittently righteous at best.

God, in His grace, seeing the simple faith of Abraham, chose to call his faith "*the righteousness of God.*" An accountant is one who balances the books and guarantees the integrity of a business. He *counts* numbers and *imputes* sums. He *reckons* on a total, and *numbers* their transactions accordingly.

God drew from His own righteousness and *counted* it to be Abraham's. According to the Divine books, Abraham was *counted* to be a sinless man; and yet more, he was *counted* as a righteous man.

Faith is right, but it is not righteousness in and of itself. It has no innate moral quality. Sinners believe and have faith in many things, including God. The devil believes and trembles, but it is not imputed unto him for righteousness.

Based on Abraham's faith, God was calling him something that he was not. The faith did not provoke God to appreciate some spark of moral beginnings and thereby award him a full measure for a small measure. Faith is not a small measure of righteousness. It is the result of God revealing Himself and His will to the understanding. Faith is the <u>channel</u> of righteousness, not a <u>seed</u> of righteousness.

It was *counted* unto him **for righteousness.**

- Faith was *counted* to be something different from itself.
- Faith was *counted* to be more than it was.
- It was unconditionally *counted* to Abraham.
- All of God's righteousness was *accounted* to him.
- The *imputation* (counting) was not linked to Abraham's righteousness or lack thereof.
- He was not given conditions to meet either to receive or to keep the gift of righteousness.
- The faith was *counted* by God, not Abraham.
- His later unbelief didn't 'unaccount' the righteousness.
- His life was marked, though in an imperfect way, by obedience to that declared righteousness.

4:4 Now to him that worketh is the reward not reckoned of grace, but of debt.

If a man works to get gain, when he is rewarded for his labor it is a simple matter of a debt paid, not grace given. It would be an insult to a workman to tell him that his pay was grace. *"And if by grace, then is it no more of works: otherwise grace is no more grace. But if it be of works, then is it no more grace: otherwise work is no more work (Romans 11:6)."* Works and grace are mutually exclusive as a basis for imputed righteousness. Grace will produce works, but as such, works are subservient to, and lesser than, the grace. The lesser cannot be a substitute for the greater. The effect, or the product, cannot become a part of the cause. To unequally yoke our feeble and incomplete works to the grace of God, expecting them to pull together, is an insult to grace. The grace of God will not share its glory with the feeble works of mortal men.

4:5 But to him that worketh not, but believeth on him that justifieth the ungodly, his faith is counted for righteousness.

This is the other side of the principle stated in verse 4. If one were justified by performing good works, the justification would not be justification at all; it would be adjudication resulting in exoneration, exculpation, and vindication—an earned recognition. On the other hand, if one is to have God's righteousness *counted* to him, personal righteousness is not a precondition. The only two conditions are **worketh not** and **believeth.**

This is amazing. Not only are good works unnecessary, they would actually prevent one from being justified by faith. The first condition is to cease from works of righteousness. The second is to believe.

In actuality, the *working not* and *believing* are one act and not two separate conditions, but we will analyze them separately.

This concept of *working not* as a condition for imputed righteousness runs all through the New Testament. Good works would not be an impediment to favor with God except as they are done in view of gaining that favor, in which case they are an affront to the grace that is offered. God is not rejecting goodness. He is rejecting the attitude behind the attempt to pay for past sins by present works. Does the sinner believe that his past sins are of so little consequence that present obedience wipes out the guilt? Present obedience is owed for the present. It has no bearing on the guilt or consequences of past sins. If a murderer were pulled from death row and offered a pardon, and he were to respond by volunteering to do one month of community service, it would be an insult to all concerned. At the very least, it would demean the value of the pardon. It would trivialize the crime. It would demonstrate a lack of appreciation for the pain he had inflicted on others. With the criminal making the offer, it would suggest that he thought one month of community service would answer to the value of the pardon.

The proper attitude, the one that society would demand of the guilty man receiving a pardon, is that of humble thankfulness and contrition. In the face of the offer of a gracious pardon, true goodness would express itself in an attitude of amazement that one so guilty and deserving of damnation as I should be pardoned by one so worthy, high, and holy. The end result should be worship, adoration, and surrender to the service of him who has given back a life that was deservedly lost. Thus the free gift of life is given only to those that are so convinced of their own moral bankruptcy as to have no hope in any self effort. In the state of hopelessness the believing sinner casts himself upon the mercy of God. Upon being pardoned, he is ever in a state of humble gratitude and worship. He feels himself to be totally bought with a price beyond repayment. He is eternally in the debt of him who gave the pardon—a most constructive attitude on which reformation can come to pass.

"For he that is entered into his rest, he also hath ceased from his own works, as God did from his (Hebrews 4:10)." God finished creation before He created Adam. Then Adam, though he may not have been conscious of it, spent his first morning on earth resting in the finished creation. Adam had done no labor, so he was resting from the work God had

just completed. He entered into God's rest.

Christ finished redemption, expecting us to rest in His finished work. If Adam had tried to complete or make additions to God's creation, it would have been an insult to the Creator. If man tries to secure salvation by engaging in good works, he is taking the Law lightly, not understanding his own sinfulness, and insulting the redemptive work of Christ.

"Therefore leaving the principles of the doctrine of Christ, let us go on unto perfection; not laying again the foundation of repentance from dead works, and of faith toward God (Hebrews 6:1)." The foundation of salvation is repentance *from* dead works. One must repent *from* his own works of righteousness in order to qualify to receive Christ's righteousness. The condition for receiving Christ's righteousness is to come without demanding conditions or offering any.

To profess trust in the gift of Christ's righteousness while continuing to perform works which we hope will make us acceptable is not *repentance from dead works.* Dead works are those works performed by dead men seeking to raise themselves to new life. When we see the depth of our own depravity, we will know the utter futility of offering our works.

Our works are not only to be left out of our reconciliation, but are to be viewed as a stain on our conscience. *"How much more shall the blood of Christ, who through the eternal Spirit offered himself without spot to God, <u>purge your conscience from dead works</u> to serve the living God (Hebrews 9:14)?"* When we rightly see ourselves, we will feel guilty for our best works. Our best moral moments when our humanity bleeds for others and our bodies are sacrificed in service are none the less occasions to repent in dust and sackcloth. When the prophet Isaiah saw God in all His glory, he said, *"Woe is me! for I am undone; because I am a man of unclean lips, and I dwell in the midst of a people of unclean lips: for mine eyes have seen the King, the* LORD *of hosts (Isaiah 6:5)."* The Psalmist said, *"...verily every man at his best state is altogether vanity (Psalm 39:5)."*

"In my hands no price I bring, simply to thy cross I cling, O Lamb of God I come."

...but believeth on him that justifieth the ungodly. Here is the second part of the condition for receiving the gift of righteousness. Keep in mind that *working not* and *believing* are inseparable.

"Then said they unto him, What shall we do, that we might work the works of God? Jesus answered and said unto them, This is the work of God, that ye believe on him whom he hath sent (John 6:28-29)." Many self-appointed defenders of the faith have been dissatisfied with this simple condition God has laid down. The large number of professing believers that demonstrate no relationship to Christ causes us to want to make the way narrower and the entrance exam more exacting. Nevertheless we must allow God to police His own kingdom. The illustration of Abraham

believing is sufficient to demonstrate the simplicity of what God means when He says, *"Believe on the Lord Jesus Christ and thou shalt be saved... (Acts 16:31)."* Abraham believed God concerning the birth of a child. We are to believe God concerning the Lord Jesus Christ. Any condition that would modify belief into some form of commitment or some degree of repentance from sin is to add works to grace. If faith is not faith and belief is not belief, what can a morally bankrupt sinner possible pull together that would make him more acceptable?

...but believeth on him **that justifieth the ungodly....** God justifies the ungodly. God does not justify the ungodly who have begun to be godly. He does not justify the ungodly who are sufficiently sorry for their ungodliness. He does not justify the ungodly who make Jesus the Lord of their lives. That would be a godly thing to do, would it not? He does not justify the ungodly who have repented of all their sins. Who ever heard of an ungodly man repenting of all his sins?

There is one word that best describes the attitude, actions, motives, and works of the one who is justified—**ungodly**. He is not like God in any way. He does not think like God, feel like God, love like God, or have the same commitments. An ungodly man is everything he shouldn't be and nothing he should be. He is without hope, promise, or possibility. He is dead in trespasses and sins. He is controlled by the world, the flesh, and the devil. He is in bondage, without strength of will or resolve. He can't lord it over a simple habit, much less "make Jesus the Lord of his life."

While in that state called **ungodly**, like a drowning man who finally gives up the struggle, he ceases to work toward acceptance with God. Sin so strangles him that he cannot make a move toward help. His hands are tied with guilt; his feet are immobilized by fear; his heart is failing from shame; his mind is too depraved to think a godly thought. Yet, the beauty of holiness attracts him. He longs to have what is beyond his moral reach.

In his condemned state he hears of Heaven's Darling who became flesh, endured all temptation, and qualified to be the first man to enter heaven fully accepted by the Father. His shame and sense of inadequacy only increases with the coming of this news. And then he hears the incredible: his sin is already paid for. Condemnation is lifted. The wrath of God rode the nails deep into the flesh of Jesus. The blood shed on Calvary poured out all the guilt, and His torn face bore all the shame. All guilty hands were nailed and all wandering feet were brought to bay when He was nailed. The body of sin was put to death, and with His last breath the Law was satisfied. With His resurrection, death was swallowed up in victory and Satan's hold was forever broken. He has sprinkled heaven with His blood, making it ground on which sinner and Savior can meet. He has now sent out a call for all that are ungodly to believe on Him.

Paul was not ashamed of this gospel, because by simple faith in Christ the vilest sinners are made clean. No one is too ungodly to come. Full provision is made for the very worst of sinners.

...his faith is counted for righteousness. See comments under 4:3. If God did not count faith for righteousness, the sinner has nothing else to count. Faith is all that is left to the sinner. Not faith within—as a resource, not faith that strengthens and gives courage, not faith that restores and lifts up, but faith that looks without, beyond to a promise of righteousness with no merit but the merit of Christ.

4:6 Even as David also describeth the blessedness of the man, unto whom God imputeth righteousness without works,
4:7 Saying, Blessed are they whose iniquities are forgiven, and whose sins are covered.
4:8 Blessed is the man to whom the Lord will not impute sin.

David also describeth.... Paul called Abraham as his star witness for the defense of the gospel. He now calls King David himself, the one known for his great sins, yet still the praise and glory of all Israel. David is a role model of repentance, yet he never suggested that his repentance in any way commended him to God.

Imputed righteousness

...imputeth.... This technical word is still quite common in legal circles. To those who are familiar with it, it is one of the most thrilling words in the Bible.

The Greek word translated imputeth (*logizomai*) carries a meaning broader than any single English word. The Greek mind was able to differentiate between the several shades of meaning inherent within this word, according to the context, just as the English mind readily differentiates between the various shades of meaning in the word love. In the Greek language one could not say "I love pizza, I love my friends, and I love God" without using three different words for love. However nothing is lost to the English mind when we use one word. We automatically understand the difference in love of pizza and love of God.

This one Greek word *logizomai* is translated in the King James Bible as: *impute, reckon, count, account, suppose, reason, think, number,* and several miscellaneous.

- Webster's dictionary defines *impute* as: To estimate, charge, think, to attribute, to reckon, to consider, to regard.
- It defines *account* as: To reckon or impute.
- It defines *number* as: To account, impute, or reckon.
- Though these words are nearly synonyms, there are subtle differences that enrich the meaning.
- *Impute,* as used by Paul, is not us reaching for reality, it is God act-

ing to define reality, not according to what we deserve, but according to His gracious forgiveness.

In the following paragraph we will use the various English synonyms that are employed to translate the one Greek word, *logizomai.* Perhaps this will help the reader to see both their similarities and their differences. The Bible uses them in a similar fashion.

If the accountant is *counting* his assets to see how much is available for purchasing, he *reckons* on those *numbers*. If there is not enough in the account, he withdraws from one account and *imputes* it to another. Once it is *imputed*, it can be *reckoned* to be the sum that has been *imputed,* and can be *counted* as such by the accountant. When a sum has been *imputed*, it has become a part of the total and can be *reckoned* to be so by both the accountant and any that would review his books.

God sent heaven's righteousness (Jesus) to live in human flesh. His body of flesh became the first and only sinless flesh, thereby qualified to enter heaven. In mortal flesh dwelt an immortal soul of eternal righteousness. Divine righteousness had become human righteousness. But instead of ascending to heaven, this one righteous man had the filth of all human sin laid on Him. *God made Jesus to be sin.* Sin was imputed to Christ that righteousness might be imputed to the sinner.

Jesus was *numbered/reckoned* among the transgressors (Isaiah 53:2; Luke 22:37), *made to be sin* (2 Corinthians 5:21), that God might *not impute sin* to the sinner (Romans 4:8). Rather, God *imputes righteousness* to those who believe (Romans 4:6) that we might *reckon* ourselves *"to be dead indeed unto sin but alive unto God (Romans 6:11)."*

...imputeth righteousness without works.... See 4:5 on works. Works are not only of no avail, they will actually prevent the imputation of righteousness.

4:7 Saying, Blessed are they whose iniquities are forgiven, and whose sins are covered.
4:8 Blessed is the man to whom the Lord will not impute sin.

He has quoted Psalm 32:1. See Psalms 85:2. Again Paul has confirmed by the use of Old Testament quotes that justification based on imputed righteousness was foreseen in both Abraham and David. David personally experienced the blessing of having his sin **forgiven** and **covered**. God forgives sin, but only on sound legal basis. The covering to which David alludes is a description of what occurred in the Levitical sacrifices. Sin was not removed; it was temporarily **covered** by the blood of animals. Nevertheless, based on the promise of a future sacrifice that would permanently cover sin, God was within the parameters of common justice *not imputing their sins unto them.*

Sin is not imputed to those in Christ, because Christ has already been *made sin for us (2 Corinthians 5:21).* God handles our sin as a single sum. Once Christ pays sin's debt, it cannot be accounted to another.

That would be double indemnity. As Christ bore the curse of our sin, we bear the blessing of His righteousness.

"*And the scripture was fulfilled, which saith, And he was* <u>*numbered*</u> *with the transgressors (Mark 15:28).*" This word *numbered* is the same Greek word, *logizomai,* that is translated as *impute, reckoned,* and *accounted.* So it was that Christ was *numbered, imputed, counted* among the transgressors, so we can be *counted, imputed, reckoned* among the righteous.

Christ did not actually do the sin that enabled Him to be *numbered* among the transgressors, and so it is that we the sinners do not actually do any of the righteousness that causes us to be *numbered* among the righteous. In a moment's time, by faith Christ received our sin; so in a moment's time, by faith sinners become righteous saints by the *gift of righteousness.*

4:9 Cometh this blessedness then upon the circumcision only, or upon the uncircumcision also? for we say that faith was reckoned to Abraham for righteousness.

10 How was it then reckoned? when he was in circumcision, or in uncircumcision? Not in circumcision, but in uncircumcision.

Is this blessing of imputed righteousness reserved only for those under the Law (the circumcision)? The timing is pertinent to Paul's argument. If Abraham was *reckoned/imputed/counted* to be righteous after he was circumcised, then circumcision could be construed to be a condition for the imputation of righteousness. If however—as was the case—he was declared to be righteous before he was circumcised, then circumcision is not a condition for justification.

In Genesis 15:6, before Ishmael was born, righteousness was imputed to Abraham. After the birth of Ishmael (recorded in Genesis 17:11), Abraham received the command of circumcision. Though Abraham is the father of the Jewish people, he died several hundred years before the Law was given. Abraham was never under the Law. His imputed righteousness occurred prior to (outside of) that legal system.

Furthermore, Abraham received the imputation of *righteousness by faith* long before he was circumcised. Therefore, *righteousness by faith* predates both circumcision and the Law, making it independent of either. Since Abraham was made righteous by faith and not by the works of the Jewish Law, it stands to reason that a gentile without that Law and circumcision can be made righteous as well.

4:11 And he received the sign of circumcision, a seal of the righteousness of the faith which he had yet being uncircumcised: that he might be the father of all them that believe, though they be not circumcised; that righteousness might be

imputed unto them also:

This word for **sign** is also translated *wonder*. It is a special indicator or attestation to. Circumcision is a sign pointing to the fact that God has chosen the Israelites. Signs are given to point to things that already exist. Abraham was already counted as righteous.

Circumcision is also called a **seal**. A seal is that by which a thing is confirmed, proven, or authenticated. It is placed to show ownership. Abraham already belonged to God, and was already justified by faith when the sign and seal were placed in his flesh.

This **righteousness of the faith** is the same as discussed in 4:3. He had this gift of righteousness many years before he was circumcised.

...that he might be the father of all them that believe, though they be not circumcised; He has made the point that Abraham received the imputed righteousness of faith before he was circumcised, *that he might be the father of all them that believe*, including uncircumcised gentiles. If Abraham had received the gift of righteousness after circumcision, he would have been the father of the circumcised only. Abraham was not the father of the Jews until after his circumcision and the birth of Isaac. Until then, he was still part of the gentile race.

Abraham becomes the father of the Jewish race through natural descent, but he also becomes the father of all them that believe by being the forerunner of righteousness by faith. One should not confuse the physical descendants of Abraham with the spiritual descendants.

4:12 And the father of circumcision to them who are not of the circumcision only, but who also walk in the steps of that faith of our father Abraham, which he had being yet uncircumcised.

This verse says that Abraham is father in two ways. He is the physical father of all Jews who follow him in circumcision, and he is the spiritual father of all who follow him in faith. So Abraham can be the spiritual father of a much greater number than just those that have been circumcised. Abraham is the father of all believers, circumcised or not, Jew or gentile. Paul is including the circumcised Jew that is also a believer in the spiritual descendants of Abraham, just as he is including the uncircumcised gentile.

To be very clear, so as not to blur a distinction meant to be maintained, gentiles can enter the faith line of Abraham by believing, but gentiles cannot enter the bloodline by believing. There is no such thing as a gentile becoming a spiritual Jew. Only a Jew can be a spiritual Jew, and that upon believing. A believing gentile is of the seed of Abraham only in a faith sense. Remember, Abraham was not a Jew. Gentiles are never called *the seed of Jacob*, from whence come Jews. Let a circumcised Jew remain a Jew and let a believing Jew or gentile who shares the faith of Abraham be of the seed of Abraham by faith.

4:13 For the promise, that he should be the heir of the world, was not to Abraham, or to his seed, through the law, but through the righteousness of faith.

See comments under 4:10.

When Abraham received promise of future blessings extending to many nations (Genesis 12:3), the Law of Moses had not yet been given—it would be more than 400 years. Since the promise was established before the Law, it cannot come under the Law's jurisdiction nor depend upon it. And since the Law comes out of the promise rather than the promise coming out of the Law, the promise is more enduring. Righteousness of faith began before the Law and extends to the present. Paul has demonstrated the superiority of the *promise* over the *Law*—a difficult concession for Jews, but a great blessing for gentiles.

4:14 For if they which are of the law be heirs, faith is made void, and the promise made of none effect:

Paul concedes that if the natural descendants of Abraham (the Jews) are automatic recipients of the blessings (the blessings of salvation), then the promise which preceded the Law (that God would bless the world through the seed—Christ) is no longer in power. If the promise is fulfilled through the Law, then we have nothing, because the Law is a conditional covenant. The blessings of the Law are conditioned upon obedience, whereas the blessings of the promise are unconditional. Paul has already proven in chapter 3 that the Law has been universally broken. A broken law cannot deliver its blessings. Therefore if the promise is part of the Law, then the blessings of the promise would no longer be available. In a conditional covenant, when the law is broken the promise is broken.

4:15 Because the law worketh wrath: for where no law is, there is no transgression.

The presence of the Law makes obedience absolutely essential, otherwise condemnation and wrath are all it will produce. The principle is simple: the Law, delivering wrath, cannot also deliver a blessing. Therefore the Law cannot be the source of blessing.

....for where no law is, there is no transgression. In contrast, since the promise is without law, unconditional, there can be no transgression to bring wrath and get in the way of the blessing. With no laws, they cannot transgress their side of the covenant. The promise was given before the Law, without conditions, and is therefore still in effect, not negated when the Law was broken.

4:16 Therefore it is of faith, that it might be by grace; to the end the promise might be sure to all the seed; not to that only which is of the law, but to that also which is of the faith of Abraham; who is the father of us all,

Therefore... As if in a courtroom, Paul gives the sum of all the evidence presented thus far.

Therefore **it is of faith,** (the blessing of salvation) **that it might be by grace** (thus being free from the limitations of Law). Since the promise was before the Law, since the promise is unconditional, since the Law worketh wrath, since circumcision came after the promise, since David describes the *blessedness* of imputed righteousness, since grace excludes the possibility of boasting, since all can be justified by grace, and since the Scripture foresaw just such righteousness of faith, therefore it is of faith, **that it might be by grace.** Grace is God's free provision for us. The only way to institute a just grace is the path Paul has proposed. *"For the law was given by Moses, but grace and truth came by Jesus Christ (John 1:17)."*

The righteousness of faith is by *promise*, not Law. It is by faith and grace, **to the end the promise might be sure to all the seed; not to that only which is of the law, but to that also which is of the faith of Abraham; who is the father of us all.**

Paul adds a closing argument. This amendment is not demonstrative proof of his point, or he would have given it before his conclusion. It is actually a result, or by product, of what he has proposed. He gives it as added incentive to encourage his reader to give a verdict in favor of the gospel of Jesus Christ. The end result of righteousness being given by grace through faith is that there is absolute assurance of receiving the promised blessing. This assurance is not only to those who are under the Law but equally to those who have never been under Law. Anyone who is of the faith of Abraham, that is, believes God as did Abraham, receives the blessing and can claim Abraham as Father in the faith.

4:17 (As it is written, I have made thee a father of many nations,) before him whom he believed, even God, who quickeneth the dead, and calleth those things which be not as though they were.

Quoting Genesis 17:4, Paul begins a description of Abraham's faith. The quote, **"As it is written, I have made thee a father of many nations,"** is given to show that God originally included *many nations* in this promise of righteousness by faith, thereby making Abraham the father of all such as should believe.

Read verse 16, leaving out the parenthetical phrase of 17, and the sense is clear. *"...who is the father of us all...* **before him whom he believed, even God...."** Abraham is the father of all who believe God as he did. Abraham is the forerunner of justification by faith without works. He is the first to whom God chose to reveal His grace in this manner.

...who quickeneth the dead.... The **dead** were Abraham and Sarah in their inability to produce children. This is a parallel to the unregenerate man's inability to produce spiritual life. We were *dead* in our sins (Ephesians 2:1-3).

In that dead state Abraham **believed** in the God who could **quicken,** make alive in a childbearing sense, their dead bodies.

...calleth those things which be not.... God can **call** a dead body something it is **not**—alive. God called Abraham the father of a great nation when Sarah and he were yet unable to produce children.

...as though they were.... In this we see the very nature of faith. Faith is believing God in His statements about the as yet unseen. God calls the believer righteous when he is yet a sinner. The sinner, who has never seen a day of righteousness in his life, is told to believe that he is recipient of the gift of righteousness, and is therefore without sin in God's sight. God calls the sinner *"the righteousness of God (2 Corinthians 5:21)"* when experience demonstrates the opposite. Abraham had to believe what he couldn't see 25 years before it became seeable. Likewise the sinner must believe what he cannot see (the righteousness of Christ imputed to his account) an entire lifetime before he ever sees its reality.

4:18 Who against hope believed in hope, that he might become the father of many nations, according to that which was spoken, So shall thy seed be.

Hope is the joyful anticipation of a yet future event—the event being counted as a certainty. If you are not vitally familiar with the background story of Abraham, you should read it now. In Genesis 12:3, the promise is first given to Abraham. It is periodically restated and confirmed: 13:15-16; 15:5-6; 16:10-12; 17:2-8; 18:18; 21:18; 22:17-18; 26:3-4; 28:4; 28:13-14; 32:12.

Who against hope believed in hope.... God called a man to be the father of a great nation. The promise was that through his descendants he would become a blessing to all nations. The man was Abraham, 75 years old (Genesis 12:4), and married to a woman that had been barren all her life (Genesis 11:30). At that time, Abraham was still fertile, but Sarah wasn't. It would have taken a miracle to give them the promised child.

God gave Abraham a piece of property, Palestine, and told him to walk over it. He walked over it for 11 years, and still the promise was not fulfilled. Sarah remained barren. It was obvious that Abraham himself would soon become incapable of producing seed.

He lost hope in a miracle to restore Sarah, and attempted to fulfill God's promise through Sarah's Egyptian handmaid. Born to him was Ishmael, who would become the progenitor of the Arabic people. When Ishmael was 13 years old (now 24 years since the promise was given), God again confirmed to Abraham that he would have the promised child through his barren wife Sarah. Abraham thought it was so funny that he fell down laughing (Genesis 17:17), for he was 99 years old and now past seed production himself. Sarah had long since grown too old, so Abraham now had no hope of bearing a child through anyone, how much less through Sarah?

Nevertheless, God assured Abraham that out of his loins and Sarah's womb would come a great nation. It would take a double miracle. It was **against hope,** but Abraham considered Him who was making the promise and **believed in hope**. That is, **against** the natural possibility of it happening, **against** the hope of such, he believed God, and thereby had hope based on the promise of God.

Righteousness had been imputed to Abraham before he was 85 years old, before Ishmael was born, when Abraham could still produce seed. God counted Abraham righteous by faith at a time when it was easier to believe than it would be at 99 when he would be beyond seed production. The unbelief that followed, expressed in producing a child through Hagar and laughing at God's announcement, did not render him unrighteous. That which God had given by unconditional promise could not be taken back. Abraham was still accounted righteous.

...that he might become the father of many nations, according to that which was spoken.... All nations that have believed the gospel and followed Christ do walk in the faith of Abraham.

So shall thy seed be. *"Now to Abraham and his seed were the promises made. He saith not, And to seeds, as of many; but as of one, And to thy seed, which is Christ (Galatians 3:16)."* The promised seed of Abraham is the same promised seed of Genesis 3:15, which seed (singular) is neither Jew nor gentile, but Christ alone. By believing on Christ, one is baptized by the Spirit into the body of Christ, and thus, becoming part of that one body, one becomes a part of that promised seed (singular) of Abraham.

4:19 And being not weak in faith, he considered not his own body now dead, when he was about an hundred years old, neither yet the deadness of Sara's womb:

It was funny and ridiculous to Abraham until God spoke His promise; then it was fact. Faith is not an inner resource. It is not a power we possess. All men have faith in many things. Faith is simply believing the word of another concerning the yet unseen. In order to believe what we do not yet see, we must have confidence in the source of our information. Our faith cannot be any greater than our confidence in the one making the promise. Nor will our faith be any less than our confidence in the one making the promise. So our faith or lack therefore is not a reflection on our power to believe, but on our confidence in the source of information. If a man doesn't believe God, it is not because he is weak in faith, it is because he doesn't regard the integrity of the God who made the promise.

Abraham considered both sides. On the one side was his old body, dead to seed production, and Sarah's body, never capable of having children, and now well past age. On the other side was the promise of God.

Weighing the impossible against the word of God, he didn't even bother to consider the impossible. He believed God.

4:20 He staggered not at the promise of God through unbelief; but was strong in faith, giving glory to God;

At 99 years old, Abraham probably staggered at everything else, but he did not **stagger at the promise** of God. At this point, when the word of God was clearly stated and understood, failure to believe would not have been the same as lack of faith; it would have been **unbelief**. Lack of faith is that absence of a response, maybe the result of being ignorant of a promise to believe. But *unbelief* is an aggressive act in itself. It is an exercise of the will to reject God's promise. To be **strong in faith** is to value the word of God above the sight of the eyes. That kind of belief gives glory to God because it is a vote of confidence in His character. It is letting *"God be true and every man a liar (Romans 3:4)."*

4:21 And being fully persuaded that, what he had promised, he was able also to perform.

Abraham had no confidence in his faith. He did not think that he would create reality with his faith. He did not believe that believing would cause God to act. He was not trying to "hold on until the blessing came through." This was no partial, struggling attempt to believe. He was not looking within for the strength to keep believing. He was **fully persuaded** that the thing God promises to do, He is **able also to perform**. God's promise was the object of his focus, not his faith. Faith was a byproduct of the promise. The promise was not a byproduct of his faith.

A promise based on the will and work of God is a certainty that draws faith out of the otherwise faithless. As such, faith is not a condition for the fulfillment of the promise; it is a condition to personally entering the blessings associated with the promise. The promise is unconditional; the personal blessings are conditional. Abraham was not persuaded of the effectiveness of his faith; he was persuaded of the effectiveness of the God who made the promise. Doubtlessly Abraham did not feel the weight of responsibility, as if his faith were the bridge on which God would accomplish His work. Abraham felt himself to be an observer of events, not a catalyst. It was God's ability and willingness **to perform** His own promise that drew faith out of Abraham.

4:22 And therefore it was imputed to him for righteousness.

The promise of God caused Abraham to believe, and the faith was counted for righteousness. It has all the appearances of a free, grace endowment. See 4:6-8 for a discussion of imputed righteousness.

4:23 Now it was not written for his sake alone, that it was imputed to him;

4:24 But for us also, to whom it shall be imputed, if we believe on him that raised up Jesus our Lord from the dead;

It was not for Abraham's sake that God recorded this event of Abraham becoming the heir of righteousness by faith. God anticipated the many that would eventually participate in this same righteousness through faith in Jesus Christ.

Abraham believed God concerning the birth of a child. We believe God concerning Christ's resurrection.

4:25 Who was delivered for our offenses, and was raised again for our justification.

The focal point and ground of our justification is the vicarious death of Jesus Christ, which paid for our offenses, and the resurrection, which secured our justification.

Christ was **delivered** (as a criminal is taken from prison and judgment Isaiah 53:8) by the judicial arm of government to the executioners.

...for our offenses.... We offended God through our carnality and unbelief. The sentence is announced that we should be executed. The sword of justice is prepared to shed our blood; but alas, Jesus is *delivered* to the place of execution in our stead.

Christ **was raised again for our justification**. The cross of Christ did not justify the sinner. The cross meets justice in paying the price for sins, but though forgiveness of sins will remove any breach caused by the sin, it does not imply elevation to a state higher than that from which sin plunged us. The offended party may forgive the offender, but the offender is not thereby instated into the family as a son. But since the believer is baptized into the body of Christ, and thereby becomes a participant in Christ, the resurrection of Christ becomes the resurrection of everyone who is in Christ. God receives sons, not as they walk away from the cross, but as they come out of the tomb. His resurrection is our justification.

5:1-11 Fruits of Justification

Paul continues his systematic presentation of the gospel. Having concluded his proof of man's sinfulness (1:18-3:23), and then presented God's program of justification (a righteousness that is by faith, imputed to the believer by God), he now moves into what is commonly, though not altogether accurately, called "sanctification."

Keep in mind Paul's overriding purpose. Though his initial readers may be sympathetic with his position, they have doubtlessly been lambasted with all the best arguments of the unbelieving Jewish community. For the benefit of the believing community, he is answering the charges levied against the gospel. It basically comes down to Law versus grace, faith versus works, Moses versus Christ.

He now defends his position offensively. He will extol the fruit and blessings of the gospel. He has anticipated this approach ever since 1:16 when he proclaimed that the gospel was the *power* of God unto salvation—not just a proscribed way, but a means to actual deliverance from sin. He now enumerates the fruits of the gospel.

5:1 Therefore being justified by faith, we have peace with God through our Lord Jesus Christ:

The present discussion is not of justification; rather, he is proclaiming the fruit of justification—the first fruit being **peace with God**. This is not the inner peace of one's personal experience. It is objective peace. When we were enemies of God and the wrath of God abided upon us, Jesus Christ brought in a reign of peace through His mediation as sacrifice and advocate. *"For he is our peace, who hath made both one, and hath broken down the middle wall of partition between us; Having abolished in his flesh the enmity, even the law of commandments contained in ordinances; for to make in himself of twain one new man, so making peace; And that he might reconcile both unto God in one body by the cross, having slain the enmity thereby: And came and preached peace to you which were afar off, and to them that were nigh (Ephesians 2:14-17)."* See also *Colossians 1:20-22; Hebrews 13:20.*

This **peace** is a gift of God to the sinner when he is yet without any sense of peace. It actually precedes any personal experience of peace. This *peace* was made by Christ when he silenced the demands of justice by the blood of His cross. It is then offered to the sinner as a gift. This *peace* is singular. It is not the many states of personal peace felt by individuals. The one *peace* was made by Christ before any of us were born. All who have the peace of God have become beneficiaries of that singular conquest of Christ.

But the outer peace (that is believed) definitely makes for an inner peace that is felt. If there is one thing that would commend the gospel to the common man it is the promise of personal peace. Theology aside, all men have a longing to be at peace. No other religion or philosophy is efficacious, as is the gospel, in bringing complete peace.

5:2 By whom also we have access by faith into this grace wherein we stand, and rejoice in hope of the glory of God.

By whom also we have access.... Sinners are denied access to a holy God. Adam was shut out of the garden, and the daily visits from God ceased. As representative man, Jesus earned access to the Father. In Him we too share that ready access. It is not a reluctant access. We are welcomed into the Father's presence through the Son. All barriers are removed. The former rebels are now welcomed as family members into God's presence and provision. This peace and *access* is experienced in Christ alone.

...by faith.... It is not by the works of the Law, thus not for Jews only. Faith opens the door for *whosoever will.*

...into his grace.... The struggling sinner, having spent his life as an enemy of God, is not only given the gift of peace, but he is given unequivocal *access* into the assisting **grace** of God. Faith is the channel; grace is the destination.

There is a general misunderstanding as to grace. Grace is not similar to mercy. It is not God's sentiment toward us. Grace is the actual provision of God through the work of Christ. All that is ours through the work of Christ is the grace of God. *"For the law was given by Moses, but grace and truth came by Jesus Christ (John 1:17)." "And he said unto me, My grace is sufficient for thee: for my strength is made perfect in weakness. Most gladly therefore will I rather glory in my infirmities, that the power of Christ may rest upon me (2 Corinthians 12:9)."* See also: Ephesians 2: 5-7; Ephesians 4:7-11. The gifts of grace include the ministers to the church (1 Peter 3: 7).

...wherein we stand.... Having been placed into this relationship of access and grace, we stand—abide there as one occupying a position of authority. The word **stand** is used 289 times in the Holy Bible, and it rarely refers to someone in the vertical, immobile position. The believer *stands* on the ground of God's grace as a man in court *stands* on evidence that will clear him. *"That your faith should not <u>stand</u> in the wisdom of men, but in the power of God (1 Corinthians 2:5)." "Moreover, brethren, I declare unto you the gospel which I preached unto you, which also ye have received, and wherein ye <u>stand</u> (1 Corinthians 15:1)."* See also: 1 Corinthians 16:13; Galatians 5:1, 6:11-14; 1 Peter 5:12.

...and rejoice in hope of the glory of God. We *stand* in anticipation (**rejoice in hope**) of the coming glory. The eye of faith sees the coming glory as a certainty. The ever-present anticipation of sharing in that glory causes the believer to **rejoice.**

In 2:7, describing the aspirations of all men, Paul says they, *"seek for **glory** and honour."* Fallen man ever has a desire to be back in the presence of the original glory. Jesus is called, *"the Lord of **glory** (1 Corinthians 2:8)."*

*"But if the ministration of death, written and engraven in stones, was **glorious**, so that the children of Israel could not stedfastly behold the face of Moses for the **glory** of his countenance; which **glory** was to be done away: How shall not the ministration of the spirit be rather **glorious**? For if the ministration of condemnation be **glory**, much more doth the ministration of righteousness exceed in **glory**. For even that which was made **glorious** had no **glory** in this respect, by reason of the **glory** that excelleth. For if that which is done away was **glorious**, much more that which remaineth is **glorious** (2 Corinthians 3:7-11)."* See also: 2 Corinthians 3:18; Hebrews 2:7-10; 3:3; 1 Peter 1:11.

5:3 And not only so, but we glory in tribulations also: knowing that tribulation worketh patience;

...**not only** is the believer given peace and access into grace, but he is caused to **glory** when he suffers tribulation for his faith. Paul is commending the gospel in its ability to make use of what would normally be thought of as a negative experience—tribulation. That which is despised under the law is turned into a blessing under the gospel. One of the strange marks of the early church was the eagerness with which the confessors embraced their crosses, burning stakes, and the beasts of their own destruction. During the first three centuries, to become a Christian was to accept the probability of a martyr's death.

- *"For our light affliction, which is but for a moment, worketh for us a far more exceeding and eternal weight of **glory** (2 Corinthians 4:17)."*

- *"If I must needs glory, I will **glory** of the things which concern mine infirmities (2 Corinthians 11:30)."*

- *"But the God of all grace, who hath called us unto his eternal **glory** by Christ Jesus, after that ye have suffered a while, make you perfect, stablish, strengthen, settle you (1Peter 5:10)."*

This is a little touch of the practical inserted into Paul's great theological work. Yet it is part of his argument on the superiority of faith and grace over the Law and circumcision. No one living under the Law had peace, access, lived in grace, rejoiced in hope of a coming experience of the glory of God, and finally—and most certainly—no one under the Law could glory in tribulation. To glory in one's **tribulation** could only be the manifestation of an inner life far superior to what the letter of the Law could produce.

The believer glories in tribulation knowing that **tribulation worketh patience**. That is tribulation, the trials and difficulties of this life, especially those that arise as a result of being a believer, will actually produce a very desired virtue—**patience**. *"But in all things approving ourselves as the ministers of God, in much **patience**, in afflictions, in necessities, in distresses, In stripes, in imprisonments, in tumults, in labours, in watchings, in fastings; By pureness, by knowledge, by longsuffering, by kindness, by the Holy Ghost, by love unfeigned, By the word of truth, by the power of God, by the armour of righteousness on the right hand and on the left (2 Corinthians 6:4-7)."* See also: Col. 1:11; 1 Thessalonians 1:3; 2 Thessalonians 1:4; Hebrews 6:12, 10:36; James 1:3-4, 5:10-11; 2 Peter 1:6; Revelation 13:10, 14:12.

Obviously, for one to glory in suffering because it *"worketh for us a far more exceeding and eternal weight of glory (2 Corinthians 4:17),"* one would have to value the eternal more than the temporal. Such becomes the true test of a believer. *"Where your treasure is there is your heart also."* When we identify our treasures we have located our hearts.

We also can identify our treasures by admitting to what thrills and depresses us. Treasures are hidden in the heart before they are mounted in public.

5:4 And patience, experience; and experience, hope:

Tribulation produces patience **and patience** produces **experience....** Tribulation is at the head of a chain of blessings. Many seek to avoid the very fountain from which comes spiritual maturity. Others mistakenly have sought tribulation as a way to enter a deeper walk. Tribulation is involuntary. If it is sought or induced, it ceases to be tribulation. It becomes spiritual sadism. There are those who fall into a kind of asceticism and seek hardship as a way to be sanctified. This stoicism is self-rewarding, and has its end with all works of the flesh.

Other than the normal trials of life, it is the struggle of darkness against light that produces tribulation. Believers who walk in holiness are a source of embarrassment to those who claim that sin is inevitable. It is a wonder how the unregenerate can hate the truth. In every government there will be those in power who feel it is their duty to stamp out the truth of Christ. Where there is genuine Christianity, there will be persecution, which produces tribulation. Yet some tribulation comes from the natural course of life as a result of the curse upon all flesh.

Where genuine tribulation is met with faith, the assisting grace of God uses the suffering to produce **patience**. There is a chain reaction—starting with tribulation; the virtues follow. Patience comes from the eye of faith, which sees beyond the immediate into eternity. Patience causes one to endure. When in faith one patiently endures trials, over time it creates many **experiences** of the grace of God. The many experiences of life are woven together to create one's personal tapestry. We are the accumulation of our experiences.

Hope is produced as we see the provisions of grace and keep our eyes on the future glory. Biblical hope is not wishful desires. It is confident anticipation of that which is yet future, still unseen, but we know it is coming. There is absolute certainty in Biblical hope. *"Remembering without ceasing your work of faith, and labour of love, **and patience of hope** in our Lord Jesus Christ, in the sight of God and our Father (1 Thessalonians 1:3)." "For we are saved by **hope**: but **hope** that is seen is not **hope**: for what a man seeth, why doth he yet **hope** for? But if we **hope** for that we see not, then do we with patience wait for it (Romans 8:24-25)." "If in this life only we have **hope** in Christ, we are of all men most miserable (1 Corinthians 15:19)." "For the **hope** which is laid up for you in heaven, whereof ye heard before in the word of the truth of the gospel (Colossians 1:5)." "Beloved, now are we the sons of God, and it doth not yet appear what we shall be: but we know that, when he shall appear, we shall be like him; for we shall see him as he*

Isaiah And every man that hath this **hope** *in him purifieth himself, even as he is pure (1 John 3:2-3)."* See also 2 Corinthians 3:12; Ephesians 1:18; Col. 1:27; 1 Timothy 1:1; Titus 1:2, 2:13; Hebrews 3:6, 6:18-19; 1 Peter 1:3

5:5 And hope maketh not ashamed; because the love of God is shed abroad in our hearts by the Holy Ghost which is given unto us.

We glory in tribulations because *tribulation* produces *patience*, and patience produces *experience*, and experience produces **hope.** No other belief system is able to capitalize on something as negative as tribulation and turn it into virtues. Most belief systems are designed to protect one from adversity, whereas Christ employs even tribulation to work good for the believer. If even the bad things can be used for good, then nothing could come into the life of a believer that would make him **ashamed** of his association with Christ.

In other words, when we place our confidence in the promises of God, and with hope wait for the fulfillment, we will never be ashamed of our confessions. God will not leave us empty.

The Law failed to realize its promise of life (Romans 7:10) even in a single individual. As a plan of salvation, the Law was a total failure. You would be ashamed if you brought someone to the Law and offered him forgiveness and life. The Law gave no assistance to the frail sinner. The Law was *weak through the flesh (Romans 8:3)*. But what the *law could not do, the law of the spirit of life in Christ Jesus* is able to accomplish.

The early Christians were persecuted unto death on a charge of atheism. They had no visible God, no earthly temple, no object of worship, nothing by which they could say, "Come, see my religion." The Jew was busy with his observance of special days, of fastings, and set times for prayers. The sound of trumpets and the garments of their priests testified to their deep religious devotion. There was a law for every event of the day. But the hope of the Christian was unseen. They all *"died in faith, having not seen the promise."* There was only one present reality that sustained the believer, and it was unseen, internal—**the love of God shed abroad in our hearts**.

It is not our love, but God's great love to us that causes us to glory in tribulation for His sake. *"Herein is love, not that we loved God, but that he loved us, and sent his Son to be the propitiation for our sins (1 John 4:10)."*

The Law commanded love, but it could never induce love. The superiority of the gospel over the Law is the ever-present love of God flowing like a river from one believer to another throughout the Roman empire. *"By this shall all men know that ye are my disciples, if ye have love one to another (John 13:35)."*

It was by the **Holy Ghost** that the love of God was experienced. See 1 John 4. There must be a continual experience of the Spirit of God in order for this love to be manifested. We will cover this more thoroughly in chapter 8.

5:6 For when we were yet without strength, in due time Christ died for the ungodly.

For.... The love of God is in our hearts, *for (because)* when we were powerless to help ourselves, Christ died in our place.

We *glory in tribulation* and are *not ashamed* because we know that when we were **yet without strength** to overcome fear of death, to do the righteousness of the Law, to commend ourselves to God in any way, Christ nonetheless **died** for us.

...yet without strength.... He is emphasizing that Christ made His offering when we were still in a hopeless state, *without strength* to obey the Law. There is no such offering in the Law, a foreshadowing yes, but no efficacious provision for the ungodly. It is understandable that God should be gracious to the sinner that is struggling to come into line with God's program, but to die for one who is still enslaved, one who has made no move to seek God, is a wonder indeed.

Christ died for the **ungodly.** Did he not die for the repentant, for the humble, for the sincere, for the elect? No! Christ died only for all that are **ungodly.** Their character, all their thoughts, their deeds, all were ungodly. It is lust and unbelief that renders them ungodly. They are rebels and enemies of all that is righteous. The parade of ungodly includes Sodomites, murderers, child molesters, rapists, thieves, preachers, and mothers. They are *all as an unclean thing*, and yet He died for each and every one, bearing the sin of the whole world (1 John 2:2).

In **due time** Christ died. Some have wondered why Christ did not come and die sooner. *"But when the fulness of the time was come, God sent forth his Son, made of a woman, made under the law (Galatians 4:4)."* Christ came at the most opportune time, at a time when conditions were ripe for the reception of the message. His coming was prophesied, and in *due time* He came as promised by Daniel. So the timing was according to God's planning. Christ came when the ground was able to receive the seed. Political and spiritual conditions had to be right lest the gospel message be laid aside and forgotten. Most probably, if Christ had come at another time, the church would not have survived.

It was the dispensation of Law that brought the Jewish nation to a condition suited for the message of the gospel.

5:7 For scarcely for a righteous man will one die: yet peradventure for a good man some would even dare to die.

Paul is emphasizing the significance of Christ dying for the ungodly. Remember, this section is not to teach the sinner about salvation. It is directed to the believer already in Christ. To impress upon us the depth of our position and the provision that is in Christ, he presses the point that it was a great act of grace that put us into God's favor.

He draws our attention to the fact that it is rare to hear of someone giving his life to save another, even when the one in peril is a **righteous man**. Yet, perhaps, you have heard of a remote incident where someone gave his life to save a **good man**. It occurs, but it is rare. Note he assumes that no one has ever heard of someone dying to save an evil man from his destruction. What would be the purpose in saving an evil enemy who was committed to the ruin of all that is holy?

5:8 But God commendeth his love toward us, in that, while we were yet sinners, Christ died for us.

But, in contrast to what is expected, God **commendeth** (to advance or set forth, to recommend) his **love toward us**. The import of this act is that **while we were yet** (still in our state of rebellion) sinners, Christ died **for us**. Wonder of all wonders! The Most Holy is dying for the most unholy.

5:9 Much more then, being now justified by his blood, we shall be saved from wrath through him.

Who would believe such could be true, that the thundering God of Sinai, the righteous judge of all the earth, would die for miserable sinners? How wonderful!

Already Paul has proven that the gospel is superior to the Law, yet there is much more than what he has already proclaimed. Verses 6-8 were given in anticipation of the *much more* of this verse. Justification is not the end. It is that which sets the past right, but God has a plan for the future, that we **be saved** (future) from wrath **through him**. The penalty of sin is lifted and Hell has lost its power over those in Christ.

...being now justified.... God has justified all who believe. The word *justify* is used in different ways in the Scripture: God justifies Himself; man justifies God; man justifies himself; and then the more popular understanding, God justifies the sinner. The word itself simply has to do with being absolved of blame, guilt, or penal consequences in a matter. When God justifies one, that one is declared by the highest court to be righteous. He is cleared of all blame and all charges. There can be no higher commendation. See comments under 3:24.

...justified by his blood.... This justification was declared in regard to one known to be guilty. The Law was broken and cried out for vengeance. Agreeing with the just demand of the Law, Jesus took on himself flesh and blood so that He might die and shed His blood on behalf of those whom He would save. Without just payment for sin, there could be no justification.

Our justification is not the result of a biased Sovereign, playing loose with the Law, signing his name to a pardon without regard to the legal consequences. Jesus took on himself the likeness of sinful flesh so He might die a real death on behalf of sinners. The blood of Christ is not incidental to salvation. *"And almost all things are by the law purged with blood; and without shedding of blood is no remission (Hebrews 9:22)."* See comments under 3:25.

"Forasmuch then as the children are partakers of flesh and blood, he also himself likewise took part of the same; that through death he might destroy him that had the power of death, that is, the devil; And deliver them who through fear of death were all their lifetime subject to bondage (Hebrews 2:14-15)."

5:10 For if, when we were enemies, we were reconciled to God by the death of his Son, much more, being reconciled, we shall be saved by his life.

Paul is demonstrating from history that God is fully committed to our ongoing deliverance and blessing. Two wonders are connected with our present state of reconciliation. First, it was while we were still enemies that God made the move to save us. Second, it was at the high cost of the very blood of God's son. Now if God made such an investment when we were still enemies, how much more is he now willing to do toward our ongoing salvation now that we are in fact reconciled to God. The high cost was paid at the beginning. With such an investment, surely God will continue this salvation until its consummation.

...much more... The *much more* reflects back to the extraordinary statement that we were reconciled while still enemies. What could be more astounding? Doing thus, surely God has done all. Yet, as magnanimous as that is, God is prepared to do *much more*. To be justified does not exhaust the benefits of grace. God is still involved in the process. Over and above being reconciled, we can be assured that in the future we will **be saved** from the power of sin through His resurrected **life**. He who died for us now lives for us with the same dedication. His death saved us from the penalty of sin, and now his life will save us daily from the power of sin.

"Wherefore he is able also to save them to the uttermost that come unto God by him, seeing he ever liveth to make intercession for them (Hebrews 7:25)." See also John 14:19-20; Ephesians 2:19.

5:11 And not only so, but we also joy in God through our Lord Jesus Christ, by whom we have now received the atonement.

With verse 10, it seemed that all was said that could be said. What more is possible? Was there ever such a gospel as this? But when it appears that he has heaped more on us than we can imagine, he reveals that there is more. Reconciled while enemies, saved by His life, **and not only**

so, but also..., and Paul continues to enumerate the blessings of grace.

And not only are we *justified by faith*, have *peace with God*, *access* into the provision of *grace*, made to *rejoice in hope of the glory*, caused to *glory in tribulation*, assured that the *hope* will *not make us ashamed*, the *love of God* Himself is planted in our hearts, we have been given the *Holy Ghost*, Christ did all this when we were *without strength, ungodly, yet sinners*, and *enemies*, and all of this *justification* was based on God's own *blood*, we *will be saved* from future *wrath*, we will be saved from the power of sin by his continuing *life, and not only so, but we also joy in God through our Lord Jesus Christ by whom we have now received the atonement.* Paul has impressed me. I readily lay aside the Law and stand in Jesus Christ alone.

Atonement—answering the critics

Bible critics say the word *atonement* is "an unfortunate translation." Though the Old Testament uses it 81 times, mostly in reference to the old covenant sacrifices, they say it should never be used in regard to the work of Christ.

This one and only usage of the English word *atonement* in the New Testament is a translation of the Greek word *katallage*, which appears ten times in Greek, and is translated *reconcile* nine times out of the ten. "Inconsistent, cry the critics." But that is just a smokescreen, for those even lightly familiar with Greek know that seldom is a Greek word translated with a single word in every usage. This is true in any cross language translation. From one language to another, words seldom have a singular exact counterpart. Context dictates the shade of meaning. It is not unusual to see a single Greek or Hebrew word translated with ten to fifteen different synonyms—in any English translation. No linguists would question the general wisdom or necessity of this practice, regardless of the translator's bias.

But the real problem, they say, is that use of the word *atonement* in this passage is "doctrinally incorrect." They tell us that the Old Testament animal sacrifices provided a mere *atonement* (covering) for sin, whereas Christ's blood provided *reconciliation*, which we are told is complete removal, a far higher state.

I have seen professors and preachers who think they have found an error in the King James Bible rejoice more over that "error" than over one sinner that repenteth. Those who do not believe that the Holy Spirit is still active in the transmission of Scripture are greatly handicapped in their interpretations.

I bother to answer the critics on this point for two reasons. One, the King James translation as it stands is essential to the original intent of the passage. Two, this is possibly the most celebrated "error" in the King James Bible. To answer it is to demonstrate the ineptitude of Bible critics at a point most celebrated by them. "Unfortunate translation," they say?

We will show that the preservation of this text, as with all the words of God, had nothing to do with fortune; it was the Holy Spirit. With close examination, the venerable old text never fails to rise to the demands of inspiration.

Their argument hangs on four assertions: 1) that the root meaning of *atonement* is a mere *covering*, 2) that atonement and reconciliation are so different as to represent different methods in different dispensations, 3) that Christ did not provide atonement, 4) that Christians do not receive the atonement; they receive reconciliation.

1. Answering the assertion that the root meaning of atonement is a mere covering:

Yes, the root meaning of the Greek word *katallage* (*atonement* in this passage) is *"covering,"* just as the root meaning of the Greek word translated *reconcile* is *"the business of changing money for an equivalent value."* To restrict the definition of a word to its root meaning, and then finding fault with a translation when it fails to conform to that narrow definition, is shoddy academics at the least. Actually, it is outright dishonesty. For example, the root meaning of Spirit (Greek-pneuma), as in Holy Spirit, is *"wind movement or air,"* from which we get our word *pneumatic*, as in air operated tools. Does the root meaning of *pneuma* (air powered) accurately define the nature of the Holy Spirit? In most instances the root meaning of a word is far from its definition in a given cultural context. This is not a matter of debate. Any student of linguistics would agree.

The method of accurately determining the definition of *katallage* (atonement/reconciliation), or any word, for that matter, is to examine all contexts in which it is used. The Old Testament Scripture provides us with an abundance of examples. Let the author of a book define his own terms in the context he employs.

2. Answering the argument that atonement and reconciliation are so different as to represent different methods in different dispensations.

The argument is that this old covenant atonement, based on the blood of animals, was a lower state than new covenant reconciliation based on the blood of Christ. At first glance, this seems perfectly plausible. We know for a fact that in this present dispensation those that are "in Christ" are in a more elevated relationship than were those under the Law, but we repudiate the assumption that the difference is expressed in the meaning of these two words—*atonement* and *reconciliation*.

We further reject the assertion that the word *atonement* should be reserved to describe only the old covenant, and the word *reconcile* be used only to describe the work of Christ under the new covenant. This supposedly new covenant phenomenon *(reconciliation)* did in fact occur under the old covenant. In the English text of the Old Testament the word *reconcile* is found nine times. Six times it expresses the work of the blood of animals in temple service. It is not set in distinction to atonement. To the contrary, it is found in the same passages as atonement and expresses the results achieved by the atonement. <u>Atonement is what is accomplished by the sacrifice in regard to the sin debt. Reconciliation is the result.</u> Ezekiel 45: 15-17 is an account of reconciliation (book of Hebrews – *kaphar*) based on animal blood. The emphasis is on the results achieved, not the sacrifice itself, so the translator's choice of *reconcile* is more appropriate than *atone*. Only the context dictates whether the passage is about the event of atonement or the result, which is reconciliation. See Leviticus 6:7-30; 16:17-24; and 2 Chronicles 29:24. In each passage you will find the words *atonement* and *reconciliation* in close proximity, atonement describing the offering, reconciliation describing the effect of the atonement, both based on the same animal offering.

The Hebrew word *kaphar* (*reconcile* in the book of Hebrews) appears 102 times in the Hebrew Old Testament. In the majority of cases (71) the King James Bible, as most versions, translates it as *atonement.* Though in the King James Bible it is also translated: purge 7, <u>reconciliation 4, reconcile 3,</u> forgive 3, purge away 2, pacify 2, atonement...made 2, merciful 2, cleansed 1, disannulled 1, appease 1, put off 1, pardon 1, pitch 1.

<u>No translation always translates the Hebrews *kaphar* as *atone*.</u> Obviously our English word *atone* is not an exact counterpart for *kaphar*. It takes several English words to express the various implications of this one Hebrew word, as all translators admit by the various renderings in their translations. So it is entirely inappropriate to fault the King James text for practices common to all.

The critics won't yield the throne on this point; they will continue with the pen knife of Jehudi (Jeremiah 36:23) and tell us that not only is the King James Bible in error when it uses *atonement* in the New Testament, but it is equally in error when in the Old Testament it translates the Hebrew word *kaphar* as *reconcile*. Their tune is "*atone* for the Old Testament and *reconcile* for the New Testament."

In the King James Bible (Old Testament) the same Hebrew word *kaphar* is translated *reconcile* seven times. Critics say the translation of *kaphar* as *reconcile* is incorrect, but then the ASV and the NRSV both translate the same Hebrew word *kaphar* as *reconciliation* in Daniel 9:24. Why do they make this exception? Because Daniel is prophesying of the ministry of Christ, saying He will "make an end of sins." If they translated this as *atonement* (something they fault the King James Bible for doing) then they would have a prediction that Christ would provide an atonement, exactly as our passage in Romans 5:11 says. So they break their own rules in order to maintain their presupposed doctrinal bias, and in so doing are found guilty of the same "error" that according to them is found in the King James Bible.

On the other hand the NIV sticks to its guns and translates Daniel

9:24 as *"to atone for wickedness."* Christ is to <u>atone</u> for wickedness? By being consistent with the rules they impose upon the King James Bible, they have produced a translation that is in agreement with and substantiates the King James translation of Romans 5:11. So according to the NIV, Christ did atone for sins. You can't reweave a perfectly woven tapestry.

Finally, in regard to the assertion that *atonement* and *reconciliation* are unique to their dispensations: Since *atonement* is the act of paying the price, and *reconciliation* is the restored relationship built on that sacrifice, to relegate *atonement* to the old covenant and *reconciliation* to the new is to have the payment made long ago by the blood of animals and the relationship restored many centuries later by the blood of Christ. Where is the reconciliation of the old covenant, and where is the atonement of the new? Both the old and the new covenants must contain both atonement and reconciliation—just as the King James Bible teaches. Granted, the first atonement is only typical and the reconciliation conditional, whereas the second atonement is sufficient in covering all sin forever, and the reconciliation complete and final, but in any dispensation, atonement producing reconciliation is the complete picture. Under the old covenant both the atonement and the reconciliation were only shadows of the real atonement and reconciliation which was to come in Christ.

3. Answering the argument that Christ did not provide atonement.

"For the life of the flesh is in the blood: and I have given it to you upon the altar to make an atonement for your souls: for it is the blood that maketh an atonement for the soul. (Leviticus 17:11)." <u>Blood makes the atonement that is the basis of *reconciliation.*</u>

This is where it gets ridiculous. If Christ did not provide atonement, we have thousands of songs, confessions, and theology books that need to be rewritten. We can no longer sing, "Christ has for sin atonement made, hallelujah...." Look in the index of any book on doctrine or theology and observe the many times *the atonement of Christ* is discussed. In theology, they study and debate the "theories of Christ's atonement." The King James Bible uses this great word one time, and suddenly it is doctrinally incorrect. Now, I can appreciate holding a view in contradiction to the prevailing opinions, but what is ridiculous is that the same books that reject the King James rendering of atonement also have extensive discussions on the atonement of Christ. You can't have it both ways. <u>If Christ did provide an atonement, why remove the only verse in the New Testament that speaks of that atonement? If Christ did not provide atonement, then why build all theology, songs, and confessions around the term?</u> Muslims, Mormons, and evolutionists don't have a monopoly on professional ignorance. Bible critics will take the prize every time.

The old covenant atonement based on animal blood typified something yet to be. The lamb typified Christ, the blood typified His *"better blood."* The atonement typified His atonement, and the reconciliation typified His reconciliation. It was the forbearance of God that covered (atoned) sins until the time appointed when Christ would shed the blood that could actually atone (completely and thoroughly cover) sins once for all.

It is true that the old covenant based on animal blood could not actually remove sin, *"for the law having a shadow of good things to come, and not the very image of the things, can never with those sacrifices which they offered year by year continually make the comers thereunto perfect. For then would they not have ceased to be offered? because that the worshippers once purged should have had no more conscience of sins. But in those sacrifices there is a remembrance again made of sins every year. For it is <u>not possible that the blood of bulls and of goats should take away sins</u> (Hebrews 10:1- 4)."*

The blood of the animal only typified the promised payment. The believing old covenant saint was forgiven, as it were, on credit. The blood of animals actually accomplished nothing of permanence, not even an atonement, but it anticipated all that the blood of Christ would eventually accomplish in atonement and reconciliation. Meanwhile, that typical sacrifice, when offered in faith, was real enough to forgive sins and impart eternal life to the point that upon dying men went to paradise.

That old atonement stopped plagues, lifted judgments, and by it men came into fellowship and communion with God. In short, sin was put away and forgiven so as to leave the man reconciled to God. That this was based on a type does not lessen the fact that the atonement did indeed place them in a reconciled state. The typical old covenant atonement did typically reconcile men to God in an efficacious manner, howbeit on the contingency of Christ's actual atonement and reconciliation.

To deny that Christ provided atonement through His blood is to suppose that the Old Testament type typified nothing. <u>If it was a typical atonement, where is the true atonement?</u> The critic answers, "Reconciliation instead of atonement." No, <u>reconciliation by means of the atonement of Christ</u>. You cannot answer that old covenant atonement typified new covenant reconciliation, for there was both atonement and reconciliation under the old system, just as there is under Christ. Atonement and reconciliation are different phases of any sacrificial system. Why attempt to create a problem, pretending there is a danger in this word *atonement*? Would someone make all this fuss just to fault one old tried and proven text? Does the King James Bible bother them that much?

The long sought after atonement is found in Christ alone. What the old covenant promised is delivered as reality in Christ.

4. Answering the argument that Christians do not receive the atone-

ment; they receive reconciliation.

Remember the thoughts of 3:25-26, *"Whom God hath set forth to be a propitiation through faith in his blood, to declare his righteousness for the remission of sins that are past, through the forbearance of God; To declare, I say, at this time his righteousness: that he might be just, and the justifier of him which believeth in Jesus."*

There was no sufficient and worthy basis for the remission of sins in past ages (Hebrews 10:3-5). God had remitted past sins (the sins of those who had lived in the past) based on promise of a worthy atonement. In the meantime God instituted a type of that coming atonement. The old system was called *atonement* because, seeing the faith of the participant, God forgave their sins on promise of future payment. By the forbearance of God their sins were atoned until the promised lamb could provide the eternal atonement based on better blood. By His death, Christ justified God in the remission of those past sins. In Paul's day especially, when the debate between old covenant and new covenant was so current, that first generation of believers could say, "We have now received that atonement. It is no longer just a promise; it is now reality."

This is the most important statement in this entire thesis on *atonement,* so take note. To create a link between the old covenant type of atonement/reconciliation and the new covenant fulfillment, it was absolutely essential to use the same word that the Old Testament text employed on the type, *atonement.*

The text says, *"...we also joy in God through our Lord Jesus Christ, by whom we have **now received** the atonement."* *"Now received,"* when for so long it was only a promise bound in a type. *"Now received,"* through the Lord Jesus Christ, not through the Law of Moses, not through animal blood, not by works, but by faith we *now*, at this time, have finally *received* the long predicted atonement.

Finally, Romans 5:10, the Greek word *katallasso* appears twice, translated reconciled, then in the following verse the Greek word *katallage*, from the same root, appears again, this time translated atonement. *Katallage* is translated reconciliation and reconcile the other three times it appears in the New Testament, but here it was translated as atonement. "Unfortunate translation," they say? The King James translators did not make this translation by accident or through poor scholarship. They carefully choose to translate the same word two different ways when it was used three times in the same passage. Why? Because the one Greek word carried with it the meaning expressed in the two English words. When the context of verse 10 is what happened to us, it is translated *reconciled.* When the context is the historical event, which we have received, then the appropriate translation is *atonement.* Thank God for translators that followed the leading of the Holy Spirit to give us an English text consistent with the original intent of the author. Let God be true and every man a liar.

5:12-21 Adam and Christ
Overview

We have before us a comparison of Adam and Christ. Adam is said to be *the figure* (type) of Christ (5:14)—this being the only time Scripture designates anyone as such. To understand the individual parts of this section we must approach it as a whole. When we understand the point of Paul's argument we can be consistent in our interpretation of the evidence he presents in support of his main thesis. Paul compares Adam and Christ for the purpose of demonstrating how Christ is the solution to all that befell the human race in Adam. In Adam the race experienced a great fall into disfavor and death. In Christ we experience a greater ascent into favor and blessing. *"For as in Adam all die, even so in Christ shall all be made alive (1 Corinthians 15:22)."*

After laying a foundation (12-17), Paul comes to the heart of his subject in verses 18-19.

> **18-19 Therefore as by the offence of one judgment came upon all men to condemnation; even so by the righteousness of one the free gift came upon all men unto justification of life. For as by one man's disobedience many were made sinners, so by the obedience of one shall many be made righteous.**

Observe the word *one*, appearing four times in the above passage. The first verse in this section (v.12) begins this discussion with, *"as by one man."* The reference to *one man*, either Adam or Christ, continues to be the common theme. It is used 12 times in this section, being the indispensable thread that ties all the thoughts together.

Adam and Christ were both in unique positions. For a while, Adam was the entire human race. What he did, all of humanity did. As goes Adam, so goes the race. Likewise, Christ came to act on behalf of the entire race. What He did affected the many. As goes Christ, so goes all His posterity. Thus Christ, being the head of a new race, was called *the last Adam.* *"And so it is written, The first man Adam was made a living soul; the last Adam was made a quickening spirit (1 Corinthians 15:45)."*

The one indispensable concept of this entire section (5:12-21), the conjecture on which any interpretation must be built, is that one man sins and one man obeys; in both cases it has repercussions on the many. To depart from this assumption at any point is to reduce Paul's argument to inconsistent nonsense and destroy the analogy of Christ.

The following section, 5:12-21, compares the fruits of Adam's sin to the fruit of Christ's work of redemption, expanding further his presentation of the great provision of sanctification in Christ. He shows how the free gift of righteousness and the blessings described in verses 1-11 are the work of one man alone, and that all, gentiles as well as Jews, are made partakers just as all were partakers of the death resulting from the sin of the one man Adam. It is a natural continuation of his thoughts on what we have inherited in Jesus Christ. He is not concerned with the origin of sin, but with the cure for death.

Paul's intent is revealed by the conclusions he draws from this section: *"even so might grace reign through righteousness unto eternal life..."* The subject of this section is eternal life triumphing over the reigning death of Adam.

Viewing 5:12-21 in context

To understand Romans 5:12-21, we must go back to verse 9 and view it in context. *"Much more then, being now justified by his blood, we shall be saved from wrath through him (5:9)."* With this *Much more*, Paul begins a discussion of all that accompanies justification from sin. All he has said up until this point has immersed us in gratitude and wonder. We are amazed at the great provisions of grace enumerated in 5:1-8. But, to our amazement he says, "There is *much more* than justification; Christ died for us, yes, but the grace that saves also preserves from wrath to come and will eventually deliver us from death."

- There are eight **contrasts** in this section:
  1. The one man Adam contrasted to the one man Christ
  2. Disobedience contrasted to obedience.
  3. Sin contrasted to righteousness.
  4. Law contrasted to grace
  5. Condemnation contrasted to justification
  6. Death contrasted to life
  7. The offence contrasted to the free gift
  8. Death's reign contrasted to the believer's reign in life
- There are four **reigns**:
  1. Death reigned
  2. Sin reigned
  3. Grace reigns
  4. The believer shall reign in life
- **"Much more"** occurs 5 times, showing the greater effect of Christ's work.
  1. Much more, we shall be saved from wrath (v.9).
  2. Much more, we shall be saved by his life. (V.10).
  3. Much more, the gift hath abounded (v.15).
  4. Much more, the believer shall reign in life (v.17).
  5. Much more, did grace abound (v.20).
- Five times Paul says that **death** is due to the sin of **one man**.
- Twelve times he speaks of **one man**, in his headship, referring to either Adam or Christ.

Historical speculations

There are many philosophical speculations arising from these verses, beginning with Augustine of the fifth century. His conjectures became the foundation of much modern theology. Philip Schaff, in his notable work, *History of the Christian Church*, says of Augustine, "He was a Christian philosopher and a philosophical theologian to the full [Vol. 3, page 997]." Amazingly, Schaff intended this statement as a commendation. Yet Schaff reflects the perspective of a large segment of Christianity. Perceived brilliance and philosophical speculation have been the hallmark of Catholicism and Protestantism alike. Augustine is the fountainhead and champion of some of the most speculative absurdities ever to come out of the Christian Church. The majority of commentaries on Romans are tainted with Augustine's imaginations.

In response to how others have handled this passage, I must caution: we should seek to go no further than the obvious intent of the writer. In order to do this, we must have absolute confidence in the completeness of the words of Scripture. By this I mean, we cannot come to a passage that doesn't fit our preconceived theology and assume that for some reason the text does not read as it should to communicate the message we suppose was intended. To do this is to place the text itself subservient to our imagined opinions. The book of Romans is either the fumbling work of a man who was less than proficient in his ability to say what he should have said, or it is the inspired Word of God, said as best as could be produced and preserved by the mind of God.

Most commentaries view this section apart from its context. The mind given to philosophy finds this section fertile ground for speculation. Luther and Calvin crashed and burned in Romans 5:12. To many, it is a revelation of how men came to be sinners. But viewing it in its context, it is obvious that the purpose of this comparison has absolutely nothing to do with revealing how sin and death originated. Neither is it given as additional proof that all men are sinners. Paul has already advanced his argument well beyond that point, showing in great detail, with carefully laid arguments in chapters 1-3, that all men are sinners by choice and practice, and that each has individually sinned against his own conscience. Mankind's involuntary participation in Adam's sin would be a poor foundation to convince a man of his guilt.

5:12 Wherefore, as by one man sin entered into the world, and death by sin; and so death passed upon all men, for that all have sinned:

Wherefore (*by reason of*, or *on account of*). *Wherefore* links what has just been said in verses 1-11 with the following. He has just said: *Much more, being reconciled* (5:10) [this sums up his message up until chapter 5], *we shall be saved by his life* (5:10) [this introduces the coming message of our deliverance from death, as will be discussed in the remainder of this chapter]. He continues: *We joy in God through our Lord Jesus Christ, by whom we have now received the atonement* (v.11). We have *received the atonement* and *will be saved* (from future judgment and death) *by his life, wherefore* (on account of, or, by reason of) the great work Christ did in delivering us from *Adam* (5:14), *disobedience* (5:19), *sin* (5:19), *law* (5:20), *offences* (5:15,20), *condemnation* (5:16), *judgment* (5:16,18), *abounding sin* (5:20), and *death* (5:21).

...as begins a comparison that is interrupted by a parenthetical explanation (v.13-17) which is completed in verse 18 with *even so.* He introduces a discussion of how the sin of one man brought death on the entire race, for the purpose of showing how Christ can bring life on the entire race. Since all shared in the death, all can share in the gift of life. He is showing the universal significance and efficaciousness of Christ's work.

...as by.... Just as (in like manner) one man brought the death penalty upon all men through his one act, so he will eventually tell us in verse 18-19 that one man by his one act of obedience will bring the gift of life upon the many.

...one man.... That one man is Adam, the first man, the embodiment of the entire human race, a type of Christ. For a time he controlled the destiny of the entire race.

...sin entered into the world.... Satan had previously sinned, but the new world created for man was yet without sin until Adam and Eve sinned. Sin made its fateful entrance when Adam ate the forbidden fruit and it drove a wedge between God and all of Adam's future descendants.

...and death by sin.... This death is physical as seen by all the many verses that speak of it. See below, *death passed.* See the Appendix under Death.

...death **passed....** The Greek word here *(dee-er'-khom-ahee)* is most appropriately translated *passed.* It means: to pass, as one who travels, passing through a region. It is not speaking of an instantaneous event, but of a history of overtaking. Death made its way to each individual member of the human race. The one act of Adam introduced death, but the men died each in his own time as death *passed* his way. Death passed through history, taking each one with it. Obviously, people could not die who were not yet born, but from that moment on, all who were born were born to die.

...death passed.... The meaning of this phrase is quite clear. The human race was without death until its first member disobeyed God. It resulted in the curse of death on Adam and all his descendants. It is a simple explanation for why death came into our world and why it reigns so thoroughly.

The death that *passed* **on all men is physical**, the dissolution of the body, as seen by:

- The common meaning of the word *death* as used in Scripture is dissolution of body. The word *death* is found 372 times in the Bible. With but three exceptions, it always refers to physical death. See the Appendix under *death*.

- The penalty for Adam's sin was physical death. God had told Adam that "*in the day ye eat thereof ye shall surely die (Genesis 2:1)*." The death with which Adam was threatened was the death that *passed* on all men. In fact, the entire human race became subject to death that day, though none, not even Adam, immediately expired.

  Adam's death was physical as seen by the fact that the Bible repeatedly represents the cure for Adam's death as yet future for all believers. "*For since by man came* **death**, *by man came also the resurrection of the dead. For as in Adam all* **died**, *even so in Christ* shall [yet future] *all be made alive (1 Corinthians 15:21-22)*." It is a physical death that anticipates a future resurrection. If the death incurred in Adam was something spiritual, then those now in Christ would already be delivered from it. But the Scripture is emphatic; the cure for our corporate death in Adam is yet future. The new birth is not the cure; the new body is.

  Romans 8:19-25 speaks of a future hope when believers will receive the redemption of the physical body and be delivered from the "*bondage of corruption*." It is the cure for death in Adam. Likewise 1 Corinthians 15:35-58 speaks of a future deliverance when "*death is swallowed up in victory*."

- The last verse in this chapter makes a final reference to *death* that could not be other than physical. "*That as sin hath reigned unto death, even so might grace reign through righteousness unto eternal life by Jesus Christ our Lord (5:21)*." Note that sin *reigns* unto death, which indicates that this *death* is not synonymous with sin. In other words, this death is not the cause of sin, as would be the case with so called "spiritual death," but this death is yet future and is a result of the sin. It could not be anything but physical death, as occurs at the end of natural life.

  Further, this *death* is not cured by grace and righteousness (as it would be if death were a spiritual condition), but by the advent of *eternal life*. Both the death and the eternal life occur at the end of a *reign*—a reign of sin on the one hand, and a reign of grace on the other.

- There is no such condition in all Scripture as being "spiritually dead." We are not denying that there is such a condition as being *dead in trespasses and sins*—estranged from God. We just deny that depravity is "spiritual" death. Figuratively, we could call it moral death or judicial death. Though it could be misleading, we could even call it *spiritual death,* if by that we simply meant that on a divine plane the man was totally out of touch with God and righteousness. But the fallacy in choosing this non-scriptural terminology is seen in the fact that it has led many to believe that the human spirit is somehow dead or inoperative. Uninformed Christian writers and theologians have even incorporated that false concept into their writings.

Though the *death* spoken of here is physical, it is a result of God's displeasure. Granted, that God should forsake the human race, leaving them subject to fear of death, has implications beyond mere dissolution of the body. To be turned over to death necessarily implies separation from life—separation from God. Nothing in right standing with God can die. Therefore to be in a state of death does have spiritual implications, but the death is physical nonetheless. When one believes on Christ, he receives the gift of eternal life immediately. But that life is found in a sure hope, yet to be realized.

There are not two conditions of *death* in Scripture—one physical and one spiritual. This may seem cross grain to popular teaching, but it is plain Scriptural truth. All one need do is look up all 372 references to *death* in the King James Bible. If you read Greek, that will work just as well, but the Authorized Version is perfectly accurate. Also look up die, died, and dead. The word *dead* is used figuratively several times, (*faith without works is dead*) but it is always a figure drawn from physical death. See *Dead* in Appendix.

Inherent death not inherent guilt

The Scripture is very clear in its assertion that the death of the human race dates to the sin of the one man. But it seems inconsistent with our sense of justice and propriety that all should bear the consequences of a deed that occurred before we even existed and, therefore, for which we had no say. But much of this subjective objection is removed when we understand that the Scripture does not teach that Adam's descendants bear the blame or guilt of his sin, just the penal and natural consequences, which is physical death. The *condemnation* (verse 18) of death passed upon all men, not the guilt. Guilt is personal and cannot be transferred. He is saying nothing more than that men die a physical death due to the sin of the one man Adam.

We can discount any view that says men die for their personal sins only. Infants who have not personally sinned, nonetheless die. Furthermore we are told in verse 14 that death reigned over those *who had not sinned after the similitude of Adam's transgression.* Also we have several clear statements such as, *"through the offence of one many be dead (verse 15)."*

Levi paid tithes

What relationship does the human race sustain to Adam that

would cause his death to become the death of all?

There seems to be no question that the entire human race was in fact present in Adam's loins when he sinned. Hebrews 7:9-10 supports this concept. We need not conjure up "covenants, gifts of righteousness, or federal headship" to understand this simple, straightforward truth. In time, biological science will discover that in the loins of a man is the essence of all his future descendants. The soul of a child comes from the substance of the soul of the father. That original soul which God placed in Adam was the soul of the race. When Adam acted, the entire race acted. It would not be sufficient to say that Adam "represented" the race. No such arbitrary relationship was ever established, nor could it have been, without the consent of those represented. Nor were Adam's descendants actually present so as to have responsibly acted. It is nonsense to speak of the human race becoming blameworthy in Adam's sin.

Though Levi paid tithes (Hebrews 7:9-10) while unborn in the loins of his great grandfather, there is no virtue ascribed to the fact. It is understandable that consequences can be passed along to succeeding generations, but not moral character or accountability. Unless one's consciousness is involved, no act could have moral quality. The human race was present in Father Adam, but not consciously so. So there is a sense in which all sinned, though not under the normal conditions of responsible choice. The first man Adam was indeed the entire human race. What he did, the race did. As goes Adam in his relationship to the Creator, so goes all that are in his loins. In that limited sense only, did all sin, just as all Levites paid tithes in Abraham.

Based on the working of this principle, he later tells us that "*in Christ all died... if one died for all then are all dead.*" The believer is accounted righteous after being baptized (not water) into the body of Christ, thus becoming a participant in all in which Christ participated. His doing and dying is then accounted to all that are in Him. *"For as by one man's disobedience many were made sinners, so by the obedience of one shall many be made righteous (Romans 5:19).*" Adam's sin is our sin in the same manner that Christ's righteousness is our righteousness. Christ's righteousness gives us life just as Adam's sin gave us death. No one would ever claim that our participation in Christ's righteousness makes us actually responsible for that righteousness. Likewise it would be foolish to claim that Adam's sin made us actually blameworthy.

Given the unusual conditions, as we are told in verse 13, God does not impute the sin of the one to the many. That is, as a result of Adam's sin, none but he are under a threat of damnation—death yes, but not damnation. The manner in which mankind was actually in Adam could pass along consequences of the first sin to succeeding generations, but not the guilt. There can be no cry of injustice simply because one's lifespan is limited. Man still has an allotted number of days in which to express his heart in obedience or disobedience. If one of Adam's descendants faults his Great Grandfather Adam for the direction he took the race, he still has the option of reversing Adam's rebellion and walking in humble submission to the Creator.

The entire human race was indeed in the loins of Adam. His soul was the soul of all future descendants. This relationship was organic. As goes Adam, so go all his descendants. But when he sinned, he alone made a moral decision. He alone consciously acted against spoken law.

From several texts it is clear that <u>God asserts the first sin to be the sin of one man, not many</u>. So we conclude that the sense in which the race was in Adam was sufficient to make it partaker of the consequences of Adam's sin, but not sufficient for the race to share actual responsibility for the act. No one will be damned on the basis of Adam's sin alone, but all do die a physical death due to the sin of the one man. This is the point that is clear to the believer with common sense who is led by the Holy Spirit and believes the book just as it is written, without the creation of any missing links.

Why was the human body the target of judgment?

The body of flesh is sinful like a garbage can is dirty. It is the content and use made of it that renders it unclean. The body is depraved like a book is depraved. The cover, type, paper, and ink of a pornographic book are the same substance as that of a Bible. Yet the Bible is holy, and the pornographic book is sinful, not based on their physical substance, but based on the content and use some moral being has made of the physical elements comprising the two books.

When Adam sinned, he didn't sin in the area of ideas alone; he sinned through the misuse of his body of flesh. The flesh is not sinful in itself. It is no more to blame than is the paper and ink of a book, but the sin indelibly affects the pages on which it occurs. It is not only the evil mind that comes under condemnation, but the medium of expression is also corrupted. The human body became depraved through the use Adam made of it in sinning. Sin cannot be other than the misapplication of moral nature. It is not the hand that sins, rather the mind that guides it. However it is the thief's hand that is cut off; as it is the paper and ink of a pornographic book that is destroyed.

When Adam sinned and his soul was separated from God, his body, the tool of sin, became contaminated. Likewise the earth, the ground on which the sin occurred, though it bears no guilt, also came under a curse, as did the animal kingdom. Any future descendants of Adam would be born into a world that was under a curse. They would be born with depraved bodies of corruptible flesh—just like Adam after he sinned. They would be born of Adam in a world of souls forsaken of God. The descendants of Adam, through their organic link to both his soul and his body, will of necessity bear the consequences of any decision he makes.

This is not exceptional in the nature of the relationship between father and son. Now, and throughout all ages, children bear the consequences of the sins of their fathers—not the guilt or blame, just the natural consequences as the relationship dictates.

The exceptional thing about Adam and his posterity is the great height from which his posterity fell. No other father has ever been in a position to lose so much on behalf of his posterity. Adam walked with God. He was without fault or blame before God. Morally, the earth and all its inhabitants constituted an entirely sterile environment. God was at home walking among the trees, talking with Adam and Eve. It was a marvelous relationship that Adam could have bequeathed to his posterity. But when he gave his body over to disobedience, he became the enemy of God. The earth and its inhabitants, like a sterile laboratory now contaminated, was no longer a fit environment for the holy God. God released the hand that Adam pulled away, and all future descendants of Adam were born without God. With the life of God removed, all that remained was temporal life with a death sentence on it. In Adam all died.

All were in Adam, but not consciously. The one man sinned, and, being forsaken of God, the death sentence was pronounced upon him. Natural life was left to run its course in futility. But all who would come forth from the corrupted loins of Adam would come to share in his death. His banishment from the kingdom was the exiling of all his posterity as well. King Adam abdicated the throne and all his descendants ceased to be royalty on that day. One man sinned, and all died. Even the ones who did not sin as he did, died just the same, for death had passed upon all men. Only in that impersonal sense were all constituted as sinners.

...for that all have sinned. There is significant variance among writers and theologians on just when and how **all** sinned. To understand the problem, read this verse in its context and compare the phrase _all sinned_ with the phrase _one sinned_. _"Wherefore, as by one man sin entered into the world, and death by sin; and so death passed upon all men, for that all have sinned:"_

The beginning of the verse seems clear. _One_ man sins; obviously sin has made an entry into the world. No problem there—all would agree. Following the chronology of events, the causes and effects, it goes on to say that as a result of the one man sinning, death entered the world. Again this is clear to all. _The wages of sin is death._ The death penalty falls on Adam, so death has entered the world.

Up to this point it has been Adam alone acting, with the consequences of sin and death falling on Adam and Eve. But he then speaks of further consequences, not on Adam, but on Adam's posterity. Here is where it gets difficult. One man sinned, and death passed, not just on the one man, but on all the world. Adam sinned, and all died. It may be difficult accepting the statement that death passes on all due to the sin of one man, but the real twist comes when he tacks on this last phrase, _"for that all have sinned."_ Is he saying that death passed on all men because all sinned? Taken with the statement that death is due to the sin of one man, this amendment that *all sinned* could seem to be a contradiction in thought. It is as if he were confusing his evidence. Which is it? Did one sin or did all sin? Is the human race suffering the consequences of Adam's sin or its own sin?

Now we have already discussed death passing on all men, but we haven't discussed whether all died because of some blameworthiness in them or because all share the consequences of Adam's blameworthiness.

That last phrase, *"for that all have sinned,"* has been the hook on which strange ideas have been hung. There are those who teach that only Adam sinned, but all receive the blame because Adam was appointed to act on behalf of all his posterity. Others explain the phrase, *"all have sinned,"* by saying that all were organically present in Adam's semen, so that the sin of Adam was actually the sin of all. Still others teach that *all sinned* later as a result of Adam's sin, either through his influence or due to some inherent tendency—like a "sinful nature."

But if the statement *"for that all have sinned"* is taken to be an explanation as to why all die, this would be completely inconsistent with his main argument that all died for the sin of the one man. This would put Paul in the position of trying to prove something with evidence that proves the opposite. You can't prove that all die for the sin of the one man if you offer as evidence that it wasn't his sin alone but actually the sin of all. Nor can you prove that all die for the sin of the one man if you go on to establish that all are worthy of death because all are sinful in nature. If any condition is set forth which establishes the blame of all, then Paul is talking nonsense.

It is at this point that the philosophers come to our "rescue." Scripture and common sense ceases to be the rule, and imagination puts on the scholar's mantle. Some tell us that this may be the single most important verse in the Bible. This passage just happens to be the point at which the Christian philosophers express their imaginations most recklessly, the ground on which theological battles have been staged. Its significance is not taken from its simple content, but from the armies of theologians who have come to it to fire off their opinions. This verse will not determine your theology, but it will reveal it. The position you take here will have powerful implications on the rest of your beliefs. We will now examine some of the creative approaches to this passage.

Commentators

Reading the commentaries, you often wonder if the commentators are considering the same verse—so much is read into the text. Judging by their comments, here is how the average writer must be reading this verse:

"For by one man's sin, all became sinners in nature, and spiritual death (the human spirit died) passed on all men by the sin of the one man Adam, for that all men were in Adam by a covenant God made with Adam, and so by proxy all participated in the first sin."

As anyone can see by reading several commentaries, I am by no means misrepresenting the average view. Though none have been so bold as to paraphrase the verse as I have, their commentaries, with some variations, assume something akin to this misguided paraphrase.

How could such an unfounded and fictitious interpretation come about? It is clear from the text that the death of all finds its origin in the sin of the first man. But theologians are not willing to leave it at that, for the simple reason that it is obvious that humanity's problems are something more than physical death. There is the reality of universal sinfulness. We also know that at this point, in some way, sin got its roots into the human race. The paramount issue is in what way is universal sinfulness owing to the sin of Adam? By what means does the sin of the first man affect all? What is the mode of transmission?

In stating the various, following positions, it is not the author's intention to imply the credibility of any of them. Biblical truth will be found outside the mainstream of popular opinion, but since these ideas are so widely believed and aptly defended, we will treat them with as much seriousness as the individual positions will permit.

1. Adam influenced his posterity to sin

Some answer it by saying that the sin of the many was a result of the influence of the one. But the Scripture clearly links the death of many to the sin of the one in a more intimate way than influence. If this is all we make of it, then the parallel in Christ would be that His righteousness did nothing more than influence us to righteousness.

If only Adam sinned, and his sin did not affect his posterity in any way but influence, then the fall was not the fall, babies are born perfect, just as Adam was created, and passages like *"in Adam all died"* are hyperbole.

2. All actually sinned in Adam

Some commentators tell us that when Paul says, *"for that all have sinned,"* he is actually saying, *for that all sinned in Adam*—that all were actually present in Adam, so that it was not his act alone, but the act of all, therefore all die for actual sin. Was the human race organically present in Adam so that all were accomplices in the first sin? If so, then all would be guilty; all would be blamed. If this is so then the sentence of death passed on all men because all actually sinned. If this were the case, could it be rightly said, *"by one that sinned"*? This is the seminal view. If all sinned in Adam, then all became sinners at the very same moment as did Adam.

This position presents no problem with our sense of justice, but it destroys the foundation of his comparison of Adam and Christ. Paul is preparing his reader for this comparison. His argument is that the work of Christ is like the work of Adam, in that what the one did was accounted to all. If man dies because of his own sins, then, in parallel, he must live because of his own righteousness. If Adam's act did indeed *make* us sinners, then we must conclude that Christ's act of righteousness did indeed *make* us responsibly righteous.

And if the condemnation of Adam's descendants is retribution for their participation in actual sin, then the eternal life bestowed upon saints must also be a deserved reward for participation in righteousness. To dispense with the concept of one man's disobedience compared to one man's obedience is to lose the basis of the entire argument through the rest of chapter five and six. He clearly says that *"one man sinned, and so death passed upon all men."*

The Scripture says that those who died *did not sin after the similitude of Adam's transgression.* Here is a clear statement that when Adam sinned his posterity did not likewise sin.

The implications are bewildering. If all sinned in Adam, then all are <u>born guilty</u> of their own sins. In other words, the fetus, still in the womb, would have past sins. If this sounds ridiculous to you, welcome to the Bible believer's club. See *Sins of the Fathers* in the Appendix.

3. Covenant sinners—Federal Headship

Of those who teach that in Adam all sinned, some teach that all sinned only in a covenant sense, which means that Adam's descendants did not sin; they are just *accounted* to be sinners. They tell us that God appointed Adam to be the "federal head" of the human race. Unknown to Adam, God made a covenant with him that he should act on behalf of all his descendants. If he should obey, then his obedience would be imputed to all his posterity, so that eventually he would have been glorified and all his descendants would have been confirmed in righteousness. But if he should disobey and choose evil, then the whole race would bear the consequences with him. His disobedience would then be imputed to all his posterity.

According to this popular but exotic view, all are blamed, though all are not to blame. All are punished though all are not personally guilty.

This argument finds its strongest support in its close compatibility with the analogy to Christ. It supports the reality of only one man sinning, just as Christ was the only one that obeyed. It also supports the concept of one man acting on behalf of all. Its strongest point is that you can well illustrate imputation with this view.

The covenant concept is conceived as a way of explaining how it is that the sin of one father affects the many, whereas the sin or righteousness of subsequent fathers does not affect their descendants. Some hold this unfounded view so highly that they desire to be known by it. They call themselves Covenant Theologians. They go to Covenant Churches, and establish a covenant with God that guarantees the salvation of their children. You have God blaming men, women, children, and fetuses for something for which they are not to blame.

One horrendous ramification of this view, which is held by so many, is the teaching that infants are born blamed by God, though not personally blameworthy. God is angry at the human race for being passive recipients of a failed covenant that God himself imposed upon an unknowing Adam. All representatively sinned in Adam, that is, all are accounted as sinners, though they share no guilt.

4. Sinful nature?

There are those who explain the subsequent sin of the many as a result of some inherent pollution caused by Adam's sin that is now resident in all Adam's descendants. Some imaginative persons have coined the bizarre term "sinful nature." That it has come to be popular doesn't lessen its alien quality. That it is a nonsense term doesn't seem to deter its use.

Proponents of this view are not teaching that all sinned, but that all *became sinners*. As they see it, the damning factor is not in the condemnation passed down in the original sin, but in the effect original sin had on the nature of Adam's posterity. It is taught that when Adam sinned his "nature" became corrupted so that he passed that depraved condition on to all his posterity. Sin is viewed as a disease, a kind of nonmaterial genetic mutation acquired in Adam and then passed down from generation to generation. It is a reverse evolution of the nonmaterial. Like organic evolution, it requires the creation of missing links to substantiate it. In this case, the missing links are fabricated terms and concepts not appearing in Scripture.

Since Augustine, a heretic of the fifth century, the level of absurdity has grown with increasing philosophical speculation, from Luther to Calvin, and down through the Puritans to Hodge, and now a whole string of modern parrots. They say that all men die because, though they didn't sin either personally or in Adam, yet all are born evil in the very essence of their souls.

But we have not reached the bottom yet. Infants, by the very composition of their souls, are said to be loathsome to God from the moment they are conceived. They come out of the womb despised by God and deserving of the fires of Hell. Those who believe in inherent evil cover the dastardly implication it has on infants by quickly pointing out that God does not damn the child who has not yet reached accountability. Yet some confidently assert that every child is born under the wrath of God unless his original sin is removed by a covenant with the parents through infant baptism. This is the view of most Protestants and all Roman Catholics.

Not only is the idea of inherent sin foreign to Scripture and reason, but it would do violence to the parallel. The initial disobedience of Adam alone is the issue on which his argument is built. For the analogy to be accurate, it must be true that the death of Adam's posterity has nothing to do with their personal condition. If mankind is despised of God because of some inherent tendency or moral impurity received from Adam, then they are deserving of death in their own right, and the analogy is destroyed. For the analogy would imply that Christians are counted righteous because of some implanted goodness.

The inherent sin concept would be more consistent with the semenal view, since Adam's descendants would have an organic link with him in his sin. But the representative (covenant /federal head) view necessarily assumes no organic link to Adam or his sin other than that of representative.

If—according to the covenant view—all came under condemnation because of a judicial ruling (that Adam should act on the behalf of everyone) then there would be no organic link to produce inherited depravity. On the other hand, according to the seminal view, if the human race organically participated in the sin, then the guilt is direct and personal, and depravity would be the result of the moral act of all—occurring simultaneously in Adam. But if there is no organic participation in the sin of Adam, and condemnation is a covenant relationship only, then moral depravity (sinful nature) must be the creation of God.

If only Adam sinned, and none but he are to blame, yet his posterity are born with natures that cannot please God, then you have a situation where men and babies are damned through no fault of their own, faulted for not being what they could not be.

Inherent condemnation, yes; inherent moral depravity, no.

Read this passage in Romans 5:12, considering only what it says without reading between the lines. The subject is not inherent depravity, but inherent condemnation. Nothing else could be consistent with the analogy. This author is amazed at how something so simple could have become so clouded. It is as if the theologians have traded their common sense in for an ascetic's imaginative visions. It would be embarrassing to hold the Calvinist's view.

All died, not all sinned

No place does it say, "In Adam all sinned." It says, Adam sinned and all died. *All* share the consequences, not the sin. The very wording of verse 12 does everything it can to avoid saying that in Adam all sinned. There are three parts to verse 12: (1. Sin enters the world through one man. (2. Death enters the world as a result of the one man's sin (3. For all have sinned. If Paul wanted to teach that Adam's sin was the sin of all and not just the one man, he definitely missed a good opportunity. And he never even intimates—not here, and not anywhere in all the Bible— that death comes on all because of the sinfulness or depravity inherited at the moment of Adam's sin.

Inherited Guilt?

Some insist that the condemnation of death passing on all men is testimony of their guilt, either the guilt of participation in Adam's sin or guilt of an evil nature inherited from Adam. Aside from the irrationality of it and the total lack of any Scriptural testimony, the concept of inherited guilt would do violence to Paul's argument that death is not of their own doing or deserving but the imputation of the doing and deserving of another.

Furthermore if death is testimony as to the guilt of the human race, how do we explain the death of animals? Are they bearing the blame of a deed for which they participated, or are they bearing the consequences of the deed of another? The only rational answer is to agree that <u>death in the animal world is a result of sharing the physical curse on Adam's sin, not a result of being blamed</u>. Then know that <u>according to Romans 8:20-21 the curse on animals is the same curse, on the same basis, as the curse on man—and it has the same cure, effected at the same time, on the same basis</u>. See *Sins of the Fathers* in the Appendix.

What the verse does teach

We have used up a lot of paper discussing error; we now look at the simple truth.

The plain sense of Scripture makes the most sense. Father Adam sins, and when the death sentence falls on him it falls on all that are in his loins. There is nothing here about guilt or blame or sinfulness. Physical death is the lot of all flesh on a planet that has forsaken the God of life.

- Sin entered the world through the **one act of one man** *("one man's offence; one that sinned; one man's disobedience; judgment was by one).*

- **Death came into the world** because of the one sin of the one man *(death passed upon all men; death reigned; all died; many be dead; to condemnation).*

- **All sinned** later as a result of their estrangement from God *(sin abounded; sin reigned; many offenses).*

There is sufficient Scriptural support throughout all the Bible for the following three concepts:

1. A man is damned only on the basis of his personal and willful violation of truth—truth understood. Until he is made consciously responsible, he is not held accountable.

2. The death penalty passed on all men because the race was in Father Adam when he sinned. Understand there is a great difference between imputing someone else's sin, with its guilt, and imputing the temporal consequences—death.

3. In consequence of Adam's sin, the whole world has in fact actually and personally sinned. One man sinned, all died, and it resulted in all sinning.

Finally, in what way was the fall of Adam the fall of the entire human race?

Adam alone sinned. He only was guilty. He alone was to blame, for he was the only one that consciously acted. But when he slipped off the edge, he took the entire future race with him, not immediately into sin, but into separation from God. Adam was sole proprietor of planet earth. At that moment he was the entire race. When he sinned God forsook Adam and all that pertained to him, which included his future descendants. When Adam was driven out of the garden, it was a foregone conclusion that his children would be born outside the garden, beyond the presence of God, which Adam had enjoyed there in the garden. The consequence on him and his posterity was not a fault in nature; it was a <u>fault in relationship</u>. All who are born are born separated from God—without the Holy Spirit

A newborn baby is born into separation from God, with the penalty of death. Because of this separation, there are manifold influences to evil. Adam's race must also content with a natural body possessed of many carnal passions, and a body weakened by generations of sin.

In addition, the fall was a fall into the kingdom of darkness. Satan exercises great control and influence over those in the kingdom of darkness.

To sum it up, a soul comes into this world without God, destined to die. <u>This estrangement,</u> coupled with natural tendencies to indulge, <u>is sufficient to account for the universality of sin.</u>

All mature persons are wicked, but men can only repent of real sin done in real time, sin that is part of their conscious history, not theological sin, doctrinal sin, sin one must accept by faith, against the dictates of his own conscience.

Why go beyond Scripture where it necessitates creating missing links to defend a nonsense doctrine? The plain sense of Scripture is profoundly simple and straightforward with no deep, unfathomable mysteries. The concept of mysteriously inherited sin comes from Origin and Augustine, and should be discarded with the rest of their heathen ignorance.

5:13 (For until the law sin was in the world: but sin is not imputed when there is no law.

...sin was in the world before the giving of the Law, for God said of those during the days of Noah, *"the wickedness of man was great in the earth, and that every imagination of the thoughts of his heart was*

only evil continually (Genesis 6:5)." Romans 5:16 speaks of *many offences*, which must be the accumulation of all actual sins. And in verse 20, he says, *"sin abounded,"* which obviously refers to the increase of individual sins. The *reign of sin* in verse 21 is in connection with the *abounding sin* of the previous verse. So, in answer to the assertion that the phrase *"for that all have sinned"* is not a reference to actual sin, we see that in this section there are five references to actual personal sin— though actual sin is never given as the cause of death.

      ...**sin is not imputed....** Which sin was not imputed to them before the Law, the sin of Adam or their personal sins? Neither. No sin was imputed to them which resulted in the death sentence. The substance of this passage is to show that all died for reasons other than their own doing, which is essential to make his comparison to the righteousness of Christ, which is imputed without participation from the sinner. It is therefore necessary to prove that neither the sin of Adam nor any subsequent personal sin can account for the universality of death from Adam to the giving of the Law under Moses. That is why verse 12 mentions both the sin of Adam (effecting the many) and the personal sin of the many, which sin was not imputed to them. That leaves the reader hanging, waiting for an explanation as to how all came under the death sentence, which is exactly where he was leading his reader. The answer affords him the opportunity to point out the similarity between Adam and Christ as heads of their races—the act of the one effecting the many.

      Of course, there was a means by which they could come to hold the truth of the Law and thereby make themselves accountable. Paul has already discussed that in chapters 1 and 2. Accountability came in measure, depending on the individual and the circumstances. Accountability didn't begin until a person's soul matured to the point of understanding good and evil. Infants and small children who died never reached a condition of accountability. Their personal sins were not imputed to them, just as the personal sins of heathen are not imputed to them unless they hold truth through one of the several sources. This is a Biblical principle taught elsewhere. Romans 2:12, 4:15, 5:13, 7:8-9; John 5:41, 15:22; James 4:17; Leviticus 5:3. See our discussion of 1:18 and 2:12. His point is that the sin that was in the world, including the original sin, since it was not imputed, could not account for the universal reign of death.

      This verse is clear; the reign of death before the Law had nothing to do with the sin of those on whom the penalty fell. The sin of Adam could never be imputed to them, because they had not sinned *after the similitude of Adam's transgression*, and we are clearly told that it was his sin, not theirs. Their personal sins were not a violation of express law. So this verse leaves us without an explanation, and leads into the forthcoming answer.

5:14 Nevertheless death reigned from Adam to Moses, even

over them that had not sinned after the similitude of Adam's transgression, who is the figure of him that was to come.

This verse is best understood in light of the last phrase, **who is the figure of him that was to come.** Paul is establishing Adam as a figure of Christ. Having already read his conclusion, knowing that he will eventually show that Christ's one act of obedience provides life for all, we know where he is going with his analogy. He must establish Adam as an accurate figure of Christ by demonstrating that Adam alone is responsible for the death sentence on all men. Only then can he say that like as in Adam all died, so in Christ all live.

...not sinned after the similitude of Adam's transgression.... During the twenty-five hundred years from Adam to the giving of the Law, there was no Bible and no God-given religion. None were responsible to direct, divine law that carried a death sentence. There was much sin, but it was *not after the similitude* (in like manner) *of Adam's transgression.* Adam's sin was different in that he knowingly sinned against an express commandment that carried a death sentence, not just a sentence of execution, but a sentence of certain mortality.

That period of time before the giving of the Law, when a man committed an indecent act, no one could say, "You have broken the Law of God; now you will die." The Scripture says that *"every man did that which was right in his own eyes (Deut. 12:8),"* meaning, every man answered to nothing higher than his own conscience. All sinned, but since they were not under jurisdiction of law, there was no certain penal consequence.

All he need establish to advance his argument is that the reign of death on the whole race cannot be accounted for by individual sins; rather, what the one man Adam did had consequences on the many.

Some might question his assumption, that the death sentence is solely attributable to Adam, by pointing to apparent exception such as the flood. In contradiction to Paul's thesis, it could be pointed out that every man was a sinner in his own right, and so each died for his own sins. Was it not true even then that *"the wages of sin is death?"*

...death reigned.... There is a difference between execution—killing someone for his deeds—and the reign of death. Execution occurs on an individual basis, at a point in history, provoked by personal evil. The Sovereign rises up to fault men for their wicked deeds, and so decrees the death sentence. That death comes suddenly by unnatural means. Death is wielded as by a sword, a flood, or fire from heaven. That death cannot be called a reign, for its execution is specific, directed toward certain individuals and not others. That death sometimes can be avoided by repentance or pardon, at the discretion of the Sovereign lawgiver.

In contrast, the reign of death is a universal curse effecting all flesh regardless of personal sin. The **reign** of death began when the human race became subject to mortality. It is an all-encompassing dominion wherein death permeates every aspect of living organisms. It is inherent death, a slow creeping, natural process to which all living things proceed. It is so thorough and so certain that many people now considered it to be part of the "cycle of life." All living things move forward in a process of deterioration, toward dissolution of substance, cessation of the precious gift of life. The reign of death is absolute and dictatorial, without appeal or reprieve. It is an inherent fault in the flow of life, a predictable calamity, an unavoidable tragedy. Impersonal destruction. It is universal and without respect of persons.

Some objections might be offered to the truth of his basis argument.

• **Is he saying they didn't sin during that dispensation from Adam to Moses?**

No. When it says God *did not impute* their sin unto them, it was an admission that they had in fact sinned.

Certainly from Adam to Moses the people sinned, It is said of those during the time of Noah, *"And GOD saw that the wickedness of man was great in the earth, and that every imagination of the thoughts of his heart was only evil continually (Genesis 6:5)."*

When the text says they *"had not sinned after the similitude of Adam's transgression,"* it is not saying that they didn't sin, nor is it saying that their sin was ignored. It is saying that the sins they did commit were not committed under the same penalty of law, as was Adam's.

• **Is he absolving them of guilt, suggesting that the absence of law left them without blame?**

No, all sin is blameworthy, though that blame may not be imputed if the Judge deems that the sin was excusable on the ground of genuine, sincere ignorance, as is the case with an infant. See Romans 1:18 for a discussion of that principle.

But the adult population from Adam to Moses were not rendered innocent by their ignorance of express law. As we are told in 2:14, even without direct revelation, they *"were a law unto themselves."* A man is held accountable to his own conscience regardless of the source of his understanding. *"Therefore to him that knoweth to do good, and doeth it not, to him it is sin (James 4:17)."*

Yet beyond their own personal sin and the individual consequences of it, those who sinned during the time of Noah had a death sentence on them before they were born, as seen by the fact that some infants died in childbirth. Death reigned long before the waters of judgment plunged them into eternal damnation. He is not suggesting that because sin was not imputed, so as to place all under a sentence of mortality, that they thereby escaped the judgment wherein each would give account of himself to God.

Only if we confuse the temporal death penalty with eternal judgment will there be a problem in our understanding. When it says *sin is not imputed where there is no law,* it is not a blanket dismissal of any fault in sinning; it is nothing more than a statement that the temporal death penalty did not come on them as a result of their own sins. Their sin was sin. It was damnable. They were under the wrath of God, but they were not brought under a penalty of death as a result of their sins.

Adam's sin was not imputed to his posterity. It was the temporal result of the sin that was passed on. Had it been otherwise, had death come to each as he personally sinned and came under judgment, then children would not have died or been sick until they reached a state of accountability and personally sinned. Of course this was not the case. Death reigned, even over the fetus and the newborn, so death can only be accounted for by something that happed in the past, which maintained universal consequences.

The imputation of anything beyond natural death, say the imputation of sin, would be ethically incomprehensible.

- **How can it be said that sin was not imputed to them when we know that on several occasions they were killed for their sins?**

When he says that *sin is not imputed where there is no law,* he is not suggesting that they were entirely without law, only that they were without a law that threatened mortality as a consequence. As we saw above, *they were a law unto themselves,* accountable to their own consciences. When they were killed for their sins, it was an individual, supernatural judgment, not natural death, which is the subject.

The exceptions (those that were killed because of their sin—Noah's flood, Sodom, Egypt, etc.), do not negate the general fact that the death sentence was over the human race from before they were born, and it indiscriminately took all children and adults. The absolute thoroughness of the death sentence, even over infants, points to a prior cause of death—that is, a cause prior to the sin of the individual.

His point is that men, women, boys and girls died even without special judgments. You can account for the death of the world in Noah's day by their sin, but how do you account for the universal relentless death that took every generation, even the little children who had done no evil? God did not kill each person, each child, individually for his or her sins. Death was a universal force with momentum of its own. It was sure, thorough, and inescapable.

- **How is it that there was no law? Did not Romans 1 and 2 teach that they are a law unto themselves, and are therefore without excuse?**

Men were accountable in so far as they perceived the truth. When

Scripture tells us *"every man did that which was right in his own eyes,"* it has revealed that every man held a concept of right and wrong. The witness of nature as discussed in Romans 1-2 is still applicable to those who had no special revelation, as did those under Moses.

- **Didn't God give law in Noah's day?**

"Whosoever shedeth man's blood by man shall his blood be shed (Genesis 9:6)." This was a law that threatened execution, not death in the sense of mortality, as inevitably comes with aging and disease.

- **Is he saying that since their sin was not imputed to them that they were not viewed as sinners? Did they escape the penalty of sin because of ignorance?**

No. When they died, they had to face God and give account in proportion to their knowledge of good and evil.

Our text does not say that their acts were not estimated to be sin, it says they didn't sin in the same manner as Adam. When any man acts other than how he should, in thought or deed, in God's sight he has sinned—he is guilty. Every man is accountable for his own sins according to the truth he holds in his own conscience (chapter 1-2). But none were made liable by express commandment from God. The fact that innocent children died is testimony that the death was not caused by personal sins.

5:15 But not as the offence, so also is the free gift. For if through the offence of one many be dead, much more the grace of God, and the gift by grace, which is by one man, Jesus Christ, hath abounded unto many.

This is still part of the parenthesis—an explanation of how the offence of one brought death on all. Remember, his purpose is to compare Christ to Adam, showing how the act of one effects the many.

The **offence** (Adam's sin) and the **gift** (the gift of righteousness in Christ) are different in this respect. His comparison includes the differences as well as the similarities, because he doesn't want to leave the impression that Christ is the mere equivalent of Adam, that he just reversed the work of Adam. The differences are just as instructive as the similarities. The differences provide Paul with the opportunity to express the superiority of the cure over the disease. Whatever Adam did in bringing death, Christ did *much more* in bringing life. What Christ did far surpasses what Adam did in both depth and scope. The purpose of this verse is to make clear the universal range and superiority of what Christ has done.

Christ's work is contrasted to Adam's by the words **much more** and **abounded.** If the offence of one mortal human can cause death to so many, how *much more* (with how much greater influence, power and certainty) will the work of Christ, not just affect, but *abound* unto many?

The power of death introduced by Adam can be broken, but the reign of life is abounding limitlessly (2 Timothy 1:10). Remember, this whole argument is about sanctification, how after being reconciled we will be **much more** saved by his life (5:10).

5:16 And not as it was by one that sinned, so is the gift: for the judgment was by one to condemnation, but the free gift is of many offences unto justification.

He is again showing us how two similar things differ. He is not contrasting the persons of Adam and Christ, nor is he here contrasting the sin and the gift, or condemnation and justification. He is contrasting the one man sinning one time to the **many offences** that were put away through the free gift. In showing the *much more* of Christ's work, he points out that whereas the **offence** that resulted in the world coming under condemnation was a singular sin, the **free gift** was in regard to not just the original offence, but to an entire history of **many offences**. In other words, between the time Adam plunged the race into death through his one sin and the time Christ came to make reconciliation, the list of offences had become extraordinary. Christ did not just undo the one sin of Adam. He disposed of a gigantic list of offences committed by myriad souls.

If Adam's one offence plunged the world into death, what must the accumulated offences of generation after generation of sinners, dotting the countryside, reaching down through the centuries, have done to increase the separation and ensure death? Since the giving of the Law, there had been many sins, many acts of disobedience against express law, each deserving of death. If Christ's work had been only the equivalent of Adam's, His free gift would have been affective for original sin only, not post-fall sins as well, and certainly not future sins. But the work of Christ potentially removes all sins of all men, past, present, and future.

One man sinned one time and brought death. Many men sinned many times under law that carries the death sentence. This additional sin further ensures death. Then Christ came, and through His one act of obedience prepared a gift of righteousness that is sufficient for all sinning souls. That gift of Christ will justify, sanctify, and deliver from coming wrath. So great salvation! *Much more* indeed!

5:17 For if by one man's offence death reigned by one; much more they which receive abundance of grace and of the gift of righteousness shall reign in life by one, Jesus Christ.)

Keep in mind that this is still part of the parenthesis—the last of it—and, as such, continues to be an explanation of the thought that one man sinned and brought death on many.

In support of verse 16, and adding a new dimension, he restates himself using some of the former concepts and bringing out a final difference. He is contrasting "the **reign of death**" to "**they** who **reign in life**." We would expect the *reign of death*, which is inanimate, to be contrasted to the *reign of life*, which is also inanimate. But he contrasts the reign of death to those individuals who have received the **abundance of grace** and so **reign in life**. It is **they** who reign, not life. Adam caused death to be king. Christ instates as king those over whom death had previously reigned. Those *"who through fear of death were all their lifetime subject to bondage"* now reign in everlasting life. Grace does not merely undo the sin of Adam; it actually places the offenders into a *reign in life*.

This difference is again a matter of degree and kind. **Much more**— even more certainly. For if the one man Adam can cause me to come under the death sentence, *how much more* is Christ able to impart an abundance of grace and cause me to *reign in life*? If so weak a cause as one man can bring in a reign of death, over which the passive recipients have no recourse, *how much more* efficacious is the **abundance of grace** and **the gift of righteousness** in causing a reigning in life?

The "they which **receive**" in this verse states that whereas the descendants of Adam suffered a reign of death without their personal act, the recipients of grace are active receivers, who will therefore more certainly bring about results. Our future reign is more certain than our death, because the cause is more powerful, and it is individually received.

When death reigns, we are its helpless victims, but when righteousness reigns, we are believing participants. Christ's act of salvation had immeasurably greater impact than Adam's one act of damnation. He didn't just undo the curse; he lifted man to *reign in life*. Not only is God's gift of grace greater than Adam's original sin, but it is greater than all the accumulated sins since the Garden of Eden. Someone has said, "Christ is much more powerful to save than Adam was to ruin."

5:18 Therefore as by the offence of one judgment came upon all men to condemnation; even so by the righteousness of one the free gift came upon all men unto justification of life.

The parentheses closed at the end of verse 17, therefore this verse should be read as following verse 12. The **even so** of this verse is the completion of the comparison that began in verse 12 with **as by**. The parenthesis was an expansive explanation of both verse 12 and verse 18.

Therefore as by the offence of one judgment came upon all men to condemnation... To refresh our memories, he restates the first part of the comparison, which he began but failed to complete in verse 12. He will now continue with his analogy.

The verse simply says: In the same way that one man's offence brought the judgment of death on all men, **even so**, (in like manner) by means of the righteousness of one man the free gift came on all.

Sin resulted in the **condemnation** to death. If you took this condemnation to be anything more than the sentence of death, you would destroy

Paul's analogy. If this *condemnation* were blameworthiness, then all are rightly dying for their own deserts—in which case it could not be said, **by the offence of one.** God would not condemn (as in find one to be at fault in a moral matter) one who did not sin.

The righteousness of one is the right doing of the one man Jesus Christ. As one man disobeyed and many reaped the undeserved consequence of death, so one man obeyed and many reap the undeserved consequence of life. This is not an issue of how sin or righteousness came upon them, but how death and life came.

The **free gift** is the priceless gift of life given at no price to the recipient. The gift is as free and unrelated to the merit of the recipients as the death was unrelated to the merit of the recipients. Paul uses the word *gift* six times to refer to what Christ has done for Adam's descendants. Ephesians 2:8-9, speaking of salvation, says, *"that not of yourselves, it is the gift of God."* Any sect of the Christian religion that conditions salvation on any form of obedience has missed Christ, and therefore salvation.

...unto justification of life... This verse is not about condemnation and justification. He is not telling us how we can have righteousness imputed to us through the gift of grace; although we can certainly see that his argument is based on that truth. The subject of his discussion is how Christ imparts life to those who were under the death of Adam. Of course life could not come without justification, but he has already established his position on justification in chapter 4.

Justification by means of imputed righteousness is necessary to remove the sentence of death. By the time Christ comes to redeem, the Law has been added and sin has abounded. It is no longer just the sin of one, but it is abounding offences from which many must be justified.

5:19 For as by one man's disobedience many were made sinners, so by the obedience of one shall many be made righteous.

The verse leads out with **For** (because). This is an explanation of verse 18, telling us why the offence of one man and the righteousness of one man could have the effect it did. This is the baseline of his entire argument: One man disobeys, and all are treated as if they were the sinners. One man obeys, and many are treated as if they are righteous.

...made sinners... By one man's disobedience many were **made** (appointed) to be sinners. In most places where we find the Greek word for *made* (Greek—*kathistemi*) it is in reference to someone being *made* an elder, priest, governor, etc. It carries the meaning of an appointed office or position. This passage is not saying that many actually became sinners, but that they were appointed to be, as one is elected to an office. This is a reckoned position, not an actual condition. The English text bears this out, for when it says "by the obedience of one shall many be **made righteous**," certainly it is not saying that Christ's obedience actually caused us to do a level of righteousness that qualifies us for salvation. The believer is *made* righteous by imputation. <u>So those in Adam were *made* to be sinners in the same sense that those in Christ were *made* to be righteous.</u>

...by the obedience of one... This is His entire life of obedience, culminating in His obedience unto death (Philippians 2:8). Christ didn't obey for us; He obeyed for himself, for the man he was, thus qualifying to be a worthy sacrificial substitute. Look under 4:6-8 for a discussion on imputed righteousness.

5:20 Moreover the law entered, that the offence might abound. But where sin abounded, grace did much more abound:

Paul has already well demonstrated the Law's ineffectiveness to make a man righteous, but he reintroduces the subject here to show its place in the overall program. In this chapter he has discussed how death reigned before the Law. The Jew would then want to know how the Law fits into this system. Many felt that they had found a refuge from condemnation in adherence to the Law. The Law is a pattern for righteousness, but not a means.

The **law entered** a program already established. It entered as something that comes later, something secondary, something that entered to serve a purpose, and then at some point in the future, when it had served its purpose, to exit as it had entered.

The Law entered the program for the purpose of causing the **offence** of the one man Adam to **abound**—to grow in scope and magnitude. Before the Law, men had done that which was right in their own eyes, having no guide greater than their own consciences. The Law was added to the conscience to enforce the sense of sinfulness.

Why would God desire for the offense to grow in scope and magnitude? Paul explains this later in chapter 7 (See comments under Romans 7:8-13). It was so men might know themselves as sinners. A disease that causes no pain will kill without warning. But if a disease is accompanied with great affliction, the man will seek a cure early.

By **abound,** he is speaking of the fruits of Adam's disobedience expressed in further disobedience by his descendants. This is the *many offences* of verse 16. It is apparent that God does not impute sin unless it is committed against a consciousness of express law. With the coming of the Law, many were exposed to the clear words of God with its many prohibitions carrying the death sentence. Thus, after the Law, many sinned after the similitude of Adam's transgression. So the coming of the Law, with its prohibitions and warnings, made the sin to be much greater in its ramifications. All sin committed against clear light is imputed to the sinner in any dispensation. Thus sin abounded.

...grace did much more abound.... God's answer to abounding sin is **much more** abounding **grace.** It is momentous that the first man Adam should precipitate a landslide of depravity, increasing with each generation, exploding into a tumbling mountain of destruction with the coming of the Law; but that the second man, the last Adam, should by His one act of obedience not only stop the destruction, but should turn the destructive debris into an everlasting temple of praise, is a wonder indeed. What sin laid low, grace lifted to heights beyond the original position before the fall.

5:21 That as sin hath reigned unto death, even so might grace reign through righteousness unto eternal life by Jesus Christ our Lord.

Sin reigns, controls all aspects of life in the body, until death, the natural consequences of sin.

Sin's reign was not diminished by the coming of the law. To the contrary, **sin reigned** through the Law, whereas in   contrast, **grace reigns** through Christ's **righteousness.**

"The strength of sin is the law (1 Cor 15:56)." Not all will admit to sin, but no one denies **death.** The greatest medical doctors, the faith healers, and scientists of all disciplines must admit that death reigns.

Completing his comparison, he says that just as sin has continued to reign unto death, so grace now reigns through the righteousness of one unto life without end. All this is by **Jesus Christ,** who is our Lord. Amen! He secured for us a place of abundance in His victory.

6:1-23 In Christ

Overview

This chapter begins a theme that carries all the way through chapter 8, expounding on the believer's position in Christ. The previous chapter told us what Adam brought on his descendants; this chapter tells us what Christ hath wrought on those that are now in Him. This chapter was anticipated in the *much mores* of chapter five. God did not take the believer out of Adam to leave him without descent, without affiliation. The believer is taken out of the death of Adam to be placed into the death and then the life of Christ.

6:1 What shall we say then? Shall we continue in sin, that grace may abound?

Paul has anticipated an objection from his detractors. Or perhaps occasionally, when publicly preaching this message, Paul had been challenged in this manner. Often the gospel message has been accused of making allowance for sin. It is a fact that men who do not fear God have often excused their sins by appealing to what they perceive to be the permissiveness of grace.

The devout Jew knew the Law to be the highest concept of righteousness ever entertained by either religion or philosophy. No school of thought came close to the lofty demands of Mosaic Law. In the Jew's thinking, a person could move from the Law of Moses in only one direction—toward a lesser view of righteousness. Did not the gospel offer immediate acceptance of anyone, and that before even a single work of righteousness? To the Jew, the Law was much higher in its standards.

Actually, what Paul was faced with was an objection to the very validity of Christianity. Skeptics reasoned that if the gospel took a dimmer view of righteousness, certainly it was not worthy to replace the Law. In 3:7-8 Paul dealt with a similar objection. His objectors claimed that Paul said, *"Let us do evil that good may come."* Two factors prompted objections like these. (1. Paul did indeed teach a gift of righteousness that required no prior works of righteousness on the part of the repentant sinner. (2. The gospel was a challenge to the old ways of Judaism. They also understood the propaganda advantage of claiming that this gospel was inferior to the Law in righteousness.

As we consider this accusation, note that though the supposition is abominable, it is based on an element of truth. Paul has already told us two verses earlier, *"where sin abounded, grace did much more abound."* It is a fact that God is ultimately glorified in the great exercise of His grace against abounding sin. The fallacy in their accusation is their assumption that grace is limited to the power to forgive—that its only glory is in passing over sin. He has already told us in 4:17 that God *"calleth those things which be not as though they were."* God calls the sinner righteous when in fact he is not. However, if the gospel went no further than to pretend that a man was righteous, then indeed it would be a sham, and the Law would be morally superior.

But their challenge is not sincere. Anyone that has actually experienced the grace of God would never ask such a question. A pure heart would never attempt to use grace as a cover for continuing in sin. But it bears answering, since it is such a common objection put foreword by those who cling to the Law while rejecting the authority of the Lawgiver. Furthermore, answering this charge provides Paul with a good lead into the next logical step in the progression of his theology.

6:2 God forbid. How shall we, that are dead to sin, live any longer therein?

He answers the challenge of verse one. Shall we continue in sin? **God forbid**. This is the strongest negative possible. **How shall** indicates that it is not a question of *shall we continue*, but **how** CAN we continue. Paul's assumption is that something fundamental has occurred in the believer that makes continuing in sin an impossibility. Continuing in sin is not an option for those that are **dead to sin**—dead to the power of sin to reign over the body of flesh.

He is introducing an amazing, new concept. We understand what it means to be dead IN sin, but he says *dead to sin*. He will show us that those that are taken out of Adam and placed into Christ are now as dead TO sin as they were once dead IN sin. The issue is not *should we*, but **how can we** who are dead to sin continue sinning? Those who are dead cannot be induced to respond. He will explain the nature of this death in the coming verses.

6:3 Know ye not, that so many of us as were baptized into Jesus Christ were baptized into his death?

This is not water baptism. Water baptism is an immersion into water. This is an immersion into Christ. The word *baptize* is by no means limited to water. In current usage the word baptism is most often associated with water. Most are unaware of its broader usage. In 1 Corinthians 10:2 the children of Israel were baptized unto Moses, but no one got wet. In Luke 12:50 and Matthew 20:22-23, Jesus spoke of His death as a baptism—an immersion into death. In Matthew 3:11 Jesus spoke of a baptism with fire. That is, the flames of Hell will baptize the damned. No one gets wet. Acts 1:12 speaks of a baptism with the Holy Ghost. The baptized are immersed into the Holy Ghost by Jesus himself, and this when they are no where near water.

John's baptism and New Testament water baptism do indeed involve water. But with the many other non-water uses, it is easy to see that the word *baptism* does not imply the element into which one is immersed. Only the individual context defines the nature of the baptism.

Any baptism requires a baptizer, a baptizee, and a baptizing element. In John's baptism, John was the baptizer, the sinner was the baptizee, and water was the element. In Christ's personal baptism the element was His own death. Rome was the baptizer, and Christ was the baptizee. In Moses' baptism, the baptizee was the nation of Israel. God was the baptizer, and the element was Moses himself. In the baptism of fire, God was the baptizer, the sinner was the baptizee, and Hell fire was the element. In John's baptism and in Christian water baptism, the believer is the baptizee, the minister is the baptizer, and water is the element.

But the most important baptism of all, the one spoken of in this passage, is described throughout Paul's epistles. *"For as many of you as have been baptized into Christ have put on Christ (Galatians 3:27)."* The element is Jesus Christ. *"For by one Spirit are we all baptized into one body, whether we be Jews or gentiles, whether we be bond or free; and have been all made to drink into one Spirit (1 Corinthians 12:13)."* Again the element is Christ's one body. The one who baptizes into the one body is not the minister, but the Holy Spirit himself. *"Buried with him in baptism, wherein also ye are risen with him through the faith of the operation of God, who hath raised him from the dead (Colossians 2:12)."* This baptism, which places the believer into the resurrection of Christ, is done by the *operation of God*; that is, God is the baptizer.

Since the baptism of this passage places the believer into Jesus Christ and thereby into His death and resurrection, we can identify this baptism with the Spirit's baptism, and not with the minister's baptism into water.

...were baptized into his death.... In chapter seven we will learn that the only way out from under the jurisdiction of the law is through death. We will also learn that the only way to be released from the cursed flesh of Adam is death. With the death sentence on Adam's descendants, and the law overseeing the execution of the sentence—a law that is unto death—the only way out is death. Christ not only died for the sinner, but he put the believing sinner to death with Him. The death of Christ becomes the death of all believers and the point at which one is freed from all that constrains one to sin.

6:4 Therefore we are buried with him by baptism into death: that like as Christ was raised up from the dead by the glory of the Father, even so we also should walk in newness of life.

Remember, Paul is explaining why it is not possible for one who is in Christ to continue in sin. Those that have died with Christ are (presently) **buried** with him. That is, by entering into Christ and becoming one with Him, Christ's history then becomes the believer's history. That which is accounted to Jesus the man is accounted to those that are baptized into Him. Therefore when Christ was buried, the believer was buried **with him** (at the same time, in the same grave).

No human minister of water baptism can place a believer into Christ's body, death, and resurrection. This can only be the work of the Holy Spirit, the operation of God. This baptism of the Spirit into one body (1 Corinthians 10:13) is synonymous with salvation, and occurs before one is baptized in water.

...that we also should walk in newness of life. His discussion of the baptism is incidental to his subject, which is that (different from the Law) those that are in Christ (and are therefore dead to sin) now walk in holiness—**newness of life**. The newness of walking comes from a new life—the life of Christ.

6:5 For if we have been planted together in the likeness of his death, we shall be also in the likeness of his resurrection:

The phrase, **"planted together,"** must allude to the concept of a seed falling into the ground to die in anticipation of a new birth. When Christ was *planted* in the grave, the believer was *planted* with Him. *"Verily, verily, I say unto you, Except a corn of wheat fall into the ground and die, it abideth alone: but if it die, it bringeth forth much fruit (John 12:24)."*

Paul argues that if God would cause us to participate in Christ's death, it must be in anticipation of our participation in His resurrection.

Death is only termination; resurrection is regeneration.

Resurrection completes the cycle.

- *"For as in Adam all die, even so in Christ shall all be made alive (1 Corinthians 15:22)."*
- *"And so it is written, The first man Adam was made a living soul; the last Adam was made a quickening spirit (1 Corinthians 15:45)."*
- *"Even when we were dead in sins, hath quickened us together with Christ, (by grace ye are saved;) And hath raised us up together, and made us sit together in heavenly places in Christ Jesus (Ephesians 2:5-6)."*
- *"Buried with him in baptism, wherein also ye are risen with him through the faith of the operation of God, who hath raised him from the dead (Colossians 2:12)."*
- *"If ye then be risen with Christ, seek those things which are above, where Christ sitteth on the right hand of God (Colossians 3:1)."*

Paul will get back to a discussion on the resurrected body in the latter part of chapter 8.

6:6 Knowing this, that our old man is crucified with him, that the body of sin might be destroyed, that henceforth we should not serve sin.

The believer's co-crucifixion/resurrection with Christ is not something to which we aspire, but a past fact we are to know—**"knowing this."**

The **old man** is the man of old, all that the natural man was in essence, relationships, and history.

The term **old man** is used two other times in Scripture. *"That ye put off concerning the former conversation the old man, which is corrupt according to the deceitful lusts (Ephesians 4:22)."* This is not a command to put off the old man. By looking at the context, it becomes obvious that Paul is showing how the believer's walk differs from that of unsaved gentiles (verse 17). Their understanding is darkened; they are past feeling (verses 18-19). But (verses 20-21) we who are in Christ didn't learn such an evil walk from Him. No, we were taught the truth in Jesus Christ, *that ye put off the old man and put on the new* (verses 22-24). Note that the text speaks of the old man as *"former."*

Lie not one to another, seeing that ye have put off the old man with his deeds...(Colossians 3:9)." Again Paul is commanding the believer to not lie based on the assumption that the old man has already been *put off*. According to 1 Corinthians 5:17, *"if any man be in Christ, he is a new creature: old things are passed away; behold, all things are become new."* The **old man** is history. Based on the reality of that Divine principle, we are assured of our freedom from the sins that were a part of that past relationship.

The believer's only reality is that of the new man.

It is important to understand the meaning of **old man** as Paul uses the term. The *old man* is not some mysterious other-self that co-exists with the new man. The old and new man are not opposing inner forces striving for supremacy. At present, this is a popular concept, but it has never been supported by any serious biblical exegesis. It is only a passing pop philosophy. Nevertheless, it has become so popular in many pulpits that we must address this fanciful idea, however unfounded.

The *old man* is not the soul, not the spirit, and not the *law of sin in my members*. It is not some *part* of the self. It is all that we were in every aspect of our being before we were regenerated and placed into Christ, thus into His death, burial, and resurrection. The *old man* is entirely replaced by the *new man*. The *old man* no longer exists in the regenerated believer.

Likewise, the *new man* is not something added to the self, some inner, divine life-force. The *new man* is not the Holy Spirit, not Christ living in me; it is not a "new nature" struggling with the *old man*. The *new man* is all that the believer is in body, soul, and spirit—after being placed into Christ's body. The believer's only reality is that of the *new man*. Every aspect of the believer is *new man*. If the believer sins, it is the *new man* that sins.

The *old man* was the *natural man*, the Adam man, *earthy, natural, carnal, dead* in personal trespasses, *weak through the flesh*, and *could not please God*. The *old man* was under condemnation. The *old man* (the self that then was) was without God and without hope. As Paul will show in chapter 7, the *old man* could *not do the things that he would*. He was *sold under sin*. The new man now sustains a relationship only to Christ, and not to Adam.

...old man is crucified with him. The *old man* **is,** right now, *crucified*. He is not challenging us to "die to self," as some have maintained. We are not told to seek crucifixion. This is an announcement of present reality, not an inducement to apprehend. Crucifixion with Christ is not the goal, but the very historical event on which we originally entered a relationship with Christ.

As long as a man is in Adam, he is under the curse of death and alienated from God. The only way out of Adam is death. Being baptized into Christ, we are placed into His death, thus freed from Adam so we can be married to Christ (7:1-3). This is a common theme of the epistles. *"I am crucified with Christ: nevertheless I live; yet not I, but Christ liveth in me: and the life which I now live in the flesh I live by the faith of the Son of God, who loved me, and gave himself for me (Galatians 2:20)."* This crucifixion results in **the body of sin** (house of the old man) being **destroyed**.

Body of sin

Only by a thorough examination of the larger contents of all Paul's writings can we determine the exact meaning of this *body of sin*. There have been many hasty and bizarre assumptions drawn from this and like passages. It is unnecessary to make wild guesses; the meaning is right on the surface. The *body of sin* is the physical body with all of its natural and accumulated lusts, tainted and depraved by a life of disobedience. Of course, when the body dies, the soul goes through a change in relationship to several things, all of which Paul will discuss in the following chapters. Death in Christ changes one's relationship to the body, to the world with all of its lust, to the Law, and to Adam. Other changes occur, but they are based on our co-resurrection. We will discuss these as we come to them in the text.

That which dies does so as a result of identity with Christ. The believer enters into Christ and thus shares His experiences. The believer's death must be identical to Christ's, since the believer's freedom from sin is a result of this union. Speaking of Christ's death, Paul says, *"For in that he died, he died unto sin once: but in that he liveth, he liveth unto God (6:10)."* His argument is that we are free from sin because of our identity with Christ's death to sin. When Jesus was crucified, nothing died but His body, which of course terminated all of its accompanying relationships. The meaning is plain if you simply reads the entire chapter and book in context. This will be discussed more thoroughly in the following verses.

6:7 For he that is dead is freed from sin.

Paul is stating the obvious. Dead people are not affected by the allure of sin. Paul is not limiting his statement to the sinner. In verse 10 he comes to his point that Christ died *to* sin. There was no sin IN Christ, so He could not die to sin in that manner. Nor is this a statement that Christ died to the sin that was vicariously ON Him. Nor is this a reference to Christ's death FOR sin.

We understand the nature of Christ's death TO sin when we see that it resulted in His own personal deliverance from the pull of sin. We are told that Christ was tempted while in the body of flesh. Now that His flesh (physical body) is dead, He can no longer be tempted. The purpose of this whole section is to prove that those that are in Christ will not continue in sin because they have died to it in the person of Christ their head.

6:8 Now if we be dead with Christ, we believe that we shall also live with him:

If we have entered into Christ so as to be a partaker of His death, we will most certainly partake of His life after death. The process is incomplete without resurrection and ascension. God would not crucify the believer and then leave him dead.

6:9 Knowing that Christ being raised from the dead dieth no more; death hath no more dominion over him.
6:10 For in that he died, he died unto sin once: but in that he liveth, he liveth unto God.

Knowing what we do of Christ's experience (which experience we have entered and do now share) becomes the criterion of understanding our own present relationship to death and sin. The believer enters the picture at the point of *knowing* something that is already history.

Death hath NO MORE dominion implies that at one time death did have dominion over Christ. His death was indeed vicarious, and as such, being in a natural, mortal, corruptible body, death overtook Christ and exercised full dominion. *"Forasmuch then as the children are partakers of flesh and blood, he also himself likewise took part of the same; that through death he might destroy him that had the power of death, that is, the devil; And deliver them who through fear of death were all their lifetime subject to bondage (Hebrews 2:14-15)."* The death Christ died was in regard to *flesh and blood.*

By becoming flesh and blood (mortal), Christ could die on behalf of those that were under the death sentence of Adam. But the emphasis here is not His death for us, but our participation in that death, so that we, as he, are freed from the power of death. As we see in Hebrews 2:14, it is through death that one is freed from it. He will explain this further in 7:1-4.

6:11 Likewise reckon ye also yourselves to be dead indeed unto sin, but alive unto God through Jesus Christ our Lord.

Likewise, in the same manner and to the same degree that Christ is *dead to sin* and *alive to God*, we are to assume the same to be true of ourselves. God is not telling us to accomplish something. He is telling us what God has done, and commanding us to believe the reality as it already exists.

This word **reckon** means to count it as reality. The command to reckon is not a command to do something. He is not telling us to enact our faith so as to appropriate something that is otherwise inactive. Reckoning does not require spiritual energy or commitment.

Some Christian-life writers have read all manner of struggle or surrender into this word. They reckon that *reckon* implies some work of grace in the heart and will, so that one can "by faith receive the blessings of sanctification."

To believe that the experience of Christ is indeed my experience is to *reckon* the words of God to be true. Nothing more is implied here or elsewhere. The weakest and most trembling can hear the words of God and believe (reckon).

Reckon yourselves to be **dead indeed** unto sin. This death of which Paul speaks is not a pretend death. It is not some emotional or spiritual death. He is not speaking figuratively about death to self-will or death to the ego. He is talking about the kind of death that destroys the human body—a death that is INDEED a death in the normal sense of the word.

If you have difficulty seeing that this death is real physical death, note in the above passages that death to sin is a direct result of the crucifixion of Christ's body of flesh and blood. *"... if one died for all, then were all dead (2 Corinthians 5:14)."* All are dead in the same manner that the one died for all. All are free from sin in the same manner that our representative is free from sin, through physical death that kills the physical body.

Reckon yourselves to be **alive unto God** through Jesus Christ. As He who died for all is now alive unto God through His resurrection, so we are to suppose ourselves to be equally alive unto God, as one is who is resurrected from genuine physical death.

...through Jesus Christ our Lord. This experience of death and resurrection is not an event independent of a relationship to Christ. It is **through** Christ that the believer can *reckon* these things to be reality. If the believer views himself apart from Christ, he will not see any signs of dead flesh or resurrection. Reckoning is believing God, as opposed to believing one's experience.

6:12 Let not sin therefore reign in your mortal body, that ye should obey it in the lusts thereof.

Let not. Only now, in the progression of his argument, has he given us something to do (other than believe or reckon). It is now within the power of those that are in Christ to not yield their bodies to the lust dwelling there.

Let not sin reign **therefore...** since we are dead to it and alive to God.

...reign in your mortal body.... Since you are dead to sin, crucified with Christ, you now have the wherewithal to *let not sin reign in your mortal body*. In this command, there exists the assumption that all believers are now free to not sin, that the body no longer controls us through lusts. Note, he links lust to the body.

...mortal body.... Over the years, there has been much philosophical speculation done in an attempt to account for universal sin and its power. Rather than believe the Bible, some theologians have created various missing links to bridge the gap between divine revelation and human experience. The Holy Spirit has been careful to use the most simple and common words to pinpoint the origin and seat of sin. Words like *flesh, body, mortal body, sinful flesh, body of sin, sin in my members, body of this death, vile body, corruptible body,* etc. Anyone can understand it. It is not deep or hidden. Any of the 24 diffent Greek bibles will confirm what you read in English. See the word *flesh* in the Appendix.

We will go by the text and assume that Paul and the Holy Spirit were able to say the truth in plain words, as God would have it said. Sin reigns in mortal bodies, in bodies of flesh and blood, corruptible bodies. *"The flesh (flesh is flesh) lusteth against the Spirit and the Spirit against the flesh... so that ye cannot do the things that you would (Galatians 5:17)." "That which is born of the flesh is flesh (John 3:6)."*

...obey it.... The *it* that is obeyed is the *mortal body*. The body is contrary to the spirit. Ever since creation, the body has been an obstacle to be overcome by the human soul dwelling within. To speak of the individual *obeying* the flesh is to recognize the independent lust of the flesh, which exerts an appeal that may be in opposition to the mind.

...in the lusts thereof. The lusts **thereof** (lusts of the mortal body). *The flesh lusteth....* The flesh left to its self cannot do other than lust. All flesh is lustful flesh. The very nature of flesh is lustful. Regenerate flesh is lustful flesh. That is not to imply that the flesh must be permitted to lust. As seen by His temptations, Christ's flesh was lust-able, though never given over to natural lusts. He never allowed his flesh to surmount His spirit and intellect. Eve saw (with fleshly eyes—the only kind she had) that the fruit of the tree was *pleasant to the eyes*. She lusted after the fruit by means of her sight. This is before she fell into sin. She deemed the fruit to be *good for food*. Again the lusts of her body were speaking to her intellect. And she judged that exercising the lusts of her flesh on the tree would give her an experience of knowledge concerning *good and evil*. She sought to learn about the world (gain knowledge), not by the word of God, but through fulfilling the lusts of her flesh (James 1:14). Flesh is flesh.

Paul knew wherein the battle lay. *"But I keep under my body, and bring it into subjection: lest that by any means, when I have preached to others, I myself should be a castaway (1 Corinthians 9:27)."*

6:13 Neither yield ye your members as instruments of unrighteousness unto sin: but yield yourselves unto God, as those that are alive from the dead, and your members as instruments of righteousness unto God.

There is no question as to the identity of the members. They are well enumerated. The eyes, ears, nose, tongue, hands, feet, reproductive organs, and the head are all called members.

- *James 3:5 "Even so the tongue is a little member, and boasteth great things."*
- *Romans 12:4 "For as we have many members in one body, and all members have not the same office:"*
- *Matthew 5:30 "And if thy right hand offend thee, cut it off, and cast it from thee: for it is profitable for thee that one of thy members should perish, and not that thy whole body should be cast into Hell."* The members of the body are the **instruments** of sin. He

speaks of the members as if they were impersonal tools to be used one way or the other.

- *James 4:1* *"From whence come wars and fightings among you? come they not hence, even of your <u>lusts that war in your members?</u>"* One's inner struggle against sin is between the lust in the members and the mind that doesn't want to sin.

- *Romans 7:23* *But I see another law in my members, warring against the law of my mind, and bringing me into captivity to the <u>law of sin which is in my members.</u>*

- *Colossians 3:5* *"Mortify therefore your members which are upon the earth;* [He enumerates some of the sins that come from the members:] *fornication, uncleanness, inordinate affection, evil concupiscence, and covetousness, which is idolatry:"*

- *Romans 7:5* *"For when we were in the flesh, the motions of sins, which were by the law, did <u>work in our members</u>* [The seat of sin is the members of the body.] *to bring forth fruit unto death."*

Now that the believer is in Christ, and therefore dead to sin, he has the power to not yield to lusts that still reside in the mortal body (now dead in Christ). Based on this reality, Paul tells us, **"Neither yield** ye your members...." With confidence that we have the resources to do so, Paul tells us to **"yield yourselves unto God."** The lusts in the members, that war against the law of the mind, cannot prevent the believer from yielding to God. This yielding is based on resurrection—*"yield yourselves unto God as those that are alive from the dead."* The power to yield does not come from our death with Christ, but from our resurrection. As he told us in 5:10, we will be saved through his life (Romans 5:10).

The members that were previously without restraint, can now be yielded to God as **instruments of righteousness**. This, the Law could not do.

6:14 For sin shall not have dominion over you: for ye are not under the law, but under grace.

Herein is an assumption that sin's dominion is in some way related to the Law's jurisdiction. That is, a person under the Law is enslaved to the habits of sin, whereas one who is under grace is freed from the dominion of sin. Remember, this chapter began with Paul answering the charge that since we were under abounding grace and not under Law, should we continue sinning? He surprises his audience by telling us that quite the opposite is true. Though you think Law so forcefully upholds righteousness, while grace is permissive, it is grace that actually delivers us from sin's dominion.

This verse is also a clear statement as to a change of dispensation. Those who are in Christ are in no sense under the Law of Moses. We will speak more of this in 7:1-4 and in 8:1-3.

6:15 What then? shall we sin, because we are not under the law, but under grace? God forbid.

This question brings us back full circle to where the discussion started in v.1, *"Shall we continue in sin that grace may abound?"* This is not an option Paul or any believer would even consider, but the enemies of the gospel thought the system to be philosophically vulnerable at this point. In their thinking, one would desire to be out from under the Law for one reason only—to sin without impunity. The apparent intent of the Law was to halt sin. It was not effectual, but that was no fault of the Law. To the Jew who knew of no other restraint, to be free from the Law was to be lawless, ungoverned, without accountability.

The Law comes as a crushing stone; grace comes as an embrace. Since the Law carries a death penalty, and grace doesn't, should we continue sinning? He is shocked at the question and answers with the strongest negative possible, **God forbid** such a preposterous thing. He raised this question in v.1 and then went on to lay the foundation for his answer. The background has been well established in verses 1-16. When Christ died to sin, the believer died to sin. When Christ was raised to a new life, the believer was raised to a new life. Paul's answer: Under the Law, one should not continue in sin; in Christ, based on the constraints of the Spirit and our participation in the death and resurrection of Christ, one cannot continue in sin.

6:16 Know ye not, that to whom ye yield yourselves servants to obey, his servants ye are to whom ye obey; whether of sin unto death, or of obedience unto righteousness?

To one who would ask the question of verse 15, Paul responds as if he is amazed that one should be so ignorant. Don't you know the obvious? The bottom line is that your lifestyle reveals your life-source. If one yields his members to sin, then he is the servant of sin, and as such will die the eternal **death** of the damned. On the other hand, if one is under grace then he has the power and the will to walk in obedience, the end being **righteousness**. So let's have no more of this absurdity about continuing to sin. Sin is overcome by all who are under grace.

This passage is not a continuation of the way of salvation or sanctification. He is reflecting on the outcome of the gospel, not the recounting the way of the gospel. This is not the means; it is the end. It is not the root; it is the fruit. The fruit is so like the root that you can identify one that is in Christ by the way he yields himself. If he yields himself to obey sin, he will die the death of the damned. If he yields himself to obey righteousness, then he reveals that he is indeed the servant of righteousness. Again, this is not a means by which one attains righteousness and life, but testimony as to whose servant you are.

This is intended to satisfy his accusers: *"Shall we continue in sin?"* His answer—don't be ridiculous; under any system, those that are servants of sin are damned.

6:17 But God be thanked, that ye were the servants of sin, but ye have obeyed from the heart that form of doctrine which was delivered you.

Thank God that servitude to sin is a thing of the past. Your heart responded to the grace of God and you were in full compliance with everything you heard. Heart obedience is the opposite of obedience to the Law. One obeys the Law in hope of pleasing God, of becoming acceptable. Whereas heart obedience to grace is the very act of embracing unmerited favor. The pressure and curse of the Law is lifted, leaving the sinner free to love God and respond in faith and thankfulness.

Note that the obedience was not to certain laws of right doing, but to the doctrine of Jesus Christ, that is, the whole message of righteousness by faith as Paul has thus far preached in this epistle to the Romans. *"Then said they unto him, What shall we do, that we might work the works of God? Jesus answered and said unto them, This is the work of God, that ye believe on him whom he hath sent (John 6:28-29)."*

…ye were **the servants of sin….** This is an indictment on the Law, in which they were formerly held. Under the Law they were *servants of sin*. He will expand on this concept throughout the next chapter.

They **were** the servants of sin—past tense. This is not an exhortation to stop sinning, nor even a warning. He is stating emphatically that *"the gospel is the power of God unto salvation to every one that believeth (Romans 1:16)."* He will eventually tell us in 8:4 that what the Law could not do in delivering from the acts of sin, Christ did. In Christ one does not fight a losing struggle against the habits of sin. Christ in a believer works to bring obedience and deliverance.

6:18 Being then made free from sin, ye became the servants of righteousness.

Three times in this chapter he tells us that we are **free from sin**. The freedom from sin was not the end of having overcome the same, but of having been placed into Christ's death and resurrection. The believer is **made** free. The freedom comes from without. The freedom is done TO the believer. This is a result of having been baptized (Spirit) into His body. Sin and Law terminated at the moment of death. Life and freedom from sin began with resurrection in Christ.

He uses the term **servants of righteousness** as a parallel to *servants of sin* (v.17). He is not saying that the believer cannot do other than righteousness, any more than *servants of sin* means that one cannot do other than sin. This is not about ability or limitations, but about relationship and orientation. One who is free from sin can still sin if he so chooses. The human person is never beyond choosing.

Paul will proceed to explain his point more fully in the following five verses.

6:19 I speak after the manner of men because of the infirmity of your flesh: for as ye have yielded your members servants to uncleanness and to iniquity unto iniquity; even so now yield your members servants to righteousness unto holiness.

Paul is about to speak in a manner that he feels is beneath the dignity of his subject. Because of the inability of his hearers to understand these high and holy realities, he will descend to the mundane and speak after the manner of common men speaking on common subjects.

...infirmity of your flesh.... He says the flesh is infirm (weak, without strength, unsound or sickly). If you are thinking too lofty here you will miss the point. Infirmity always refers to natural depravity—depravity of the substance of body. See 8:26 under infirmities. People with headaches, backaches, toothaches, or dementia don't sit and listen very well. People with low blood sugar, high cholesterol, constipation, or hemorrhoids, can't stand lengthy, verbose explanations. Young people are agitated by hormonal rushes, and old people go to sleep while the explanation is being given. The brain cannot retain the definition of words and loses the associations of modifiers and antecedents. It can't remember the difference between an adverb and a verb, so make it simple for simple folk who have been going downhill ever since Adam forsook God.

While the soul is confined to the body of flesh, the human mind perceives through the mechanics of the fleshly brain. If the body is diminished or depraved, then the mind is limited. Likewise, the will and emotions, though nonmaterial, share the limitations of the material body.

So as to be understood, in a common way he says: Just as you previously, with total abandonment, yielded your members to the complete servitude of the principle of iniquity that you might work iniquity, so now with the same zeal and abandonment yield your members to the principle of righteousness that you might work holiness.

...even so now yield.... Here is something for the believer to do. The believer is not creating reality by yielding, he is responding to reality. The reality being the work God did in Christ in crucifying the believer and freeing him from the power of sin. Yielding is now within the scope of those that are in Christ. Yielding does not imply action, but the cessation of resistance.

...as ye have yielded your members...even so now yield your members.... The battle is still on the level of resisting the passions that dwell in the human body, the flesh. The members are members of the body. The mind, will, and emotions are not members. No part of the nonmaterial self is called a member. This is not a struggle within the soul; it is a struggle between the soul and the body of flesh. *"From whence come wars and fightings among you? come they not hence, even of your lusts that war in your members (James 4:1)?"*

Before being put into Christ, the *law of sin*, which was *in our members*, warred against the *law of our minds* and brought us into captivity to the *law of sin in our members*, but the *law of the Spirit of life* in Christ Jesus has now made us free from the *law of sin and death* which dwelt in our members. Based on this reality, we are free to yield our members as instruments of righteousness unto holiness. We will see more of this in chapter 8.

6:20-23 The fruit of sin and righteousness contrasted

20 For when ye were the servants of sin, ye were free from righteousness.
21 What fruit had ye then in those things whereof ye are now ashamed? for the end of those things is death.
22 But now being made free from sin, and become servants to God, ye have your fruit unto holiness, and the end everlasting life.
23 For the wages of sin is death; but the gift of God is eternal life through Jesus Christ our Lord.

Overview of verses 20 -23
In these four verses, he will motivate the believer to respond as he has commanded.

You should reverse the former role, because when you were under the servitude of sin you had no regard whatsoever to the principles of righteousness. You didn't care what was right or wrong; you just recklessly did what you wanted, absolutely free from the constraints of righteousness. And what was the benefit of doing those things that now bring such a feeling of shame? Death, and nothing more.

But in your present state you are *free from sin* and are become *servants of God* just as you were once *servants of sin*. And is it not far better that whereas the fruit of the former life was death, the fruit of this present life is not only freedom from sin, with the joys of holiness, but life that never ends? For you know the principle: sin always terminates in death, but God gives eternal life when you are in Jesus Christ.

For when ye were the servants of sin, ye were free from righteousness. He is saying that in the former relationship you sinned as one that was entirely free from the duty to be righteous. His suggestion is that as a new creature you should apply the same principle to the new relationship. You had no regard for righteousness then, so have no regard for sin now.

Those who sustain a relationship to sin as its servants are under no obligation to walk righteously. This is a terrible dismissal. If one is not in Christ, his efforts to do good are not welcomed. He is wasting his time. He is under no obligation to obey Christ. He is none of His. Christ can say, "I never knew you." The servants of sin are slaves to their own bodily passions. As long as the sinner makes his own selfish pursuits his end, he can never do righteously. Until one repents toward God and is born-again, he is outside of God's jurisdiction. When the body is contracted out to evil, sold to the highest bidder offering the greatest indulgence, there is no obligation except to the one to whom the body is sold. Paul, speaking of his former state, said, *"I am carnal, sold under sin."*

6:21 What fruit had ye then in those things...?

By way of encouraging and motivating the believer, Paul asks a pertinent question. The answer is readily implied. This is just a reminder. In the former relationship, what fruit did sin produce? Remembering the lousy fruit of the former relationship should cause the new creature to abandon sin altogether and throw himself into righteousness as readily as he formerly threw himself into sin. It is for this carnal comparison that Paul apologized.

The root was sin, so the fruit was death. Between the root and the final fruit of death there is much reaping. The fruit of sin is more sin, guilt, shame, broken marriages, anguish, addiction, hate, misery, no peace, etc. Why would one cultivate such a crop? Because the planting of it is a thrill, an immediate pleasure, and the bitter harvest is much later than the sowing. *"Be not deceived; God is not mocked: for whatsoever a man soweth, that shall he also reap. For he that soweth to his flesh shall of the flesh reap corruption; but he that soweth to the Spirit shall of the Spirit reap life everlasting (Galatians 6:7-8)."*

...whereof ye are now ashamed.... The sinner still bears the image of God, and, so occasionally, does know shame. But upon repenting to God, the believer becomes ashamed of even his reflection in the mirror before he was saved. It is a mark of a believer to be ashamed of what one ought.

...for the end of those things is death. The end of all sin is death. It is most fitting. In a universe destined to contain nothing but the glory of God, what other end could sin have? That **death** is what Christ came to abolish.

6:22 But now being made free from sin....

The believer is not working to free himself from sin. He is working inside that freedom. The freedom is **now**. He is from without **made** free. Christ *made* us free by placing us inside of Himself and His freedom.

Three times in this chapter, Paul tells us that we are *free from sin*.

...and become servants to God.... He designates the believer as a *servant of God*, not because that is the best word to describe the entire relationship, for Jesus said, *"Henceforth I call you not servants...but I have called you friends... (John 15:15)."* The phrase *"servant of God"* is to contrast *"servant of sin."* The word *servant* defines not our person but our work in regard to God.

...ye have your fruit unto holiness.... The root is known by its fruit. The fruit of the Holy Spirit is holiness. To speak of an unholy Christian would be like speaking of a righteous devil.

...and the end everlasting life. Remember, Paul is encouraging and motivating the believer. He reminds us that as the fruit of sin is death, the fruit of being a servant of God is holiness, and in the end, everlasting life. Everlasting life is not a reward brought about by holiness; it is just the **end** of the life that Christ gives.

6:23 For the wages of sin is death; but the gift of God is eternal life....

This final statement sums up the entire comparison between servants of sin and servants of God. Yield your members to God as servants of righteousness, because the wages (the end) of sin is death, but this great gift of God is eternal life. Therefore make sure you walk in compliance with who you are.

As you can see from the context, this verse is not part of the "Romans road to salvation." The context is sanctification. This reminder of the two, great, opposing principles is given to encourage the believer.

...through Jesus Christ our Lord. The believer finds his cure from sin, not in a constitutional change that leaves him free to function with the parameters of his own powers, but in a continuing relationship to Jesus Christ.

7:1-6 The old husband now dead

1 Know ye not, brethren, (for I speak to them that know the law,) how that the law hath dominion over a man as long as he liveth?

2 For the woman which hath an husband is bound by the law to her husband so long as he liveth; but if the husband be dead, she is loosed from the law of her husband.

3 So then if, while her husband liveth, she be married to another man, she shall be called an adulteress: but if her husband be dead, she is free from that law; so that she is no adulteress, though she be married to another man.

4 Wherefore, my brethren, ye also are become dead to the law

by the body of Christ; that ye should be married to another,
even to him who is raised from the dead, that we should bring
forth fruit unto God.

5 For when we were in the flesh, the motions of sins, which
were by the law, did work in our members to bring forth fruit
unto death.

6 But now we are delivered from the law, that being dead
wherein we were held; that we should serve in newness of
spirit, and not in the oldness of the letter.

Overview 7:1-6

This is not an attempt to convey the laws of marriage. It is an analogy that looks back to what has already been said and forward to what
will be said. The entire law/grace, works/faith, flesh/Spirit, Adam/Christ,
death/life, contrast is in view in this simple illustration.

Three parties are involved (one woman and two men) in a dilemma
involving the law. It is important to note that the main character is the
woman. The drama is her marital status.

The illustration is based on the unstated assumption that the woman
is married to a most undesirable man. Apparently, she would like to be
married to another, but she cannot, for the law will not permit her to di-
vorce and remarry another man. She must continue with this undesirable
husband until one of them dies. Only death will free her from his tyranny.
The law will not change. The other man, honorable in every way, will not
marry her while her first husband is alive. There is only one possible solution—the death of her husband—though not at her hand. If he did indeed die of a cause in which she was not an accomplice, the law's jurisdiction would terminate with honor, leaving her free to marry the new
man.

The Law does not die.

It is true that the law of marriage is an impediment to her taking the
new husband, but the analogy does not in the least suggest that termination of the law is an option. An inanimate law cannot die. The dignity of
all concerned demands unquestioned reverence for the integrity of the
law. The first verse states most clearly the parameters within which this
dilemma must be solved. The woman is bound to her husband as long as
he lives. The only possible release whereby she may be married to another is the death of her husband. The analogy and that which it illustrates must proceed with respect to this fact.

Paul is, so to speak, having his day before a Supreme Court of very
serious Jewish lawyers. They are watching carefully to see that he does
not solve his dilemma with the law/Law in a way that dishonors the law/
Law. It is of utmost importance to Paul to win his argument for the sanc-
tity of the gospel on grounds that are irrefutably legal. He knows that his

case will be argued over and over again by antagonists who will study it from every angle, having, as we now know, centuries in which to ferret out any loopholes in his reasoning. He argues not only for his generation but for all evangelists and defenders of the faith who down through time will take this message to those learned in the Law.

Who or what is the old husband?

This is a notoriously misunderstood chapter. Paul begins with an analogy to explain the simple truths of chapters five and six. Using the analogy of marriage, he beautifully illustrates how in our death with Christ our flesh died, freeing us from the Law, thus enabling us to marry Christ. It is an analogy as appropriate and simple as the mind of God could conceive.

Commentators rightly agree that the woman typifies the bride-of-Christ-to-be. Most rightly agree that the law is the Law of Moses—that judicial system that rules a man or woman until the day of death. The woman (future church) is bound by the law of marriage (Mosaic law) to her first husband (which we will show is the flesh). The final goal is that the would-be church (the woman), now married to the flesh (old husband), should be married to Christ (The new man), but the Law/law will not permit this as long as the old man (the first husband/the flesh) is still alive.

The commentators

Who is this *old man* that must die? On this point the commentators fan out like spokes on a wheel. When reading the commentaries, we discover only one consensus: that Paul fouled up in his illustration and the Holy Spirit preserved this "unfortunate" analogy, which is so "confusing." I am not in the least exaggerating, as you will see.

William Barclay says of this passage, "Seldom did Paul write so difficult and so complicated a passage as this." C. S. Dodd has said that when we are studying it we should try to "forget what Paul says and to find out what he means." Frank E. Gaebelein says, "The reader is apt to be somewhat disturbed in that there is a measure of inconsistency in the way the illustration is applied." He says, "The parallel breaks down." Again he reveals his unbelief by saying, "Paul was no doubt aware of a certain incongruity between illustration and application." R. C. Sproul manifests his unbelief by saying, "Paul introduces an analogy for the purpose of simplifying something difficult. Unfortunately this analogy, which was designed to simplify, has been the occasion of much confusion and a great deal of stumbling over the centuries." Can you believe that one claiming to be a Bible believer would say that Paul's analogy is "unfortunate" and that it "has caused confusion and stumbling"? Geoffrey B. Wilson advertises his lack of faith in the Word of God by saying, "The parallel is not exactly carried through because it would have been obviously untrue to say that the Law died." Alva J. McClain, demonstrating that he doesn't even know enough to be mixed up, says, "It looks as if Paul has mixed up his illustration. But this is not an analogy, which corresponds in every point; it is an illustration." The most noted writer, Charles Hodge, also failed to believe that Paul wrote what he meant to say. "The apparent confusion in this passage arises from the apostle's not carrying the figure regularly through."

Then Hodge says, "[O]ut of respect probably to the feelings of his readers, [Paul] avoids saying the Law is dead." I submit to you that Paul never avoided boldly saying the truth out of respect for Jews, gentiles, Romans, wise, or unwise. He would stand in front of a man's idol and tell him that he was "too superstitious." He would tell a Jew that his circumcision was counted as nothing. He would tell a Greek that his wisdom was foolishness. Are we to believe that the apostle Paul chose not to be clear because he was afraid of offending those who did not believe the truth? I cannot believe this of the Paul that wrote Romans 1-3 and the book of Galatians. It is strange how schoolhouse scholars read their own timid motives into biblical writers.

There is a general failure to appreciate what Paul said, the way he said it, simply because what he actually said is not in agreement with what the commentators choose to believe. Rather than change their teaching to agree with the Scripture, they fault Paul as if his writings were not inspired by the Holy Spirit. The commentators almost universally treat the Apostle Paul as if he were just another one of "the scholars" stating his own angle. You can't have it both ways. Either the Bible is the Word of God, perfect and infallible, which means that it is written as well as God can write it, or it is just the opinion of another commentator, thus subject to criticism and improvement.

It is not that the identity of the husband "has been a source of confusion" to commentators, but that the commentators have been a source of confusion to the passage. The confusion is not derived from any ambiguity in the Scripture. It is simply that having rejected the biblical definition of *flesh*, the passage no longer makes sense as written. Most want to say that the husband is the Law, and that the believer is freed from the Law so he can marry Christ. According to the analogy, the woman is indeed freed from the law; but it was not by the death of the law, rather the death of her husband—the one over whom the law held jurisdiction.

Interpretive parallel 7:1-6 (a quick overview)
(1. You that know the law, don't you understand? The law has authority over people only as long as they are alive. Its jurisdiction does not reach beyond the grave.

(2. You who would belong to Christ are bound to your body of flesh, that old man with all of the accumulated sins. You are not free to be the bride of Christ, because the Law has indicted you for your marriage union to your sinful flesh.

(3. Until that flesh dies you cannot be married to Christ. The flesh has prior claim on you.

(4. But the fact is that you Christians are no longer under the jurisdiction of the Law, because when you were baptized into Christ's body you were baptized into His death. When His flesh died, your flesh died at the same time. Now you have indeed been married to Christ that you might live to please Him, not your old man, the flesh.

(5. Remember, when you were still married to that flesh, sin used the condemnation of the Law to give more power to the members of your body to cause you to do things that put you further under the death sentence.

(6. But that is not your present condition. You are no longer subject to the Law or its condemnation, because that old man, the flesh that once held you, is now dead; so you can now serve God from your spirit and not just through Law, which was powerless over the flesh.

7:1 Know ye not, brethren, (for I speak to them that know the law,) how that the law hath dominion over a man as long as he liveth?

Paul has not suddenly reverted to a discussion on marriage. He refers to the law of marriage because it provides a perfect analogy for what he wants to say. When he addresses himself to those **who know the law**, our first thought is that he is talking to Jews, yet we know that he is writing to Rome, which is predominately gentile. More likely, the gentile Christians had become sufficiently familiar with the Old Testament to appreciate the laws of marriage. Further, similar laws of marriage were held among most gentiles. The nature of law, wherever it is found, is that of a binding rule, and so he can build on that universal understanding of law in general.

It is important to note that the **dominion** of Law and how one is released from that dominion is incidental to his subject. It does not serve his purpose sufficiently to simply show that we are not under the Law. To seek release from the Law, or to celebrate that release, would imply that the Law was improper, evil, or outdated. If release from the Law was all he wished to teach, he could have reminded us that a man is under the jurisdiction of law until he dies. That would have been easy to communicate, and there would have been no misunderstanding. If he intended to say that the Law has somehow been replaced by a different dispensation, he could have spoken as he did in Galatians. How simply he could have pointed out that by being in the body of Christ we have entered into His death, and being dead we are therefore free from the Law. But this is not his message, as many commentators think. He wants to show how one can get out from under the Law while both the Law and the person are still alive and operative. The Law rules over flesh, over natural man, over *"earthy"* man.

God's ultimate goal is a bride for His son. But she must be legitimate, in complete compliance with the Law. There must be no question of legality or ethics. God's son must wed under the most honorable of circumstances. So the opening principle, the tension on which this unfolding drama is built, is that the law's jurisdiction is until death—no exceptions.

Presenting this principle with use of the male gender *(hath dominion over a man as long as he liveth...)* does not imply that he is talking from the perspective of the husband in the analogy. The woman is the center of interest.

7:2 For the woman which hath an husband is bound by the law to her husband so long as he liveth; but if the husband be dead, she is loosed from the law of her husband.

...the woman which hath an husband.... He anticipates the eventual development of his analogy as he makes the woman's relationship the center of our attention. Her legal condition of being bound to her husband is the constraining element that prevents the woman from being married to another—to Christ.

...bound by the law.... The law of marriage, which represents the Mosaic Law. The Law is a just and good impediment. Only on grounds that are legal can one find release from the Law's jurisdiction.

...so long as he liveth.... He also anticipates that the needful thing is the death of the husband, not the woman, and not the law. The living husband typifies the flesh to which one is wed.

...if the husband be dead.... The husband is a type of the flesh, inherited from Adam.

...she is loosed from the law of her husband.... As the death of a husband frees a wife from the law of marriage that bound her to her husband, so the death of the flesh frees the believer from the Law that governed men in the flesh. If it were the law of marriage that the woman sought to escape, she would not remarry another husband, for that would put her right back under that law of marriage. It is the old man (flesh) she seeks to escape, not the law itself.

7:3 So then if, while her husband liveth, she be married to another man, she shall be called an adulteress: but if her husband be dead, she is free from that law; so that she is no adulteress, though she be married to another man.

He takes the background principles of his analogy even further by telling us that the jurisdiction of the law is such that if this woman should marry another man (Christ) while the first husband (flesh) is still alive, she would be called an adulteress. The only answer to her (our) dilemma (a desire to be married to Christ) is the death of the husband (the flesh of Adam).

Again Paul anticipates the point he will make by suggesting that the solution lies in the death of the husband. There is no hint of the law dying or of the woman dying.

...adulteress... The concern that it not be an adulterous union typifies Paul's concern that the believer's union with Christ should be completely according to Law.

7:4 Wherefore, my brethren, ye also are become dead to the law by the body of Christ; that ye should be married to another, even to him who is raised from the dead, that we should bring forth fruit unto God.

Wherefore introduces the present reality typified in the above analogy. He addresses the **brethren** as the subject of the present reality, as the *woman* was the subject of the analogy—the *brethren* and the *woman* correspond.

...ye (brethren) **also** (in like manner to the woman of the analogy) are become **dead to the law**. The law didn't die, and the woman didn't die. It is the relationship of the woman to the Law that is dead, not the law itself. The law maintains its integrity.

...dead to the law.... Now you could become confused here if you take this word *dead (dead to the law)* to be synonymous with the death of the husband. As in the illustration above, the dead husband terminates the law's jurisdiction over the woman, so rendering her effectually "dead" to the law's control. The law remains intact.

Through verse three, the illustration has explained the necessity of the death of the first husband (flesh). Rather than continue the chronology of his story, which would be to relate the events surrounding the death of the first husband (which was covered in chapter 6), he jumps into verse four, assuming that the death of the first husband is a known fact. The illustration is clear. The first husband must die. Paul is confident that his readers, having read chapter six, are well informed as to the reality of that which has already died, leaving us free to be married to Christ.

Our death *to the Law* occurred by means of the **body of Christ**. Our participation in the body of Christ is the occasion of death. When we discover exactly what died at our co-crucifixion with Christ, we have discovered the identity of the *husband*. We have already been told in the previous chapter that we were crucified with Christ and buried with Christ in the likeness of His death. So, to state it simply, if our death (the husband that died) flows out of our participation in Christ's death, then the thing that died in the believer will correspond exactly to the thing that died in Christ.

When Christ died, exactly what part of His being died? His Adam flesh. When Jesus was crucified, it was His natural flesh and blood that terminated. Jesus no longer has a natural body of flesh, and He has no blood at all. *"Flesh and blood cannot inherit the kingdom of God."*

The purpose of the death of the old husband (flesh) was to release the woman (the believer) to be **married to** Christ. The marriage to Christ occurred after our immersion into His **body**. Entering into Christ, the believer first dies on the cross with Jesus. We are then buried with Him. At the point of death the Law's jurisdiction has ceased. When Christ is **raised from the dead** and we are raised with him, the union is complete. The Church is married to Him who is raised from the dead.

The results are that we **bring forth fruit unto God**. When *in the flesh* (as he is about to discuss), we served sin and brought forth fruit unto death. Being free from the dominion of that old husband (the flesh of Adam), we can now walk after the Spirit and bring forth fruit unto God.

7:5 For when we were in the flesh, the motions of sins, which were by the law, did work in our members to bring forth fruit unto death.

...were *in the flesh*—past tense. He looks back on the former state (when we were married to the old husband) as being **in the flesh**. Romans 8:9 says, *"But ye are not in the flesh..."* Regardless of what you feel your experience to be, the Bible declares that the believer is *not in the flesh*. How did the flesh of the believer cease? It died when Jesus' flesh died (Romans 6).

During that former condition, when we *were in the flesh*, sin gained its **motions** (its ability to freely move about in our bodies) from the jurisdiction of the Law.

...which were by the law.... The Law commands the body to be good, but it offers no assistance. When one fails to obey, the Law screams blame and condemnation. The Law upholds righteousness and condemns sin, and, in so doing, drives the sinner away from God and into the tight embrace of guilt. The estrangement created by the Law is fertile ground for the incubation of further sin. This is discussed further in verse 8.

Sin's activity **worked in our members**. We discussed *members* under 6:13 & 19. Since the members are well defined and are only identified with the body of flesh, and since we are conscious that sin does in fact get its initial propensity from the desires of the flesh, we can well understand the concept of sin *working in our members*. The fruit of our marriage to the flesh is **death**. Death is the natural and penal consequence of sin.

7:6 But now we are delivered from the law, that being dead wherein we were held; that we should serve in newness of spirit, and not in the oldness of the letter.

But now.... Now, in contrast to our past relationship to the flesh and the Law; now that the old husband, the flesh, is dead; now that we are married to the new man, Christ.

...we are delivered from the law.... In his analogy the woman was bound by the law to her husband. Her hope was to marry another. The law prevented another marriage as long as the husband was alive. The solution was the death of the old husband. With his death (the death of our flesh) we (the woman) are *delivered from the Law* (The entire Mosaic system, not moral law), which prevented us from being married to Christ.

Note again: the Law has not changed in regard to its condemnation of sin. Even in the particular case before us, the law has not in any way reversed its rulings or lessened its demands. Deliverance from the Law came when we ceased to be part of that body over whom the Law exercises jurisdiction—those living in bodies of flesh.

The law of marriage is still in effect over those that are alive. It is in this one particular case that the law of marriage has lost its control, and that due to death, which was the outer bounds of the Law's jurisdiction from the beginning. Christ doesn't free us from the Law by a new law or principle that sets aside the old. He employs the original jurisdiction of the Law. The Law's authority never went beyond the grave.

...that.... This is the most misunderstood *"that"* in all literature. We are delivered from the Law because *that* (entity) is dead **wherein we were held**—to which we were held. That man—first husband (flesh)—to which the Law *held* us is now dead. He says, <u>*that* entity to which the Law held us is dead</u>, and as a result we are **delivered from the [L]aw**. If the Law were dead we wouldn't need to be *delivered* from it.

On the other hand, following his analogy, if *that* thing that died is the *flesh* (husband), then the analogy is perfectly consistent in every detail. According to verse two, the woman was *bound by the law to her husband*. It was the husband to which the woman was **held**, not the law. Her relationship to the law was only in regard to her union with her husband. The law didn't harass her; it was the husband.

If Paul had wanted to say that we are no longer under the Law, he would have said, "We are delivered from the Law that held us." This would have avoided the confusion of saying the Law was dead. But rather, he tells us that we are now free from the Law because **that** <u>to which the Law held us is dead</u>. **That** which brought forth fruit unto death is now terminated. **That** which we received from Adam, which thing is terminated in Christ, the natural man of flesh, is dead. <u>The believer's death occurs in union with Christ's death</u>. As he died, so the old husband died—the old Adam of chapter 5.

This is most pertinent. In complete identity with Christ, **that** <u>which</u>

died in the believer must correspond exactly to **that** which died in Christ. There is no death but Christ's. The believer is a passive participant in that one death. The believer cannot die in a different way than Christ. So the question is, "When Christ died, what was terminated; what was changed; from what was the Man Christ Jesus freed?" We answer—the Adam body of flesh, which was the only source of Christ's weakness, the only source of His temptation. Likewise when Christ was crucified, the believer was in Him and so died as He died, no more and no less. Why is this so difficult to understand?

...newness of spirit.... Being wed to Christ, our own spirit is now renewed by the presence of the Holy Spirit, enabling us to serve our new master, as Paul said in 1:9, *"Whom I serve with my spirit."* Before we were married to Christ, we served the *old man*, the first husband (the flesh), under the letter of the Law. It was a cold, lifeless service, without grace, promising only death if we failed.

In chapter 6, Paul showed how believers participated in Christ's death and resurrection. In 7:1-6 he shows what part the Law played in this and how we now relate to it. Remember, many of Paul's readers are Jews. Even when he is ministering to gentiles, Paul's perspective is still Jewish. He will tell us later that he labors among the gentiles in hope of provoking the Jews to jealousy. Time and again, we see Paul anticipating and then answering the Jew's response to his gospel. After hearing his argument in 7:1-6, some of them might charge him with saying that the Law must be itself evil if it was the means by which one was enslaved to sin and prevented from being married to Christ. In verses 7-13, Paul expounds on the purpose of the Law.

...and not in the oldness of the letter. Modern cult-like movements have used this single phrase to justify their point of departure from a traditional view of the Holy Scripture. Romans 2:27, 29 and 2 Corinthians 3:6 are cited as further examples of the supposed theme of this verse. *"Who also hath made us able ministers of the new testament; not of the letter, but of the spirit: for the letter killeth, but the spirit giveth life."* They say that the old *letter that killeth* is the written Word of God, whereas the *spirit that giveth life* is that Spirit dwelling within. Those who espouse this view are marked by their reliance upon their own spiritual perceptions as the ruling principle.

Having put away the Bible as the final source of truth, they have cut themselves off from the only source of correction, and so continue being guided by their own spirits, which is a lot like looking at your face in a mirror to see where you are going. Yet the Bible is clear as always. The next verse after the one in question continues with an explanation as to the *letter that killeth*. It is not the written Word of God; it is *"the ministration of death, written and engraven in stones,"* which Moses received on Mt. Sinai.

Clearly, this *oldness of the letter* is the old dispensation instituted at Sinai, which is set in contrast to the new dispensation of Christ. Read all of 2 Corinthians 3. Reread the context of this passage in Romans and ask yourself if Paul is indeed dismissing the written Word of God for the higher calling of the Spirit within.

7:7-13 Purpose of the Law

7:7 What shall we say then? Is the law sin? God forbid. Nay, I had not known sin, but by the law: for I had not known lust, except the law had said, Thou shalt not covet.

Anticipating the Jews' rebuttal, Paul asked their question for them, "Paul, since according to your gospel the Law's jurisdiction had to be terminated in order for the believer to bring forth fruit unto God, are you saying that **the law is sin?**" He answers, "**God forbid**"—the strongest negative possible.

He proceeds to delineate the function of the Law.

...I had not known sin.... How can the Law be sin if it exposes sin? That would be a house divided against itself. Paul speaks of his own experience as a representative of all that are under the Law. His assumption is that when the Law reveals sin it is performing a righteous service.

...for I had not known lust.... Paul defends the Law by showing that it worked a deeper understanding than even the letter it represented. The Law merely said, "**Thou shalt not covet.**" When Paul applied himself to ferret out all coveting, he found that something deeper was present in his heart—**lust**. The letter of the Law caused Paul to see the spirit of his own heart. There can be no evil in a law that promotes such high standards.

We can begin to see where Paul is going. The Law is most effective in uncovering sin, even in the intentions. He will eventually arrive at the conclusion that, though the Law exposes sin, it cannot produce righteousness. Therein is its weakness. It defines the problem, but it cannot deliver a cure. It is not that the Law is evil; it is just not suited to more than its nature—which is to reveal sin.

7:8 But sin, taking occasion by the commandment, wrought in me all manner of concupiscence. For without the law sin was dead.
9 For I was alive without the law once: but when the commandment came, sin revived, and I died.
10 And the commandment, which was ordained to life, I found to be unto death.

The natural question to arise is, if the Law reveals sin and demands a high standard, then why seek something higher? Remember the issue is the integrity of the Law. Paul has not questioned the rightness of the

Law, neither has his hearers nor his Jewish enemies, but they have accused him of demeaning the Law through his position that the Law is not
suitable to produce righteousness. To the Jew who loves the Law and
cannot see anything higher, it seems that Paul is throwing the Law away
and replacing it with another religion—Jesus Christ received by faith.

He will now show the inadequacies of the Law. Sin was exposed by
the Law, but rather than losing its power when brought to the light of
day, it increased its reign.

...the commandment.... That particular commandment that forbid
coveting.

...sin, taking occasion by the commandment.... In keeping with
the issue, Paul is showing that the commandment (Law) did not produce
more sin, rather sin itself used the occasion of the coming of the Law to
increase its power. In other words, the root of sin was not in the Law, but
in the lust itself. Nevertheless, as an ongoing rule, sin always uses the
guilt that comes with knowledge of the Law as an occasion to increase
the power of lust.

So the commandment was there to reveal sin, which it did very well.
In the process of revealing sin, it magnified sin's presence by intensify-
ing guilt. Thus it furthered the sense of estrangement from God. Men
who are estranged from God do not have hope created in their breast by
further and deeper revelations of their sinfulness. The greater the guilt,
the more distant one becomes to the laws of righteousness. The greater
the estrangement, the closer one feels to his lusts and further from natural
restraints of conscience. One's resolve to do better diminishes in proportion to the moral distance between himself and his Holy Creator. **Concupiscence** (fleshly lusts) increases under the work of the Law.

Paul says there was a time when he was **alive without the [L]aw**.
He is not suggesting that he was alive in the sense of regenerated, but
alive in the sense of not being *"dead in trespasses and sins."* He was not
yet *accounted* as a sinner. Before the Law did its work of revealing sin,
when he was a young child and had no consciousness of his fault, he was
without a sense of condemnation. One cannot be *dead in trespasses and
sins* until he sins against a divine prohibition. To trespass is to pass over
a defined boundary. The Law defines boundaries. Until the Law makes
itself known, there can be no trespass, *"...for sin is the transgression of
the law (1 John 3:4)."*

Sin was dead, in that the strength of concupiscence brought on by
Law was not yet awakened. Sin does not have the power to condemn and
damn apart from the prohibition of the Law. As soon as a child is born he
goes astray speaking lies *(Psalms 58:3)*, but *"sin is not imputed where
there is no law (5:19)."* The lying child is not *counted* as a sinner. Not
having the intellectual capacity to understand duty, the child does not
feel guilt and is therefore not held accountable. When the child does

grow into knowledge of good and evil, sin *revives* and the child becomes *dead in trespasses and sins (Ephesians 2:1)*.

...when the commandment came.... The commandment came to Paul as it does to all men, when he grew into a knowledge of good and evil. Being raised a Jew, there was no time when he was isolated from knowledge of the Law, so as well as speaking on behalf of the entire race, he must be speaking of his own subjective experience. In situations where one is not taught the Law of God, or where the mature but otherwise ignorant adult suddenly receives renewed understanding of the Law, it could be said that in his experience *the commandment came*.

...sin revived, and I died. The coming of the commandment to his consciousness did not produce sin in an original sense; it **revived** sin already present. He **died** in the sense that he came under condemnation—*dead in trespasses and sins*.

Paul is speaking personally, but he is speaking as a representative of all men. The point in his experience when this commandment came and he died is probably at the point when he reached moral maturity—knowledge of good and evil—sometime in his middle youth. With the coming of the Law to one's consciousness, personal sin, which was previously not imputed because of ignorance of the Law, could then be justly counted as a transgression, and thereby the sinner experienced guilt and a sense of the separation from God (this separation having existed since Adam).

The **commandment which was ordained to life....** Here is a clear statement as to the possibilities within the Law. Again, in keeping with the flow of his argument, Paul gives recognition to the high calling of the Law. The Law is high and holy, for it was given with a promise of eternal life for those who kept it. This the Jew well understood and therefore held it up to be the only door into God's favor. Paul admits that it was designed to give life, but follows through to call their attention to the fact that it did not in fact give life. It brought death. <u>The death was a result of the sin, not the Law, but the Law was the occasion.</u> He is preparing his reader for the moment when he will present Christ as the answer to the ineffectual efforts of the Law.

As a sideline to our main thought, if one were born under guilt, blameworthy, there would be no way the Law could be ordained to give life. Romans 2:6-15 expresses this concept. See also Romans 10:5 with Leviticus 18:5; Ezekiel 20:11; Luke 10:27-28.

...I found to be unto death. Speaking on behalf of universal experience, Paul concludes that death, *"dead in trespasses and sins,"* is a result of his failure to keep the Law as he perceived it. One is not born *dead in trespasses and sins*, for no one has trespassed until he has consciously done so. One is morally condemned in proportion to his inner consciousness of condemnation (See 1:18).

It is important to note that the death Paul speaks of is not inherited, but occurs in his own history as a result of his own sins. In the transgression of Adam, when the entire human race died, Adam was the only transgressor, as we saw in Romans 5:12-19. That death that passed on the human race was not remedied by regeneration, but by resurrection and a glorified body (1 Corinthians 15:54). The death inherited from Adam was physical, whereas the death that Paul experienced in his own history was psychological and legal. See *dead* in the Appendix.

7:11 For sin, taking occasion by the commandment, deceived me, and by it slew me.

Again, Paul emphasizes that the source of the problem is sin, not the Law. The commandment, that is the coming of the commandment to the consciousness of a man, is the **occasion** of further sin.

Sin **deceived** him, as it does anyone that thinks the commandment is going to deliver him from the power of sin.

A natural man without direct divine revelation (Law) is conscious that all is not as it should be, but he does not have a clear perspective on his own condition. When the Law first comes to such a man, it is a bright ray of light. Suddenly everything falls into place. For the first time he clearly understands his duty. He no longer stumbles around in darkness groping for direction. The Law is a light unto his path; his steps are clearly marked before him. Oh the joy of knowing what God doth require. Now there is hope, *"This do and thou shalt live."* With the dawning of the Law, the deception of sin seems to disappear. At first its power appears to be broken. It cannot abide the light. Truth sets one free.

The Pharisees are an example of the heights to which the Law will carry one. They were *confident that they were a guide to the blind, a teacher of babes, and instructor of the foolish (Romans 2:19-20).* The Law removed the outward manifestations of sin but did nothing to cleanse the inward man. In fact, by the outward restraints the inward lusts were sublimated to incubate into hypocritical lusts that warred against the soul.

...and by it slew me. By means of the Law's oversight, sin slew him. Sin is the slayer, not the Law. It is just that sin gets its moral authority to bring condemnation through the righteous rule of Law. Each man experiences his own personal awareness of moral defeat at that point when he has made a commitment to keep the Law and then realizes that with his best efforts he has failed. The Law shuts him out from the presence of God. He stands alone, without strength, without God, and without hope. *It slew me; I died.* A most appropriate way to describe the experience of all men under Law.

7:12 Wherefore the law is holy, and the commandment holy, and just, and good.

He speaks of that particular **commandment**, which in his illustration was the occasion of his death. But let it be understood, regardless of the ill effects resulting from the coming of the Law, Paul wants to go on record as saying that the Law is holy; it is good. There is no fault in the Law. The Law is perfect. It is appropriate. Its justice is supreme. It is a thing of beauty.

7:13 Was then that which is good made death unto me? God forbid. But sin, that it might appear sin, working death in me by that which is good; that sin by the commandment might become exceeding sinful.

So there will be no misunderstanding, he labors the point. He asks the question his detractors might pose, "Paul are you saying that the **good** Law was a source of **death**?" To say such is to misunderstand his entire argument.

He answers with the strongest negative possible, **God forbid**—as if it were a scandalous thing to say. "The Law, the cause of death? God Himself stands against such a ridiculous idea."

But sin, that it might appear sin…. Sin, as an act, was present before the Law reached the conscience. The Law, by its very nature, revealed the deed to be sin. The effect was one of moral death. The self became aware of its sinfulness.

…working death in me by that which is good…. The coming of the Law was indeed the occasion of conscious estrangement. The Law does work death, but only because of the presence of sin, which sin occurred as an act before the coming of the Law. Knowledge of the Law manifested to the conscience of the individual the nature and extent of his condition (**exceeding sinful**), so knowledge of the Law was the *occasion* of the **death** but not the cause.

7:14-25 Inability of the carnal man to obey the Law.

Paul now shows wherein the Law is weak. The Law is weak, not because of any fault in its constitution, but because of the failure of anyone to actually accomplish it. The Law has yet to see its first man (other than Jesus) actually render full obedience

7:14 For we know that the law is spiritual: but I am carnal, sold under sin.

15 For that which I do I allow not: for what I would, that do I not; but what I hate, that do I.

16 If then I do that which I would not, I consent unto the law that it is good.

17 Now then it is no more I that do it, but sin that dwelleth in me.

18 For I know that in me (that is, in my flesh,) dwelleth no good thing: for to will is present with me; but how to perform that which is good I find not.

19 For the good that I would I do not: but the evil which I would not, that I do.

20 Now if I do that I would not, it is no more I that do it, but sin that dwelleth in me.

21 I find then a law, that, when I would do good, evil is present with me.

22 For I delight in the law of God after the inward man:

23 But I see another law in my members, warring against the law of my mind, and bringing me into captivity to the law of sin which is in my members.

24 O wretched man that I am! who shall deliver me from the body of this death?

25 I thank God through Jesus Christ our Lord. So then with the mind I myself serve the law of God; but with the flesh the law of sin.

7:14 For we know that the law is spiritual: but I am carnal, sold under sin.

...**carnal**.... When Paul says he is *carnal*, sold under sin, it is obvious that he is confessing sinfulness, but we can better receive the import of what he is saying if we first understand the broader meaning of the word *carnal*. There is a prevailing assumption that the word *carnal* is exclusively sinful, but its biblical usage ranges from the wholesomely *natural* to the *sensual*, but not necessarily sinful.

Of the eleven times that our English text uses the word *carnal,* at least five times it has no connotation of anything sinful or depraved.

- Hebrews 9:10 calls the Mosaic ordinance governing the every day life of Israel, *"carnal ordinances."*

- In Hebrews 7:16, the divine commandments under which priests were inaugurated were called *"carnal commandments."*

- In 1 Corinthians 9:11 it speaks of the remuneration given to a minister of the gospel—this would include housing, food, and clothing—as *"carnal things."*

- In Romans 15:27, speaking of the need for the congregation of saints to support the ministers, he says, *"For if the gentiles have been made partakers of their spiritual things, their duty is also to minister unto them in <u>carnal</u> things."* In other words, it is the duty of the congregation to see to it that the preachers have plenty of *carnal things* to assist them in their ministry.

- Obviously, the word *carnal* means *natural, tangible, earthy.* As Paul said concerning the flesh, *"For though we walk in the flesh* [nothing sinful here; just the natural state], *we do not war after the flesh* [that is, Paul does not enter into spiritual battle depending on the natural resources of mind and body]: *For the weapons of our warfare are not* <u>*carnal*</u> [as in the natural resources of human flesh], *but mighty through God to the pulling down of strong holds; (2 Corinthians 10:3-4)."*

Adam was created carnal. All descendants of Adam are carnal. All earthly mammals are carnal. Jesus had a carnal body, ate carnal food, lived in a carnal house, and provided for the carnal needs of others when he fed them carnal food and healed their carnal bodies.

The word *carnal* can be used to describe the composition of a person or a thing, or it can be used to describe one's orientation. To be carnal in composition is not sinful; it is just natural—fleshly. But to be carnal in orientation is to prefer the fleshly and temporal over the spiritual and eternal, which state of mind is sinful. Until we get our glorified bodies, the brain (physical substance) will always be carnal, but the mind is not carnal unless it is a mind set on fleshly gratification; then it is a *carnal mind* (Romans 8:7). Any believer still living in the flesh (still alive) has a carnal body, but he is commanded to *walk after* [an act of the will] *the spirit* and *not after the flesh*. In so doing he is not *carnally minded*; he is *spiritually minded.* That is, the believer in the carnal body does not set his mind on carnal gratification, and so does not walk after the carnal flesh.

A spiritually minded believer puts carnal money into an offering plate to provide for the carnal needs of the missionary. When a church makes rules to govern the earthly actions of believers, or a parent makes rules to govern the children and the household, they are carnal commandments. Jesus had carnal flesh, but He was not carnally minded; that is, His mind was yielded to the spirit and as such he was a spiritual man.

Three occasions only contain the six negative uses of the word *carnal*—all by Paul (This one in Romans 7:4, and again in Romans 8:7, and finally in 1 Corinthians 3:1-3). If the carnal state is the natural man residing in a natural body, why does Paul speak of it as synonymous with *"sold under sin"* or why does he say that *"the carnal mind cannot please God"*?

Adam was a composite of two planes of reality, one carnal and one spiritual. Obviously, God had created a balance wherein Adam could find expression in both areas without conflict. But only one force could sit in the driver's seat. God intended for the human spirit to live in fellowship with God and so exercise control and discipline over the carnal drives. When Adam chose to follow his carnal drives—expressed in the act of eating—he rejected God's authority and so made a decision to live by the flesh. Adam had chosen a new master, and so God stepped back and gave Adam over to his choice. From that point forward, Adam and all his descendants became wholly *carnal* in orientation—given over to the flesh. The flesh itself is not sinful, but by preferring it over the will of God it becomes our master, our god. See commentary under 8:7

I am carnal, Paul says of himself. This is a statement of inability, of being out of favor with God, totally in touch with fleshly passions. I am immersed in my own bodily lusts. I am a slave to the dictates of lust. I am **sold under sin.** As a slave is helplessly sold to the highest bidder, Paul, speaking on behalf of all natural men, speaks of his slavery to carnal (fleshly) passions of the natural body.

The *carnal man* is the *natural man*, and so is left to his own pitiful resources. *"But the natural man receiveth not the things of the Spirit of God: for they are foolishness unto him: neither can he know them, because they are spiritually discerned (1 Corinthians 2:14)."*

The remainder of this chapter is testimony as to the helplessness of a carnal man. This is not a current testimony. He is speaking of his own experience, and thus as a representative of all mankind. It is common practice in both speaking and writing to speak in the first person, as a representative of all, on matters that are universal.

7:15 For that which I do I allow not: for what I would, that do I not; but what I hate, that do I.

Paul says, "Regardless of my intentions, that which I actually do on a daily basis is not what I intended to do, for what I know I ought to do, I am not doing. Again, Paul is speaking on behalf of the entire unregenerate human race. Carnal men, that is men who are *in the flesh*, end up *walking after* the flesh even though they may have good intentions fostered by the Law. He goes so far as to say that he is even doing those carnal things that he *hates.* Certainly he is *sold under sin,* limited to the jurisdiction of the Law, without divine assistance.

7:16 If then I do that which I would not, I consent unto the law that it is good.

His own psychology is testimony to his high regard for the Law. His argument goes like this: "Even though I am not doing the Law, you can see by my failed attempt that I highly regard it, otherwise I would not be making the attempt. My very efforts, though poor indeed, prove that I hold the Law up as desirable." If a man in agony of soul loses his struggle to keep the Law, he has demonstrated his high regard for the Law as much as if he had kept it.

7:17 Now then it is no more I that do it, but sin that dwelleth in me.

Paul, in a sense only, disclaims responsibility for the source of sin, not to exempt himself from guilt, but, on behalf of all, to explain his inability to do the Law that he loved. Sin did not come about because he conceived the idea of evil, or because he chose to disregard the Law. The driving force causing him to sin was in the members of his fleshly body, which is where the Law was weak. So we see that universal sin is accounted for by the propensity of natural flesh—the carnal state.

Paul is vindicating his attitude toward the Law. He is saying, "My failure to keep the Law is not because I do not think it valuable; my failure to do the Law should not be a reflection upon how I esteem it. I do indeed exalt the Law; it is just that I find myself enslaved to something that prevents me from doing all that I would do."

Observe carefully: Paul, with the best resources of human nature, chose to do the Law of God. It was his material flesh (carnal orientation) that drove him to surrender his better judgment to passion.

7:18 For I know that in me (that is, in my flesh,) dwelleth no good thing: for to will is present with me; but how to perform that which is good I find not.

He further explains why he is not obedient to the Law. Through his failed attempts to do what he knows he ought, he has demonstrated that the will of man applied to the Law is not sufficient in itself to overcome the flesh.

He concludes with all men, there is **no good thing** in my **flesh.** The evil was not in his nature, but his flesh—the old husband to which the woman was bound until his death (7:1-4).

...to will is present with me.... Note the wording—*will is present.* If the will were in bondage, as Luther taught, when did it escape and return to Paul? In this state of enslavement to the flesh, the will was present and active. The sinner has a free will—that is, a will that chooses according to one's own values. It is foolish to conclude that the sons of Adam do not have operative wills simply because their wills are overcome by a greater force. There are those who argue that a will that is, for whatever reason, not able to enact its choice is enslaved, no longer free. Their assumption must be that the human will is omnipotent—that choice alone is sufficient to move the self to action, that nothing within or without can thwart the will, which of course is absurd to all.

The force of the act does not proceed from a single provocation. That is the will does not choose in a vacuum, in a neutral environment. One can act through either a prompting of the spirit, the choice of the intellect, an urging of the emotions, or, as in the present situation, one can act based on passions of the flesh. Paul is telling us that the carnal flesh has consistently proven to be the stronger impulse.

In practice, the will can be enslaved. This is not a constitutional inability to choose; it is a lack of moral fortitude to resist the consuming drives of the flesh. The consistent failure to do what one ought is not a fault of constitutional attributes, the will being an essential attribute of personhood.

This enslavement to sin and captivity of the will is the final result of *walking after the flesh* until it becomes a dominant habit. The natural body is so given over to indulgence that the will has lost control. This is not a malfunction in the will; it is simply a drive that has exceeded the will in intensity.

7:19 For the good that I would I do not: but the evil which I would not, that I do.

...the good that I would.... He is still choosing, and choosing good—no problem with the will itself.

...I do not.... In further explanation of how he failed to keep the Law, Paul expresses the sentiments of all unregenerate men, testifying of his failure to do as he knows he ought.

Again, this is a clear statement that the sin condition was not in "the bondage of the will" as Luther wrote. Nor was sin the result of a "propensity to sin," as most theology teaches. Paul's propensity was to do the will of God.

If a man is doing what he hates to do, what he absolutely resolves not to do, then there is another force within that overcomes the will by means of providing stronger stimuli. If a man were only an intellectual being, he would have a single seat of control, the mind and will; but, being a dual creature of body and soul, man can find himself completely resolved in the will, while the body runs away with passion. There are involuntary compulsions in the body that will act on instinct and drive unless the soul stirs itself to exercise control. His point is that the carnal man (all natural men—unregenerate) cannot always be sufficiently bestirred by the Law and the resources of soul to consistently carry out the intentions of the will.

...the evil which I would not, that I do. Paul is not implying that he never did what he wanted to do, that he always in every circumstance was prevented from doing the good he would do. We know from other passages, such as his letter to Phillipi, that he was a man who kept the law of God in its outward form. As with all men, there is that point at which human will is not enough to overcome in the most trying of circumstances. This "incapacity" only need be true one time or in one area to demonstrate the ineffectiveness of the law and flesh to deal with sin. Paul has named *lust,* in verse seven, as the point on which he failed to will himself into obedience.

7:20 Now if I do that I would not, it is no more I that do it, but sin that dwelleth in me.

It would follow that if a man is doing something different from what he wills to do, then some force is present stronger than his will. He defines that alternate force as *sin dwelling inside.*

At this point it is very critical to ask, "Inside what?" Does sin dwell inside the mind, the will, the emotions, the spirit, or the body? Certainly sin is manifested through all the above. Sin affects all areas of one's being. All that can be called *man*, any part or any combination, is going to manifest sin. Where there is sin, no part of one's moral or physical being is going to be free from it. But in this particular passage Paul has differentiated between these different aspects of our being. He has placed his will on the side of good—*"the good that I would."* He has placed his emotions in conformity to the Law of God—*"for I delight in the law of God."* He has also represented his mind as in conformity to the Law of God when he says, *"with the mind I myself serve the law of God."*

In verse 26 he will tell us what he means by *within*. Sin dwells in the *members* of the fleshly body. He has already told us in verse 18, *"in my flesh dwelleth no good thing."* In the following verse and on into chapter 8 he will speak more of the body of flesh, which contains the root of all sinful passion.

7:21 I find then a law, that, when I would do good, evil is present with me.

Remember, Paul is building a case for faith over against the Law. He has been charged with doing despite to the Law. He is preparing his readers for the moment when he will say, *"for what the law could not do, in that it was weak thought the flesh...,Christ did."*

It is important to understand where you are in his argument at any time. Having shown how he gave his best efforts to obeying the Law, yet failed, he makes a judgment about his condition: "When I would do good, but find myself compelled to follow the flesh, I can only conclude that evil is present with me. In other words, evil is not just external, as in the thing that tempts; it is now internal. There is something *in me* that corresponds to the evil without. Therefore, that which is within, the uncontrolled passions, must be evil also. There is such affinity between the temptation without and the drive within, and the failure of the will to overcome is so consistent, that it takes on the nature of a *law,* a working principle, a rule."

This is not a law as in command, but a law as in a recognized rule of action.

7:22 For I delight in the law of God after the inward man:

Over against the *law of sin within* is the *Law of God without*. Yet his *inner man*, the self that inhabits the outer body, delights in that Law of God.

The **inward man** is a straightforward term. As opposed to the outer man (the body of flesh) the *inward man* is the nonmaterial self. It is not a *part* of the soulish self; it is the entirety of all that one is apart from the body. This is not a term for the regenerate only. All men are an *inward man,* that you cannot see, and an *outward man,* that is made of flesh and blood.

Many argue that the unregenerate cannot *delight in the Law of God*, but this is opinion enduring long enough to sit on the shelf with presuppositions. What is commonly accepted as orthodoxy is often nothing more than error that has been held for several generations. David in the Psalms, and Solomon in Proverbs, along with many others, are represented in Scripture as delighting in the Law of God.

7:23 But I see another law in my members, warring against the law of my mind, and bringing me into captivity to the law of sin which is in my members.

Through his experience in the Law, he has discovered another controlling and motivating factor, which is just as real as the outward Law. This **law of sin** is in his **members**.

It must be understood: the root of sin was not in his will, his mind, or his emotions. All of these were arrayed against sin, and all failed to overcome the law of sin dwelling in the *members* of his flesh. The problem was not in his *inward man*; it was in the outer man, the body of corruptible flesh, the carnal man, the natural man, the Adam man.

...warring against the law of my mind, and bringing me into captivity.... The flesh appropriates the will. A man who is an obsessive gambler may hate his bondage, and exercise his will to cease his vice. He may promise to stop, but then find himself compelled to gamble. His will is powerless against the impulse to gamble. His will is not negated, but captivated. He cannot control himself. Yet his will is not constitutionally limited. That is, there is no law of necessity that makes it impossible for him to actually stop gambling. Captivity to sin is always voluntary even when one's will is hopelessly overcome.

To speak of the will as overcome or enslaved is to acknowledge the full function of the will, for the will was present enough to fight a losing battle. A will engaged in war with the drives of the flesh, even a will that is consistently overcome, is not a will that is by nature inclined to evil. If so, there would be no war—no contest.

There are many examples of the freedom of the will. If the compulsive gambler, in our illustration, arrived at an illegal gambling casino, only to be informed that sometime during the evening it would be raided, he would suddenly find strength of will to leave. Likewise, one who comes to fear AIDS may abstain from certain habits over which he previously had no self-restraint. We are not offering these illustrations in suggestion that there is any righteousness in these decisions. We only point out that the will is motivated by the most pressing concern. It most cases it is gratification of the flesh, but in some instances more pressing issues lead the will in a course of abstinence, as when a man exercises his will to stops drinking, for reasons of his own, be they moral, physical, social, economic, or religious.

The law of sin, which enslaves, is not a law of necessity, as is gravity. The enslavement is not constitutional. The slave is not a victim. He is

enslaved to his own love of indulgence. He can will not to want to indulge, but the body does not cooperate with the intellect. Passions remain
the same regardless of what one thinks or wills. A man can will not to sin
because his intellect dictates righteousness, but if he loves indulgence
more than the state of righteousness, on one level he will voluntarily surrender his body to sin, while on another level he wills not to sin.

To argue for the existence of a free will in all men is not to argue for
an omnipotent will. That is, the will is not the bottom line. Within the
man there can be opposing factors that overcome the will. A will overcome of a greater force is no more a cessation of the will or its freedom
than a rising elevator is the negation of gravity.

7:24 O wretched man that I am! who shall deliver me from the body of this death?

It was the Law that made him feel **wretched**.

...body of this death.... If there is any doubt as to the source and
seat of sin, it should be clear from this passage. Paul, on behalf of the
human race, cries out his lament. He seeks deliverance, not from a will
he supposes to be in bondage—not from a "sinful nature," but from his
body of flesh, the same body that died in Adam.

A man that was constitutionally sinful (if such were possible) would
not consider his plight to be wretched. If he were inclined to evil from
within his mind or soul, then there would be no sense of wretchedness. It
is the mind's revulsion at the fleshly indulgence that creates the mental
state of wretchedness.

Paul cries out as if he did not know from whence his deliverance
would come. On behalf of all philosophers and religious seekers, from
the dungeons of repentance and from the chains of binding sin, he cries
into the darkness with those who have no confidence that deliverance is
possible.

To this end—despair—Paul has been bringing his audience. He was
not an irreligious agnostic, but a devout Jew, loving the Law, yet coming
to an admission of total defeat. To this point his lengthy discussion has
been devoid of Christ, faith, and salvation. He now answers the dilemma.

7:25 I thank God through Jesus Christ our Lord. So then with the mind I myself serve the law of God; but with the flesh the law of sin.

In answer to the above question, *"Who shall deliver me from this
body of death?"* he answers: **Thank God**, not through the Law, but
through Jesus Christ. Any sincere Jew who has followed his argument
has been forced to admit that the Law has not been effectual in delivering
from sin. It has indeed brought death through sin, and leaves one without
the promised righteousness. In the next chapter, Paul will show how

Christ is indeed the fulfillment of the righteousness promised in the Law.

The "**So then**" brings us to his conclusion of this chapter. One should carefully observe the period after the first phrase of this verse. Coupled with the *so then* it is obvious that the latter sentence does not hinge on the former statement, but on the entire chapter.

...with the mind I myself serve the law of God; but with the flesh the law of sin. This chapter has been a detailed description of what he means by "serving God with his mind." It has nothing to do with walking righteously, for while he delighted in the *Law of God after the inner man*, he served the *law of sin* with his *flesh*.

Again note. The *inner man*, Paul the person, the soul that chooses between alternatives, is said to **serve the Law of God**, but the **flesh** served sin. There is no hope that the Law will ever bring deliverance. He doesn't lack teaching, conviction, commitment, repentance; he lacks inner power to overcome his body of flesh.

This is not a statement of partial victory, but of total defeat. If he had served the law of sin in his members because he didn't know any better, there would still be hope in education. If he served the law of sin because he had not yet repented, then all he need do is go back to the place of contrition. If he served the law of sin because he had a weak will, then he need only make a greater commitment. But Paul was fully committed in his mind, will, and emotions, so that he could characterize his intentions as serving the Law of God. The point he is making is that even after giving it the best a man can give, he was still a slave to sin. The best man with the best of intentions and the greatest commitment had failed to do what he knew he ought. He was *carnal, sold under sin*.

This forms the ground for his introduction to the way of deliverance in Christ. If Christ only forgave sin and didn't deliver from the act of sinning, Paul's argument would carry no weight at all.

Keep in mind Paul's basic direction. The Law, though good, was insufficient to deliver a man who had the best of intentions. The problem ran deeper than the mind, emotions, and will. The flesh, the outer man, was contrary to the inner man. History has proven that in a contest the flesh wins against the Law. In chapter 8, he will tell his readers that what the Law could not do because of the weakness of the flesh, Christ did.

8:1-4 Righteousness fulfilled in us

1 *There is* **therefore now no condemnation to them which are in Christ Jesus, who walk not after the flesh, but after the Spirit.**
2 For the law of the Spirit of life in Christ Jesus hath made me free from the law of sin and death.
3 For what the law could not do, in that it was weak through the flesh, God sending his own Son in the likeness

of sinful flesh, and for sin, condemned sin in the flesh:
4 That the righteousness of the law might be fulfilled in
us, who walk not after the flesh, but after the Spirit.

Overview 8:1-4

The common theme of the first four verses is seen in that they begin and end with the same statement—*"who walk not after the flesh but after the Spirit."* So each statement in these first four verses should be viewed in light of that single thought. The gospel is not just a philosophy transplanting the Law; it actually enables one to do righteousness. The Law made a demand upon flesh, but those who walked after the flesh utterly failed, as seen in chapter 7.

The gospel does not strengthen the flesh. As we saw in chapter 6, the gospel is the good news that the flesh is crucified. This not only ends the power of the flesh, but it ends the dominion of the Law as seen in 7:1-4. Just as the Law was in control in 7:1-4, the Spirit is in control in 8:1-4. The Law led to sin, the Spirit leads to righteousness.

Take note of the significant words repeated more than once in the first 4 verses: condemnation/condemn, Christ Jesus/Son, Spirit/Spirit of life, flesh (used 5 times), law (4 times), walk.

Also note the many contrasts in these first 4 verses.

- **flesh & Spirit** (chapter 7 was the flesh, chapter 8 is the Spirit)
- **Law & Christ** (There was no Christ in chapter 7. What the Law could not do in chapter 7, Christ does in chapter 8).
- **law of sin and death & law of the Spirit of life** In chapter 7 Paul discovered another law in his members warring against the *law of his mind.* Only a far more powerful law can override it—chapter 8 answers with the *law of the Spirit of life in Christ Jesus.*
- **walk after the flesh & walk after the spirit** The practical result of being *under the Law* and *in the flesh* was to *walk after the flesh,* as seen in chapter 7. In chapter 8 the answer is to *walk after the Spirit.*
- **sin in the flesh & likeness of sinful flesh** Chapter 7 described the workings of sin residing in the fleshly body; chapter 8 relates how Christ came in that likeness of sinful flesh in order to destroy the reign of death.
- **death & life** Death was the result of flesh under the Law, as seen in chapter 7. In chapter 8, life is the result of Christ's righteousness; and beyond that, our righteousness is a result of the life thus given by the Spirit.
- **In the flesh & in Christ Jesus** Chapter 7 concerns life in the flesh, and chapter 8 concerns life in Christ Jesus.

The overriding theme of this section is: *what the Law could not do, Christ did.* The Law, which put us under condemnation, did not produce righteousness; Christ, who took us out from under condemnation, does indeed not only declare us righteous but actually make us righteous. It is ironic that the Law, which made personal righteousness a must, failed to produce it, while Christ, who took us out from under the high demand of the Law, actually affects righteousness in the believer far in excess of what the Law demanded.

The entire sweep of Paul's argument, from the end of chapter 3 through chapter 7, culminates in these four verses.

- Verse 1 is a summary of chapter 5. Christ frees us from condemnation and the penalty of sin.
- Verse 2 is a summary of chapter 6. Christ frees us from the power of sin through sharing his death.
- Verse 3 is a summary of chapter 7. The Law cannot make us righteous because of the weakness of our flesh.
- Verse 4 is a summary of the first half of chapter 8. As the believer walks after the Spirit he actually lives righteously.

Throughout this chapter there are allusions to concepts formerly discussed in chapters 3 through 7. Words, phrases, and concepts, previously defined, are readily employed, assuming the reader's prior knowledge of former arguments.

Many commentators expound this chapter as a theological treatise on sanctification. They see it as the conclusion to a natural progression that began with a discussion of justification in chapter four. Certainly it is of great value to us as such. But what we see here of justification or sanctification is a byproduct of, and incidental to, his main point. Keeping the entire book in mind, it is readily apparent that Paul's primary concern is a defense of the gospel of grace and faith as set over against the Law of the Jews. It was necessary for him to fully examine the entire gospel message both in theory and in practice if he would prove that the gospel is affective where the Law has failed. A systematic revelation of justification and sanctification is only his means to another end—defending the gospel of grace against the Jewish detractors.

The first half of this chapter is about practical deliverance from sin—here and now. The latter half is about ultimate deliverance by way of a glorified body. This is not an exhortation to avoid carnality—the flesh; it is a declaration that righteousness by faith is effectual in delivering from not just the penalty of sin but from its very power and presence. Understand, he is not telling Christians to be holy; he is telling the Jew that the righteousness of faith is superior to the works of the Law because it certainly delivers from sin, whereas the Law only brought condemnation.

Remember, he is a Jew with a new message that threatens to set aside the former religion of the Jews. The burden of proof is on him. In Romans 1:15-17, Paul begins his epistle by defining his purpose, "*So, as much as in me is, I am ready to preach the gospel to you that are at Rome also. For I am not ashamed of the gospel of Christ: for it is the power of God unto salvation to every one that believeth; to the Jew first, and also to the Greek. For therein is the righteousness of God revealed from faith to faith: as it is written, The just shall live by faith."* Paul states the reason why he knows his message will never give him cause to be ashamed, *"because it is the power of God unto salvation."* In other words, the gospel is more than words; it carries its own power to actually change the lives of those that believe. His bold promotion of the gospel against all other religions and philosophies is not because it brings a personal religious experience or because it provides a forensic justification. The salvation of which he speaks is something that changes lives; it is a visible, tangible, practical salvation from the power of sin. Nothing else would commend it to the Jews.

- In 3:8 he quotes his accusers, *"as we be slanderously reported, and as some affirm that we say,) Let us do evil, that good may come?"*

- Then in 3:31, anticipating his detractors, he asks, *"Do we then make void the law through faith? God forbid: yea, we establish the law."*

- As he progresses in his argument, in 6:1 he again anticipates an argument against his gospel, and he asks, *"What shall we say then? Shall we continue in sin, that grace may abound? God forbid. How shall we, that are dead to sin, live any longer therein?"*

- Continuing to develop his argument, in 6:15 he answers a supposed accusation, *"What then? shall we sin, because we are not under the law, but under grace? God forbid."*

- In 7:6, answering what must have been a common challenge, he says, *"What shall we say then? Is the law sin? God forbid."*

- Then in 7:13 he answers what one might suppose him to be saying about the Law, *"Was then that which is good made death unto me? God forbid."*

Each of these challenges follows an argument and precedes a defense of the gospel of Christ. Taken as a whole, they tie together and carry along his whole argument. Chapter 8 is just the crowning touch on his defense. If you read Romans as if it were a systematic theology book, clarifying the doctrines of justification and sanctification, there will be many passages you will find difficult. On the other hand, if you don't lose sight of Paul's objective, then it all flows along in perfect harmony.

8:1 There is therefore now no condemnation to them which are in Christ Jesus, who walk not after the flesh, but after the Spirit.

Therefore (based on concepts previously expressed) there is no condemnation (as there was under the Law in chapter 7) to those who are now in Christ.

We are told by most commentators that this *therefore* refers back to chapters 5 and 6. Interpreting this primarily as a treatise on sanctification, they see no connection with the previous chapter, but with chapters 5 and 6. They read it like this: "Christ died for the ungodly (chapter 5) and the gift of God is eternal life (chapter 6) (skip 7 since it is about carnal Christians and continue with the thoughts of 5 and 6), Therefore (because of the work of Christ in 5 and 6) there is no condemnation to those in Christ (that is, the salvation you got in chapters 5 and 6 is eternal—you will never come into condemnation now that you are saved)." This makes for a nice package of fundamental truths, but the passage is not that evangelical. Aside from the fact that chapter 7 is not about "carnal Christians," there is much more here than a sermon on justification and sanctification.

The latter half of this verse (condemnation and flesh), along with the continuing flow, links this passage directly to the preceding chapter, which was full of condemnation and failure.

To see this verse in its immediate context, follow the flow of thought from the previous chapter. To maintain the flow, we skip the summation sentence. *"O wretched man that I am! who shall deliver me from the body of this death? I thank God through Jesus Christ our Lord.... There is therefore now no condemnation to them which are in Christ Jesus, who walk not after the flesh, but after the Spirit."* Verse 1 is an answer as to how we will be delivered from the flesh. The answer: In Jesus Christ we are not under the condemnation of the Law, and we are freed from the power of the flesh—we no longer walk after it.

...no condemnation.... We come out of chapter 7 with a heavy sense of defeat. The flesh is powerless to obey the Law. We well know the penalty for not obeying the Law. The end of chapter 6 told us that if we obey sin the penalty is *death*.

The statement, *no condemnation*, jumps out and pulls us in like water to a thirsty man. The sweetest truth to a believer is that we who deserve condemnation are delivered from it by the grace of God. But this chapter is not primarily about release from condemnation; it is about release from the power of sin. It is not about how Christ's righteousness is imputed to us; it is about how the righteousness represented in the Law is actually manifested through us—lived out in daily experience.

Romans 8 is an unequivocal statement of sure deliverance from sin, now and hereafter. In contrast to chapter 7, where we find man under the Law and walking after the flesh, those in Christ Jesus are not under the condemnation of the Law and do not walk after the flesh.

Most commentators see the *no condemnation* and relate it to John 4, *"...shall not come into condemnation ...."* They tell us that condemnation and justification are opposites; that since there is no condemnation then the subject must be justification. Having assumed that the subject of the chapter is justification, they then try to fit everything into that mold. That may be good evangelistic sermonizing, but it does violence to the context.

Certainly every believer thrills to the truth that we who are justified will never come under condemnation unto damnation, but condemnation of a different sort is still possible for the Christian. Note the following verses where Christians do come under condemnation.

Christians coming under condemnation

* **James 5:8-9** *"Be ye also patient; stablish your hearts: for the coming of the Lord draweth nigh. Grudge not one against another, brethren, lest ye be* <u>*condemned*</u>*: behold, the judge standeth before the door."*

* **James 5:12, 14-16** *"But above all things, my brethren, swear not, neither by heaven, neither by the earth, neither by any other oath: but let your yea be yea; and your nay, nay; lest ye fall into* <u>*condemnation*</u>*. Is any sick among you? let him call for the elders of the church; and let them pray over him, anointing him with oil in the name of the Lord: And the prayer of faith shall save the sick, and the Lord shall raise him up; and if he have committed sins, they shall be forgiven him. Confess your faults one to another, and pray one for another, that ye may be healed. The effectual fervent prayer of a righteous man availeth much."* The condemnation on the *"brethren"* turned out to be a threat of physical death, caused by sickness.

* **1 Corinthians 11:30-34** *"For this cause many are weak and sickly among you, and many sleep. For if we would judge ourselves, we should not be judged. But when we are judged, we are chastened of the Lord, that we should not be condemned with the world. Wherefore, my brethren, when ye come together to eat, tarry one for another. And if any man hunger, let him eat at home; that ye come not together unto* <u>*condemnation*</u>*."* The believers in Corinth had come together to take the Lord's table in a manner that was unworthy of the occasion. Chastisement had followed, resulting in many becoming physically weak, some very sick, and others were already dead. It was called a judgment. It was said to be chastisement, *condemnation* from God.

* **1 Corinthians 5:5** *"To deliver such an one unto Satan for the* <u>*destruction of the flesh*</u>*, that the spirit may be saved in the day of the Lord Jesus."* Here Paul is commanding the church to turn a believer over to Satan with the intentions that he would die, thus assuring the man's continuing salvation.

* **1 John 5:16-17** *"If any man see his brother sin a sin which is not*

unto death, he shall ask, and he shall give him life for them that sin not unto death. <u>There is a sin unto death</u>: I do not say that he shall pray for it. All unrighteousness is sin: and there is a sin not unto death." The one sinning is a brother, saved. If the sin is going to result in the man's death—God killing him—then it is a waste of time to pray that he will live. Certainly being killed for one's sin is condemnation, not eternal condemnation, but temporal as regards the body.

- **Romans 8:12-13** *"Therefore, brethren, we are debtors, not to the flesh, to live after the flesh. For if ye live after the flesh, <u>ye shall die</u>: but if ye through the Spirit do mortify the deeds of the body, ye shall live."* Brethren, <u>Christians, who walk after the flesh will come under condemnation</u> and die.

...in Christ Jesus.... This is a summation of chapter 6. God placed the believer in Jesus Christ and thus into His death, burial, resurrection, and finally into His ascension and glorification, as we will see in this chapter.

To be *in Christ* is a constant state of being, not a manner of walking. Being *in Christ* is the opposite of being *in the flesh*. Those *in the flesh cannot please God*. Those *in Christ* have crucified flesh and are *led by the Spirit*.

...who walk not after the flesh but after the Spirit. If you are not using a King James Bible, you may not have this part of the verse. Most so-called Bible scholars have ignorantly stated that this verse is not in the "oldest and best manuscripts." They should do more research before committing such a damnable error *(Revelation 22:19)*.

They are most vocal in claiming that it is not theologically correct, telling us that "believers cannot come under condemnation." It is their theology that needs changing, not the Word of God. That kind of error comes about when the fundamentals of the faith are removed from their context and exalted independently of their source. The fundamentals are then enshrined in creeds and worshiped as if the creeds themselves were the source of truth. A kind of religious logic comes to surround the fundamentals, and a special tradesman's terminology becomes the basis by which the Bible itself is interpreted. Under this biblical dumbing-down process the fundamentals are refined until they stand on their own innate logic rather than the revealed Word of God. All too often the end product has little resemblance to the original source. The Bible is then made to yield to official doctrinal positions by adding or removing words from the Bible, all in the name of scholarship.

...walk designates the daily, moment by moment <u>process</u> of living.

To walk **after** is to be energized or directed by. Our primary goal or motivation, that which holds our attention, gains our affection, captivates our energies, is what we will *walk after*. Those who are *in Christ* walk differently from those who are *in the flesh. Oh wretched man that I am, who shall deliver me from* this enslaving body of flesh? The flesh is carnal, *sold under sin,* and cannot obey the Law. But we are not doomed to obey the lusts of our flesh. Those in Christ have an advantage over those under the Law: they *do not walk after the flesh* as did the defeated of chapter 7.

Walking after the flesh and being *under the law,* is certain *condemnation.*

The unregenerate do not have the Spirit of God and therefore cannot walk after what they do not have (1 Corinthians 2:14). Those who are *in the flesh* do *mind the things of the flesh.* Those who are *in Christ do mind the things of the Spirit.* One doesn't walk his way into the Spirit and into favor with God; one walks in light of favor already bestowed.

This verse is a summary of chapter 5. It is not a condition to be met, but a statement of fact, a description of all that are in Christ. They do not walk after the flesh as do those under that Law (described in chapter 7). This verse is the beginning of a thought that is concluded in verse four— *"that the righteousness of the law might be fulfilled in us."*

Remember, the issue is one of righteousness. The Jew argued that the Law was the only true representative and guardian of righteousness. Paul is arguing that the Law, though spiritual and good, nonetheless failed to produce righteousness. For his argument to be effective, he must show that in Christ there is an actual righteousness accomplished in the believer apart from the works of the Law. The Law brought condemnation and left the penitent without strength to do good. So the gospel of Christ finds the sinner under the Law not only without strength but also under great condemnation.

Paul promotes the efficaciousness of the gospel by stating that it answers all the needs of the sinner and all the demands of the Law. The sinner is removed from condemnation, and the Law is satisfied because of the high level of righteousness produced by those in Christ Jesus. The unbeliever is working to get ready for judgment day; the believer is working because the judgment of sin in Christ has already made him ready.

8:2 For the law of the Spirit of life in Christ Jesus hath made me free from the law of sin and death.

The **law of sin and death** is not the spoken or written Law of God. It is true that the Law of God caused a revival of sin and brought death (7:8-9). But Paul has made a clear distinction between one law and the other, for in 7:12 he says of the Law of God, *"Wherefore the law is holy, and the commandment holy, and just, and good."* He continues in 7:23 with, *"But I see another law in my members, warring against the law of my mind, and bringing me into captivity to the law of sin which is in my members."* He concludes chapter 7 with, *"So then with the mind I myself* *serve the law of God; but with the flesh the <u>law of sin</u>."* Clearly there is another law called *the law of sin and death.*

The word **law** as used here does not imply something written down or even spoken. It is not a judicial pronouncement, but a rule of action. It is common in language to attach the word *law* to any working principle that maintains a consistency of operation. It is called law not because it precedes the act and dictates it, but because the consistent operation of the phenomenon is best defined as a law—a rule of action. For example, when we speak of the law of nature or the law of the jungle, we are not referring to any written dictate.

The *law of sin and death* is universally known and reflected in all religions. It is observable to anyone that *the wages of sin is death, the soul that sinneth shall die.*

Note the various ways law is used in Romans 7-8.

- *7:21 I find then a <u>law</u>, that, when I would do good, evil is present with me.*

- *22 For I delight in the <u>law</u> of God after the inward man:*

- *23 But I see <u>another law</u> in my members, warring against the <u>law of my mind</u>, and bringing me into captivity to the <u>law of sin</u> which is in my members.*

- *25 I thank God through Jesus Christ our Lord. So then with the mind I myself serve the <u>law of God</u>; but with the <u>flesh the law of sin</u>.*

- *8:2 For the <u>law of the Spirit of life in Christ Jesus</u> hath made me free from the <u>law of sin and death</u>.*

- *3 For what the <u>law</u> could not do, in that it was weak through the flesh, God sending his own Son in the likeness of sinful flesh, and for sin, condemned sin in the flesh:*

- *4 That the <u>righteousness of the law</u> might be fulfilled in us, who walk not after the flesh, but after the Spirit.*

Why does Paul use the word *law* in various ways? He is discussing the conflict between the Law of God and the flesh. He shows that it is not by coincidence that we are all overcome of sin. Sin finds such fertile ground in the flesh that it operates so consistently in competition with the Law of God as to qualify as a rule of law.

Uses of law contrasted

- **The law of sin**

  The law of sin is not an entity. By that I mean that the *law of sin* cannot be measured and located. It is not a thing in itself. It is not a force or a power with independent identity. It is only a manner of speaking, a way of defining a pattern of behavior.

- **The law of sin in my members**

  This is indwelling sin, indwelling the flesh. The flesh is so given to sinful indulgence that one can predict with certainty that unaided flesh will consistently indulge—thus the *law of sin in my members.*

- **The law of my mind**

  The mind is the normal function of the natural intellect. When Paul speaks of *the law of my mind* he is not saying that his mind is governed by a law of necessity outside the normal functions of the intellect. The *law of his mind* was not some alien force or some constraint foreign to his humanity; it was the normal function of his intellect. The best his natural intellect could offer, when viewed as a trend, was called the *law of his mind.*

- **The law of sin and death**

  This is the innate moral law that assures us that all sin terminates in death. Like the second law of thermodynamics, The law of sin and death operates without the need of divine oversight. And yet, though it is a law of nature, it is not without divine oversight.

- **The law of works**

  The Law of Moses was a law of works, also called the Law of God, but he is not referring to any written law, rather to the theoretical concept that one approaches God by works. Only one man has ever effectively operated under the law of works—the man Christ Jesus.

- **The law of faith**

  As we saw earlier in Romans, Paul coins another term to contrast the law of works, *"Where is boasting then? It is excluded. By what law? of <u>works</u>? Nay: but by the <u>law of faith</u> (Romans 3:27)."* The law of faith is the operating principle of faith, not a commandment.

- **The law of liberty**

  "So speak ye, and so do, as they that shall be judged by the <u>law of liberty</u> (James 2:12)." The *law of liberty* is not a commandment; it is that liberty in which a believer operates. It is the working principle of faith and grace in the believer. The *law of liberty* and the *law of faith* are in the same vein as the *law of the Spirit of life in Christ Jesus.* The *law of faith* is the principle by which we are saved. The *law of liberty* is the relationship we sustain to God. The *law of the Spirit of life in Christ Jesus* is source of our power and our authority. These terms represent different aspects of that which motivates, guides, and empowers the believer.

- **The law of the Spirit of life in Christ Jesus**

  The law of the Spirit of life in Christ Jesus is set over against *the law of sin and death* as a competing, overcoming rule of law. This term is not found elsewhere in Scripture. To say *the <u>law</u> of the Spirit of life in Christ Jesus* has made me free is not the same as saying *Christ*

Jesus made me free, or *the Spirit made me free.* Nor is it the same as saying that *the Spirit of life in Christ Jesus made me free.* When the writer put the word *law* in front of *the Spirit of life,* it stopped being the objective work of God and became a working principle, a rule of relationship. It is not on the basis of *the law of the Spirit of life* that we are declared righteous and delivered from eternal condemnation. The believer's daily relationship to his Heavenly Father, motivation and empowering, is called *the law of the Spirit of life in Christ Jesus.*

We are doing no despite to imputed righteousness, which was introduced, explained, and established in chapter 4. Imputed righteousness is objective, the work of God alone, whereas the *law of the Spirit of life* is a working principle that involves the believer in overcoming sin in the flesh. The imputation of righteousness is based on a work finished before one believes. In our walk of holiness, we are required *to yield, to submit, to put off, put on, mortify the deeds of the body, set our affections, let this mind be in you, and sin no more.*

The believer has an obligation he must meet or suffer the consequences. *"Therefore, brethren, we are debtors, not to the flesh, to live after the flesh. For if ye live after the flesh, ye shall die: but if ye through the Spirit do mortify the deeds of the body, ye shall live (Romans 8:12-13)."* Here is a command to believers and a warning. The means of mortifying the deeds of the body is *through the Spirit—the Spirit of life in Christ Jesus.*

Viewing the laws all together

The law of Paul's *mind* was to obey the *Law of God,* but the *law of sin,* which was in the members of his fleshly body, was inclined to walk after the desires of the flesh and so prevented him from reaching God through the *law of works.* The *law of sin and death* took affect and Paul came under condemnation. He cries out for deliverance from his bondage.

Christ comes in human flesh and is made under the *Law of God.* He lives by the *law of works* and overcomes. But then he took upon himself the *law of sin and death* and came under the curse of the *Law of God* and was raised by *the Spirit of life in Christ Jesus.*

The *law of faith* is preached to Paul, and upon believing, Paul is given the Spirit of God. He is taken out from under the *law of works* and is placed under the *law of liberty.* He then found that what the *law of his mind* could not do in regard to the *law of works,* the *law of the Spirit of life in Christ Jesus* does very well.

Additional verses on the Spirit of life in Christ Jesus

- *"Therefore we are buried with him by baptism into death: that like* as Christ was raised up from the dead by the glory of the Father, even so we also should walk in <u>newness of life</u> (Romans 6:4)."

- "And if Christ be in you, the body is dead because of sin; but the <u>Spirit is life</u> because of righteousness (Romans 8:10)."

- "Always bearing about in the body the dying of the Lord Jesus, that the life also of Jesus might be made manifest in our body. For we which live are alway delivered unto death for Jesus' sake, that the <u>life also of Jesus</u> might be made manifest in our mortal flesh (2 Corinthians 4:10-11)."

- "Who also hath made us able ministers of the new testament; not of the letter, but of the spirit: for the letter killeth, but the <u>spirit giveth life</u> (2 Corinthians 3:6)."

In summary of the Spirit of life in Christ Jesus:

That same Spirit that raised Christ from the dead, the Spirit of new life, that Spirit that is the life of Jesus, the very life of God, now dwells in the believer and functions in the place of his own spirit. That day to day function of that Spirit within is called *the **law** of the Spirit of life in Christ Jesus.*

8:3 For what the law could not do, in that it was weak through the flesh, God sending his own Son in the likeness of sinful flesh, and for sin, condemned sin in the flesh:

For, because. This verse is vitally linked to the former two by the connecting word *for*. It is an explanation of how we came into the state where there is *no condemnation*, of how we were *made free from the law of sin and death,* and how it is that we *do not walk after the flesh,* but are enabled to *walk after the Spirit of life in Christ Jesus.*

...what the law could not do.... The Law could not empower a man to *walk after the Spirit* instead of *after the flesh.* This phrase carries us back to chapter 7 where we have a thorough explanation of what the Law could not do in the unregenerate man. The mind, will, and emotions were all on the side of the Law of God, but without the *Spirit of life* the Law was worse than powerless; it actually made matters worse by empowering sin. *"The strength of sin is the law (1 Corinthians 15:56)."*

The Law itself did not fail. There was no want in the Law. By nature the Law is not an empowering force. The Law, which in theory was established to give life (Romans 7:10), actually brought further bondage to sin. The Law was given to represent the righteousness of God. It did its job perfectly. It just could not elicit an acceptable response in its hearers.

This statement is the last of many analyses of the Law. For eight chapters Paul has been preparing his readers for this conclusion about what the Law could not do, but Christ did.

...in that it was weak through the flesh.... Paul is clear. The fault was not with the Law. It was the weakness of flesh. Be very sure to note:

the one thing that caused the sinner to fail to obey the Law was not human nature and not an enslaved will. The problem causing sin was *flesh.*

Chapter 7 was Paul's proof that the fleshly body with all its natural passions could not be brought into subjection by the mind, will, and emotions. Human history is irrefutable testimony to the failure of flesh to conform to the Law of God.

The Law was good and its demand was fair. The flesh was all that flesh can be, but the very nature of flesh, as we saw in Eve, is to indulge. If the flesh is not closely governed, it will tend to selfish indulgence— thus the source of temptation, even in Christ. The human spirit and intellect should govern the flesh, but when the Spirit of God left Adam and Eve, the human race lost the direction and unction necessary to subdue the flesh. Man was not created to exist separate from God.

The flesh cannot please God. With ever increasing futility, the Law makes its demands upon flesh. The external commands of the Law could not bring discipline to the flesh.

...God sending his own Son.... Jesus existed before He came to the earth. He was a son *sent*, not a son born. *"Who, being in the form of God, thought it not robbery to be equal with God: But made himself of no reputation, and took upon him the form of a servant, and was made in the likeness of men: And being found in fashion as a man, he humbled himself, and became obedient unto death, even the death of the cross (Philippians 2:6-8)."*

That God should *send* His holy son in the likeness of sinful flesh demonstrates once and for all the extent to which God is willing to go for this rebellious race.

...in the likeness of sinful flesh.... Christ's flesh was like *sinful flesh* (flesh that had sinned) in that it too was *weak.* He hungered, grew tired, needed to sleep, aged, and was capable of bleeding to death. Christ's flesh was mortal flesh, as seen by the fact that it died as flesh dies.

"Because the foolishness of God is wiser than men; and the <u>weakness of God</u> is stronger than men (1 Corinthians 1:25)." There was no point at which Jesus could be said to be *weak*, except in his body of flesh. *"For though he was crucified through <u>weakness</u>, yet he liveth by the power of God (2 Corinthians 13:4)."*

For Christ to put away sin in the flesh it was necessary that He be totally identified with the flesh—the place where sin originated and set up its reign. To overcome flesh, He must dwell in flesh and be subject to its weakness and temptation.

Jesus the man, as the *last Adam* (1 Corinthians 15:45), the *second man* (1 Corinthians 15:47), was faced with temptations *in all points like as we are* (Hebrews 4:15), yet He walked according to the *Spirit of life,* and sinned not. Jesus the man overcame in human flesh where all others had failed. *"Forasmuch then as the children are partakers of flesh and blood, he also himself likewise took part of the same; that through death he might destroy him that had the power of death, that is, the devil; And deliver them who through fear of death were all their lifetime subject to bondage (Hebrews 2:14-15)."*

The authority to deal with *sin in the flesh* belonged to the human race alone. Jesus took part in flesh and blood that he might triumph in the same flesh that was the source and residence of all sin. *"Having therefore, brethren, boldness to enter into the holiest by the blood of Jesus, By a new and living way, which he hath consecrated for us, through the veil, that is to say, his flesh (Hebrews 10:19-20)."*

As a side note, this verse tells us something about the nature of flesh in general. Jesus' flesh appeared to be **like** sinful flesh (flesh full of sin). Was it His nature that appeared sinful or his fleshly body? Obviously it was only in Christ's fleshly body that God condemned our sin and by so doing lifted condemnation. Therefore this Greek word *sarx* (always translated *flesh*, as it is here) cannot be anything but a body of flesh, for there is no problem in saying that Jesus' body was flesh just like that flesh which is full of sin, but it would be heresy to say that Christ came in the likeness of *sinful nature*, which is how the NIV sometimes translates this word *sarx*.

...for sin.... Such an odd thing, that the sinless Son of God should come in the likeness of *sinful flesh*. Certainly it was not a proper context for His pure soul. Why make this showing in flesh? Because he came *for sin*, in regard to sin, because of sin. He came to put away sin through the sacrifice of His flesh.

...sin in the flesh.... We will best understand what he means by *condemned* sin in the flesh when we first understand what he means by *sin in the flesh*. This terminology has already been introduced in chapter 7 where *sin in the flesh* is the theme. *"It is no longer I that do it but sin that dwelleth in me, I know that in me (that is in my flesh) dwelleth no good thing." Sin in the flesh* is that *"law in my members (7:23)."* Flesh that has been allowed to indulge without restraint from the inner man becomes conditioned to dominate. The habits of sins in the flesh darken reason, sear the conscience, distort the affections, captivate the will, and leave the mind reprobate. Paul lamented concerning sin in his flesh, *"I am carnal sold under sin."*

It would be good to mark this verse in your mind and in your Bible. It is salient indeed. Sin has a seat. It is the fleshly body.

...condemned sin in the flesh. God condemned sin, not as a judge uttering a judicial pronouncement, but as an executioner. God *condemned sin* by crucifying the sinner with his sin (Romans 6). Remember, Paul represented sin dwelling in his members as a rule of law, a working principle, a force in conflict with his own will. He cried out against it,

159

but found no deliverance. Who will deliver me from the body of this death; who will condemn this sin in my flesh (7:23-24)? The runaway principle of *sin in the flesh*, profiled in chapter 7, is what God *condemned.*

This does not say that Christ paid for sin in His own flesh, which of course is true. It does not say that Christ lived in such a way as to express His judgment against sin, though He did that. It does not say that Christ made a judicial pronouncement against sin while He was in a fleshly body; that he did many times. Note, the condemnation of sin resulted in *the righteousness of the law <u>fulfilled</u> in us.* Read it together: Christ *"condemned sin in the flesh that the righteousness of the law might be fulfilled in us."* <u>The condemnation of sin resulted in our being able to actually do righteousness.</u> This is absolutely essential to our understanding of the entire book of Romans, and to Bible doctrine.

God had disassociated Himself from man because sin reigned in the flesh. Any plan of restoration that did not restore man to obedience would be unworthy of God and an affront to His government. By means of the Law, Jews made a great attempt to separate themselves from sin. When flesh failed to obey, the Law stood firm in condemning the sinner for his failure. Paul must show that Christ does what the Law could not do—terminate sin in the flesh. Mere forgiveness without compliance to the Law would have been an embarrassing scandal. Paul would not say, "I am not ashamed of the gospel of Christ because, though like the Law it cannot put an end to sin in the flesh, nevertheless, it abrogates the Law's demands and calls the sinner righteous." Preposterous!

Those who understand imputed righteousness know that the sinner is justified in the sight of God and declared righteous before he does a single act of righteousness. But we also know that the Law's demands were not set aside as a means to achieving that end. The Law did indeed find us guilty. Its judgment was not blunted, rather it was poured out on the whole world in the person of Jesus Christ.

Christ didn't combat the Law in court. He didn't challenge its jurisdiction. Accepting the Law's just verdict, the punishment demanded by the Law was poured out on our substitute, Jesus Christ. Paul is not negotiating for jurisdiction—an issue settled at the cross, he is commending the gospel because it works to separate the sinner not from just the guilt of sin, but from sin's very power.

We are not suggesting that the gospel must deliver the sinner from breaking the Law if he is to be free from the Law. The regenerate believer is now dead to the Law because in Christ *he* is dead. The Law does not travel beyond death (7:1-4). It is simply an issue of public confidence. Does the gospel operate only in the realm of the court? Does it declare a man righteous based on the work of another and then leave him in the same weakened predicament as the Law? Is *sin in the flesh* also master over the *Spirit of life in Christ Jesus*? God forbid! What the Law could not do in actually making a man righteous, Christ does completely. On that basis, Paul promotes his gospel as superior to the Law. In this we see the heart and soul of the book of Romans.

Two inseparable things occurred in the execution of Christ's flesh: (1. In the death of His flesh, He paid the price for our sin, (2. When His flesh died, our flesh died with Him, freeing us from sins in the flesh. Christ died for us; we died with him. That is the full gospel.

It is wonderfully true that the believer's sins were imputed to Jesus Christ and God judged them in His flesh—condemned them. The condemnation of the Law was once and for all lifted in the work of Christ for us. The condemnation of the Law buried itself in His flesh, never to rise again. But the whole discussion of chapter 8 is about the power of sin, not the forensic imputation of righteousness.

Of late, in the development of practical doctrine, there has been a strong move to separate the work of Christ into two parts, justification and sanctification. There is a great tendency to believe that the work of justification does not necessarily imply a continuing work of sanctification. Ministers tend to treat the mass of professing Christians as if they were a pool of potentially "spiritual Christians." The general consensus is that by far most Christians will never come close to going forward in their experience to be sanctified. This dangerously false trend has led to much deception.

This phrase, **condemned sin in the flesh**, is a summary of the entire sixth chapter. That is, when the flesh was crucified, the sin that resided in it was defeated. *"Forasmuch then as the children are partakers of flesh and blood, he also himself likewise took part of the same; that through death he might destroy him that had the power of death, that is, the devil (Hebrews 2:14)."* *"And you, that were sometime alienated and enemies in your mind by wicked works, yet now hath he reconciled In the body of his flesh through death, to present you holy and unblameable and unreproveable in his sight (Colossians 1:21-22):"*

It is not the power of sin in the flesh that is destroyed, but the very flesh itself. *"In whom also ye are circumcised with the circumcision made without hands, in putting off the body of the sins of the flesh by the circumcision of Christ (Colossians 2:11)."* *"Knowing this, that our old man is crucified with him, that the body of sin might be destroyed, that henceforth we should not serve sin (Romans 6:6)."*

He did not free us from the Law by condemning the Law, but by condemning the sin that gave the Law its power. And He condemned sin by crucifying the flesh in which sin lived. *"And they that are Christ's have crucified the flesh with the affections and lusts (Galatians 5:24)."*

8:4 That the righteousness of the law might be fulfilled in us, who walk not after the flesh, but after the Spirit.

This verse will conclude the thought begun in verse one. These four verses, 8:1-4, are the answer to the question asked in 7:24, *"Who shall deliver me from the body of this death?"* The answer is *Christ,* and the means is: Christ *condemned sin in the flesh* of Adam's race—destroyed its power by crucifying the flesh (Romans 6)—so that the righteousness of the Law would actually be lived by those of us in Christ who can now *walk after the Spirit* rather than *after the flesh.* What the Law could not do, Christ did.

When God justifies the sinner, it is not the righteousness of the Law *fulfilled* in the experience of the sinner, but the righteousness of God *imputed* to him. The present subject is not the imputed righteousness of Christ. He is past that point in his argument. The issue at hand is how the Spirit can be superior to the Law. He is showing that union with Christ involves the utter incompatibility of union with sin. Paul is still developing his argument of Romans 6:*14, "For sin shall not have dominion over you: for ye are not under the law, but under grace."* He has shown that a man who is under the Law cannot escape from the dominion of sin.

This is not a mere encouragement to walk after the Spirit so as to produce righteousness; it is an emphatic statement as to the efficaciousness of the gospel.

…who walk not after the flesh, but after the Spirit. This phrase could be understood to be a statement of how one qualifies to be free from condemnation: You walk after the Spirit and thereby live righteously, thus avoiding the condemnation that comes with not being righteous. But viewing it in its context, we can see this is not a practical lesson on the victorious Christian life; it is a statement of the definitive superiority of *the law of the Spirit of life in Christ Jesus.* This is an identifying phrase, not a qualifying phrase. There is no condemnation to this group, as opposed to the other. The assumption of the text is that all believers do indeed walk after the Spirit and live righteously. This is contrary to pop theology, which theology is unique to our generation alone. The Scripture stands alone, apart from our experience. It is clear. Let it speak as it will.

Romans 8:5-8 In the flesh
**5 For they that are after the flesh do mind the things of the flesh; but they that are after the Spirit the things of the Spirit.
6 For to be carnally minded *is* death; but to be spiritually minded *is* life and peace.
7 Because the carnal mind *is* enmity against God: for it is not subject to the law of God, neither indeed can be.
8 So then they that are in the flesh cannot please God.**

Just as the first four verses expressed a common idea, so verses 5-8 hang together as a unit. Verses 1-4 discussed how those in Christ walk after the Spirit and not after the flesh, whereas verses 5-8 comprise an explanation of why the carnally minded cannot obey the Law of God.

This is not a warning against carnality. It is not commanding obedience or encouraging the believer to responsibility. He is not telling anyone how to be victorious.

This continues to be a profile of the difference between two opposing states—that of *in the flesh* and *in the Spirit*. Chapter 6 is a complete statement about how the flesh was crucified with Christ. Chapter 7 shows the other side, how the flesh utterly fails to keep the Law. Chapter 8 is a summary of the two states, with a presentation of the victory of Christ over the flesh.

8:5 For they that are after the flesh do mind the things of the flesh; but they that are after the Spirit the things of the Spirit.

The source of life determines the quality. Different roots manifest different fruit. There are only two kinds of people in the world, those that are *natural, unregenerate, after the flesh*, and therefore *walk after the flesh* and those who are *born again* and are now *after the Spirit* and therefore *walk after the Spirit*.

...are after refers to the basic state, whereas *walk after* refers to the visible manner of walking. *Are after* defines the source of one's life. It has to do with organic relationship. *Walk after* defines not just the manner of walking, but the source of that walk—that which directs the way we walk and influences the choices we make.

...are after **the flesh....** A man could be defined in many ways—his education, vocation, position, accomplishments, etc., but Paul cuts through all the externals and exposes the one factor that muddies all else. The best of men are flesh, and not just flesh in residence, as was Christ, but flesh in orientation, flesh in pursuits. Human life, contrasted to all that is angelic and holy, can only be defined with the portrayal—*"after the flesh."*

To say one *is after the flesh* is not to say one is evil, but being *after the flesh* results in *walking after the flesh*, which is evil.

The flesh is amoral in itself. Christ had flesh that, like any natural man, was endowed with passions. But it could not be said of Christ that He was *after* the flesh. Adam was created flesh, but was not *after* the flesh until after he sinned. It was God's intention that Adam, by means of God's presence, should pursue life from the spiritual perspective rather than the fleshly. When Adam chose to allow the flesh to be the primary criterion of life, God departed and left Adam to his carnal choice. He and all his descendants are now *after the flesh*, unless born again, at which time the Spirit of God joins the spirit of man and he becomes *after the Spirit—spiritual*.

...do mind the things of the flesh.... To *mind* is to allocate the resources of the mind to a given end. That which has your attention, which you think on or pursue, is what you *mind*. That which you value receives the most attention and energy. What you choose as most valuable captivates your mind. The little choices throughout the day reveal that to which the heart is dedicated. If the little choices reflect an interest in the flesh rather than the Spirit, then the flesh is the ultimate goal. To mind the flesh is to think on it for its own momentary pleasure.

The root determines the fruit. As chapter 7 so well supported, those who *are after the flesh* will *mind the flesh*. There is no constraint here, but a sufficiently overriding pull so as to establish the certainty that all Adam's descendants, born of the flesh, will *mind the things of the flesh* and *walk after* it.

The unregenerate may, as Paul did, well understand their moral duty and seek to mind the Spirit. The carnally minded may, and often do, value things that are good and wholesome. It is the nature of a human to appreciate things that are intrinsically pure. Thus the fleshly minded will often be heard defending righteousness, and will be seen dedicating their time and energies to the pursuit of things wholesome and lovely. The carnally minded are able to sponge away their guilt through publicly expressing their support of the truth. But when the final score is taken and all of life is examined, those who are after the flesh will manifest to all that their mind was indeed set on the flesh. When one has walked after the flesh, it is testimony that despite his commitment to goodness, in the actual moment of choice, he followed the lusts of his flesh, probably suffering great guilt and self-incrimination at the moment.

This is not an exhortation to mind what we ought. It is a statement of fact that permits us to discern the difference between two opposing states. The fruit of being *after* the flesh (unregenerate) is to have your mind occupied with pleasing the flesh. The proof of this statement is already given in chapter 7. When Paul was *after the flesh*, he inevitably minded the things of the flesh.

...they that are after the Spirit [do mind] **the things of the Spirit.** His purpose at this point is not to discuss being after the Spirit. He has already covered that subject in 1-4 and will come back to it in verse 9. He mentions the *Spirit* here to contrast it to the *flesh*.

One must be born again if he is to mind the *things of the Spirit*. The natural man cannot mind what he does not have—the Spirit of God. He can set his mind to do good, and often does. He can mind to obey the Law of God and delight in the Law of God after the inward man, as Paul did before he was saved: *"touching the righteousness which is in the law, blameless (Philippians 3:6)."* He can, as Cornelius, be a devout man who fears God and prays to him always (Acts 10:1-2). But unless one is endowed with the Spirit of God, he cannot *mind* the things of the Spirit (1 Corinthians 2:14).

It is useless and vain to seek to direct your attention so as to *mind* what you ought. If you are *after the flesh* you will *mind the flesh*. If you are *after the Spirit* you will *mind the things of the Spirit*. The kind of fountain will determine the kind of water (James 3:11). Force of will, that changes what you do in hopes of redirecting the mind, is a futile effort.

8:6 For to be carnally minded is death; but to be spiritually minded is life and peace.

...**to be carnally minded is death....** This is similar to Paul's statement in the previous chapter, *"I am carnal, sold under sin (7:14)."*

The Greek word here translated *carnal* is sometimes translated *flesh*. To be *carnally minded* is to be *flesh minded*.

We have come to the final stage of a progression from flesh to death. First one is born *after the flesh*. Those who are born after the flesh then *mind* the flesh. Those who *mind* the flesh will *walk after the flesh*. Finally, he tells us here, those who have a carnal mind, causing them to walk after the flesh, will *die*.

A word of caution

He does not say that the penalty of being BORN IN the flesh is death. One has no choice in regard to the state of his birth. There is no fault in coming into this world without the Spirit of God. The fallen sons of Adam are born whole and entire as moral beings. There is nothing in the inner man that constitutes an involuntary compulsion to sin. Nothing of man's constitution is impaired. He has all the powers of will, mind, and sensibility that he had at creation. But without doubt, the expression of human attributes are curtailed by the presence of sin, the depraved human body, and the absence of the Spirit of God. But man remains man in nature, and is therefore responsible, and will be held accountable.

It is failure to do what one ought that establishes grounds for condemnation. It cannot be said with intelligence that one is morally responsible to do more than one is constitutionally capable of doing. Guilt comes from a failure to achieve what one knows he should have and could have done. Therefore there is fault and blame in setting one's mind on the carnal.

The state of *being without the Spirit of God* is not blameworthy, but employing the resources one does have in pursuit of the flesh is an act worthy of death. So he is careful to define the cause of the condemnation that leads to death. It is to be *carnally minded*. One is always responsible for the focus of his own mind. So all carnal mindedness is worthy of death.

...**to be spiritually minded....** *"To be carnally minded is death; but to be spiritually minded is life and peace."* Spiritual-mindedness is not a plane of achievement or a higher level of anointing; it is the state of all believers. To have one's life characterized by a constant focus of the mind on spiritual reality is the duty of all moral beings. But one cannot be spiritually minded who is not *in the Spirit* or, as stated another way, *after the Spirit.*

Certainly, the term *spiritually minded* is a statement about the set of one's thoughts. It is cast in contrast to *carnally minded.* But having followed the flow of thought, we know that it is more than a statement about the content of one's thoughts; it is a statement about the thinker himself. *"For as he thinketh in his heart, so is he (Proverbs 23:7)." "O generation of vipers, how can ye, being evil, speak good things? for out of the abundance of the heart the mouth speaketh (Matthew 12:34)." "For where your treasure is, there will your heart be also (Luke 12:34)."* Thoughts don't land in our brains like stray birds. They are like the shells, rocks, and litter lining a beach. What a man brings home in his pocket is what caught his imagination, and he deemed it worthy to be viewed again.

Carnal-mindedness and *spiritual-mindedness* are both causes and effects. I am what I think, and I think according to who I am, though I became who I am by what I thought. I continue to be responsible for what I think, and yet my thinking has rendered me irresponsible. The bottom line is that I remain liable as I continue to select my thoughts. I will be held accountable. If I find, as Paul did in Romans 7, a *law in my members* bringing me into captivity to the *law of sin in my members,* then I can believe on the Lord Jesus Christ and be baptized into His death, at which point the *carnal mind* is crucified and the *spiritual mind* takes its place.

When one chooses Christ, he has *minded* the things of the Spirit, but that choice alone does not render him *spiritually minded,* since spiritual-mindedness is a state as well as a choice. The state of spiritual-mindedness comes with the giving of the Holy Spirit to the one who has chosen to *mind the things of God* rather than *the things of the flesh.* Understand, if upon believing (making a spiritually minded decision) the individual were left to the resources of his mind, will, and emotions, he would soon *mind the things of the flesh.*

The human mind is naturally without God. It finds expression only through a physical brain in a depraved body. Through a lifetime of choices, sin dwells in the flesh, and has proven to be the strongest inducement.

After one has set his mind on the Spirit (repented towards God) and has been crucified and raised to receive a new Spirit of life (become spiritually minded) he still maintains control and responsibility for the direction and content of his thoughts. In other words, a *spiritually minded* person still has the capacity to *mind the things of the flesh.* Paul will come to this in verse 12.

...**is life and peace.** To *be spiritually minded is life and peace.* The state of spiritual-mindedness is the state of *life and peace.* Peace is both objective and subjective. Judicially, Christ established a peace with God through the blood of his cross. See Romans 5:1.

Peace is also subjective. The nature of man is such that, unless his conscience is seared, he has an internal demand to conform to the Law of God, which Law is written in his own nature. There is no peace until a man judges himself to be in conformity to that Law.

8:7 Because the carnal mind is enmity against God: for it is not subject to the law of God, neither indeed can be.

Because refers back to the two previous statements and is an explanation of why *they that are after the flesh do mind the things of the flesh* and why *to be carnally minded is death.*

...**carnal mind is enmity against God....** He is not speaking of the constitution of the mind, but of the content of one's thoughts. The carnal (constitutional state) think on carnality (voluntary mental intentions) and not the Spirit, because their very minds are in a state of declared war (enmity) with God and His purposes.

Furthermore the carnally minded are destined to death, because with their very thoughts they have made themselves enemies of God. One need not assault God to be His enemy. One may even speak in defense of God, but if the mind is set on the flesh, it is committed to an end that is in direct opposition to God's program. To make one's self the servant of flesh—which would of necessity exclude being a servant of the Spirit—is to make oneself the enemy of God.

...**for it is not subject....** It is not just the person but the mind itself that cannot be in subjection to the Law of God. Remember, he is speaking of mental states—the mind. The mind is not an organ that can be diseased, as is the brain. The mind is not matter. When we speak of a diseased mind, we are speaking of consistently bad choices. Depravity of mind is depravity of thought, not substance. The depravity of mind one inherits at birth is a mind left to its own devices without the fellowship of God. It is not a mind twisted or altered, but a mind forsaken of God. There is nothing inherent in the mind at birth that inclines one to evil thoughts. It is the mind yielding to fleshly passions and then tainted by the accumulation of evil thoughts and habits that becomes the sinful mind.

By placing the adjective *carnal* before the noun *mind,* he is telling us that it is not strictly the mind itself that is not subject to the Law of God, but the *carnal* mind. That is, the mind set on pleasing the flesh. A mind already claimed by the flesh is not available to be in subjection to the Law of God. All reversals of action are first a reversal of mind. One does as he thinks. The mind thinking *flesh* cannot be in subjection to the

Law of God.

That the carnally minded cannot be subject to the Law of God (as expounded in chapter 7) is the background on which Paul acclaims Christ as worthy to succeed the Law. As a man thinks in his heart so is he. A mind that is bent on satisfying the flesh will do nothing else. No amount of religion or reformation will ever cause the carnally minded to obey the Law.

This is not to say that the carnally minded have no control of their own wills. They can will to do what the Law says, as Paul did in chapter 7, but the power of the flesh will overcome the force of their wills. There are times when the will triumphs over immediate passion, but the overall pattern of the carnal (unregenerate) is to walk after the flesh.

Furthermore, the carnally minded would never choose to mind the things of the Spirit if God were not gracious in His pursuit of them. Since the carnal mind cannot know the things of God, the heart of the sinner must be turned through the preaching of the Law, by the message of the gospel, and the conviction of the Holy Spirit.

...to the law of God.... *...the carnal mind is not subject to the law of God....* This reference to the *law of God* takes us back to chapter 7 where Paul carefully chronicled his journey in the flesh and his failure to be in subjection to the Law of God. The Law of God is more than the Mosaic Law. It is any and all revelation as to the will of God.

...neither indeed can be. The mind, having fixed itself on an end, is then dedicated to that end and no other. All resources are then allocated to the realization of that cause. The very nature of mind is such that one cannot hold two different and opposing ends at the same time. Where two things are mutually exclusive—as is the flesh and the Spirit—the mind cannot choose both as an end at the same time. It should be well established by now; the carnal mind, that is, the mindset of all natural men, is devoid of any hope to keep the Law of God.

- *"Ye adulterers and adulteresses, know ye not that the friendship of the world is enmity with God? whosoever therefore will be a friend of the world is the <u>enemy of God</u> (James 4:4)."* To be at enmity with God is to be in the posture of an enemy.

- *"No man can serve two masters: for either he will <u>hate the one</u>, and love the other; or else he will hold to the one, and <u>despise the other</u>. Ye cannot serve God and mammon (Matthew 6: 24)."* Nor can one serve *the Spirit of life in Christ Jesus* and the *flesh* at the same time.

- *"But if thine <u>eye be evil</u>, thy whole body shall be full of darkness. If therefore the light that is in thee be darkness, how great is that darkness (Matthew 6:23)!"* The focus of the eye, that is the direction of the mind, determines the direction of the whole man.

- *"But the natural man receiveth not the things of the Spirit of God: for they are foolishness unto him: neither can he know them, be-*

cause they are spiritually discerned (1 Corinthians 2:14)." Look at the context around this verse. The natural man can know the things of another man through the human spirit that each possesses, but the spirit of the natural man cannot know the things of God because he is devoid of God's Spirit, and his spirit is in subjection to the drives of his flesh.

8:8 So then they that are in the flesh cannot please God.

This he proved in chapter 7. It is not that humanity is incapacitated; it is just that humanity alone, separated from Deity, cannot maintain the moral sphere demanded by God.

He does not conclude with, "So then they that are carnally minded cannot please God," which would be true, but he has gone behind the carnal mind to the source of that carnality, which is the state of being **in the flesh**. That state of being IN the flesh is the incubator of human sin. One is born *in the flesh*—the Spirit of God not being present in those born. And with the coming of moral maturity, when one chooses his own course, those **in the flesh** *do mind the things of the flesh.*

...cannot please God. The point Paul is making is that since those *in the flesh*—the condition of all natural men—cannot please God, as Paul tried to do in Romans 7, then the Law is useless to make men righteous, and something more is required, something that can deal with *sin in the flesh*. That brings us to the answer revealed in the next section.

8:9-11 *In the Spirit*

9 But ye are not in the flesh, but in the Spirit, if so be that the Spirit of God dwell in you. Now if any man have not the Spirit of Christ, he is none of his.
10 And if Christ be in you, the body is dead because of sin; but the Spirit is life because of righteousness.
11 But if the Spirit of him that raised up Jesus from the dead dwell in you, he that raised up Christ from the dead shall also quicken your mortal bodies by his Spirit that dwelleth in you.

Overview 8:9-11

Verses 9-11 announce freedom from the flesh. Two levels of freedom are discussed. The first is a summary of all that has gone before, starting with chapter 6. Simply stated, it is that those who are *in Christ* share His crucifixion of the flesh and His *Spirit of life*. The second level of freedom has not been previously discussed. He introduces it here, then goes on in the remainder of the chapter and expounds upon it. It is the ultimate freedom of a glorified body. The gospel message is twofold: (1. In the here and now there is freedom from the flesh through sharing Christ's crucifixion. (2. In the future there is final freedom from the flesh through sharing Christ's resurrection.

169

8:9 But ye are not in the flesh, but in the Spirit, if so be that the Spirit of God dwell in you. Now if any man have not the Spirit of Christ, he is none of his.

But... in contrast to the absolute bondage of those in the flesh—as described in all of chapter 7 and the previous four verses.

...ye.... For the first time in this chapter Paul has become personal. Up to this point he was discussing general doctrine. He now turns and addresses the believers reading his book.

...are not in the flesh.... No believer is ever *in* the flesh. This is not a description of one's walk, but of the seat of one's life. The natural man's life emanates from the *flesh* and cannot do other. The believer's life emanates from the Spirit and cannot do other. The believer was circumcised out of the flesh when he was buried with Christ into His death.

This must sound strange to those of you not familiar with this marvelous biblical truth. Certainly, the loose language of Christianity needs to be brought into conformity to the words of God.

...but in the Spirit.... We have an emphatic, all-inclusive statement: All believers are positioned *in the Spirit*. The source of the believer's life is no longer the flesh, it is the Spirit of God. This is not a statement about the *quality* of one's life, but about the *source* of life. The natural man is *in the flesh*. The regenerated believer is *in the Spirit*. There is no back and forth, no mixture.

...if so be.... This clause is inserted to distinguish to whom he speaks when he says, *"ye are not in the flesh but in the Spirit."* It is also designed to cause one to examine whether he qualifies to be among those of whom Paul speaks. Merely holding to correct doctrine is not the same as actually being possessed by the Spirit of God. One is in the Spirit *if so be....*

...that the Spirit of God dwell in you.... The missing factor in every natural man (all children born into this world) is the *Spirit of God.* The human spirit is sufficient to express humanity, but not sufficient for humanity to express God. The human spirit will lift us to lofty heights in poetry, music, and art, but it will never reach to heaven. The puny compass of the human spirit is sufficient for man to plot his course and venture the seas of life, but it is not sufficient to keep him from wandering off course when the Sirens call to his flesh. Adam's spirit was sufficient to rule the flesh as long as he stayed in communication with the Spirit of God. The Spirit of God restored to humanity is humanity enabled to fully express humanity.

The Spirit of God comes into the believer immediately upon regeneration.

- *"For by one Spirit are we all baptized into one body, whether we be Jews or gentiles, whether we be bond or free; and have been all made to drink into one Spirit (1 Corinthians 12:13)."*

- *"Who hath also sealed us, and given the earnest of the Spirit in our hearts (2 Corinthians 1:22)."*
- *"Now he that hath wrought us for the selfsame thing is God, who also hath given unto us the earnest of the Spirit (2 Corinthians 5:5)."*
- *"And because ye are sons, God hath sent forth the Spirit of his Son into your hearts, crying, Abba, Father (Galatians 4:6)."*
- *"In whom ye also trusted, after that ye heard the word of truth, the gospel of your salvation: in whom also after that ye believed, ye were sealed with that holy Spirit of promise (Ephesians 1:13)."*

Now if any man have not the Spirit of Christ, he is none of his. Where the Spirit does not dwell, Christ does not dwell, and there is no life, just carnality. Having the Spirit and being justified from sin are inseparably linked. One who has the Spirit needs a constant *filling* of the Spirit and an occasional *anointing* for ministry.

8:10 And if Christ be in you, the body is dead because of sin; but the Spirit is life because of righteousness.

And if Christ be in you.... He is not offering the believer some side benefit to the Christian experience. If you are saved, Christ is in you. If Christ is in you, your body is dead to sin. If Christ be in you, two things are true, set one over against the other: 1.) The body is dead 2.) The Spirit is life.

We have a marvelous twofold cure for the human sin problem. 1.) The seat and source of sin, the body, is destroyed 2.) The life of God is restored through the *Spirit of life.*

...the body is dead.... The *body* (the human body of flesh, the source of sinful lusts) is *dead because of sins*—physical death. The body at no time was ever *dead in sins*. The soul—the man—is *dead in sins* (personal sin). The problem was that the body was all too alive to lusts. All of chapter 6 was a detailed explanation of how the lustful flesh was baptized (nothing to do with water) into Christ's death. That co-crucifixion destroyed *sin in the flesh,* so that he tells the believer to *"reckon ye also yourselves <u>to be dead</u> indeed unto sin, but alive unto God through Jesus Christ our Lord (6:11)."* In Christ our human body is dead. That which was crucified in Christ is that which the believer shares. Paul says, *"I <u>am crucified</u> with Christ: nevertheless I live; yet not I, but Christ liveth in me (Galatians 2:20)." "...if one died for all, <u>then were all dead</u> (2 Corinthians 5:14):"* All are dead in the same manner as the one died for all—physical death.

Experience would never teach that *the body is dead* and free from sin. Take it further: personal experience would never teach us that we who have believed on Christ are now resurrected and seated in heavenly places. The gospel of Christ is supernatural. God defines reality in His own terms, not ours. The Christian experience begins and continues through believing the unseen. According to the Word of God, the natural body of a believer is dead in Christ. God's word is the starting point for reality.

...because of sin.... The body is dead *because* of sin—not dead in sin, but dead on account of sin. Sin was not the death; it was the occasion that necessitated the death, which death was affected by our participation in Christ's death.

Sin in the flesh made the body a target for divine extermination. Remember Paul's cry after that terrible description of human carnality, *"O wretched man that I am! who shall deliver me from the body of this death (7:24)?"* Then the answer, God *condemned sin in the flesh (8:3)* by crucifying the flesh. It is like condemning termites by getting rid of the wood. God condemned sin in the flesh by terminating the place where sin resides—the flesh (the message of Romans 6).

...but the Spirit is life because of righteousness. In the first part of this chapter we are told that *the Spirit of life in Christ Jesus hath made me free from the law of sin and death.* He says *the Spirit is life*, not, "the human spirit is brought to life because the person is righteous." Because of the need for *righteousness*, and because of the *righteousness* of Jesus Christ and the provision He has made, the Spirit of God has become, not just the source, but the very life of the born-again believer. The presence of the Spirit of God in the believer is the presence of life, divine life, eternal life, walking-righteous life.

Neither is he saying that the human spirit came to life because of righteousness. Contrary to popular belief, man did not lose his spirit; neither did he lose the function of it when Adam sinned. Adam was created whole and complete, yet very alone. His body lacked nothing in the way of humanity; it functioned perfectly, but he couldn't reproduce. Adam was created to be part of a union—a union with Eve. Likewise, spiritually Adam was created to be part of a union with God. Without that union man would feel a sense of incompleteness and would be sterile spiritually. When Adam fell, the Spirit of God departed from him and all his descendants. The world had become an unfit place for the Spirit called "Holy."

As we have seen, man left to the devices and resources of his own humanity is a carnal being. The human spirit falls subject to the passions of the body. So it can be said, without God man is spiritually dead—not dead to his own spirit, but dead to the Spirit of God, and dead to righteousness. When a man is regenerated, the Spirit of God joins the human spirit and the two spirits are wed in a way that enables man to function in fellowship with God. *"But he that is joined unto the Lord is one spirit (1 Corinthians 6:17)."* The introduction of the Spirit is life.

...because of righteousness.... *The Spirit is life because of right-*

eousness. Certainly it is not the believer's righteousness that makes the Spirit life.

- *"That as sin hath reigned unto death, even so might grace reign <u>through righteousness</u> unto eternal life by Jesus Christ our Lord (Romans 5:21)."*
- *"For Christ is the end of the law for righteousness to every one that believeth (Romans 10:4)."*
- *"But of him are ye in Christ Jesus, who of God is made unto us wisdom, and righteousness, and sanctification, and redemption (1 Corinthians 1:30)."*

Jesus alone is righteous before God. His righteousness is God's gift. It is not the righteousness worked inside of us by the Spirit of life that saves. It is the righteousness lived by one man, Jesus Christ. Romans 5:17 speaks of *the gift of righteousness.*

Righteousness lived out in the experience by the aid of the Holy Spirit is not a *gift of righteousness.* The gift is whole and entire, sufficient to declare us entirely righteous before God. As any gift, it is given without any contribution or compliance from the sinner. This gift of righteousness immediately puts one into perfect standing before God. *The Spirit is life* because of righteousness in Jesus Christ, not man.

8:11 But if the Spirit of him that raised up Jesus from the dead dwell in you, he that raised up Christ from the dead shall also quicken your mortal bodies by his Spirit that dwelleth in you.

...Spirit of him.... We have a guarantee. If the same Spirit dwells in us that dwelt in Christ when He was raised from the dead, we can expect the exact same treatment. This point is already well taken in Romans 6:4-5, *"Therefore we are buried with him by baptism into death: that <u>like as Christ was raised</u> up from the dead by the glory of the Father, even so we also should walk in newness of life. For if we have been planted together in the likeness of his death, we shall be also <u>in the likeness of his resurrection:</u>"* Having become a recipient of the work of Christ on the cross, we are assured of a continuing work. *"Being confident of this very thing, that he which hath begun a good work in you will perform it until the day of Jesus Christ (Philippians 1:6):" "For as in Adam all die, even so in Christ shall all be made alive (1 Corinthians 15:22)."*

...quicken your mortal bodies.... The word *quicken,* as used in the New Testament, is reserved for that act of resurrection wherein the mortal body is raised from the dead. Spiritual renewal is never called a *quickening.* The word *quicken* is very similar to *make alive,* but unique. Life that has come into a state of degeneracy and is restored is said to be quickened. *"...that which thou sowest is not quickened, except it die (1 Corinthians 15:36)."*

- *"For Christ also hath once suffered for sins, the just for the unjust, that he might bring us to God, being put to death in the flesh, but quickened by the Spirit (1 Peter 3:18):"*

- *"And you, being dead in your sins and the uncircumcision of your flesh, hath he quickened together with him, having forgiven you all trespasses (Colossians 2:13);"* When Christ was raised from the dead all those that were baptized into His body were raised *(quickened)* with Him.

- *"And so it is written, The first man Adam was made a living soul; the last Adam was made a quickening spirit (1 Corinthians 15:45)."* The first Adam was given life in his soul by the breath of God. Jesus, likewise the head of a race of regenerated people, thus called the *last Adam*, was *made a quickening spirit*. Speaking of the resurrection body he says, *"And as we have borne the image of the earthy, we shall also bear the image of the heavenly (1 Corinthians 15:49)."*

- *"As it is written, I have made thee a father of many nations,) before him whom he believed, even God, who quickeneth the dead, and calleth those things which be not as though they were (Romans 4:17)."*

- *"But God, who is rich in mercy, for his great love wherewith he loved us, Even when we were dead in sins, hath quickened us together with Christ, (by grace ye are saved;) And hath raised us up together, and made us sit together in heavenly places in Christ Jesus (Ephesians 2:4-6):"* The believer's participation in Christ's resurrection occurred at the same time as Christ's own resurrection and is therefore spoken of in the past tense. In the passage above, even our ascension into heaven is viewed as past reality.

...mortal bodies.... *...shall quicken your mortal bodies....* Once again it is brought to our attention that the enemy of all righteousness, the seat of sin, the object of the judgment unto death, is the *mortal body*. Likewise the final act of salvation is the donning of a new, glorified body.

8:12-13 The Believer's responsibility

12 Therefore, brethren, we are debtors, not to the flesh, to live after the flesh.

13 For if ye live after the flesh, ye shall die: but if ye through the Spirit do mortify the deeds of the body, ye shall live.

...brethren.... Starting with this verse, for the first time in this chapter Paul is addressing the *brethren* concerning their responsibility. This is a marked change and should be noted.

Therefore, because of this promise of a quickened body (v. 11) we are *debtors* where it concerns the flesh. *"What? know ye not that your* *body is the temple of the Holy Ghost which is in you, which ye have of God, and ye are not your own? For ye are bought with a price: therefore glorify God in your body, and in your spirit, which are God's (1 Corinthians 6:19-20)."*

...we are debtors.... A debtor is beholden to someone. He is a recipient of something of value, and is under obligation to his benefactor. The greater the value of that which is received, the greater his obligation. We who were dead in trespasses and sins were placed into Christ and quickened in his quickening. We owe all. We must give all.

...not to the flesh, to live after the flesh.... *"I beseech you therefore, brethren, by the mercies of God, that ye present your bodies a living sacrifice, holy, acceptable unto God, which is your reasonable service (Romans 12:1)."* The former state, when we *were in the flesh*, was one of servitude to the flesh. *"But God be thanked, that ye were the servants of sin, but ye have obeyed from the heart that form of doctrine which was delivered you. Being then made free from sin, ye became the servants of righteousness (Romans 6:17-18)."* Again keep in mind that Paul is now addressing believers and is stating their responsibility.

A natural (unsaved) man is *after the flesh* and *in the flesh*, whereas a *spiritual man* (saved man) is *after the Spirit* and *in the Spirit*. It is not the believer's duty to be *in the Spirit*. But it is the believer's (one who is *after the Spirit* and not *after the flesh*) duty to <u>walk</u> *after the Spirit* and *not after the flesh*.

A command to do something implies that one must give himself to the means if that thing is to come to pass. If a believer could not do other than *walk after the Spirit*, it would be a waste of breath and paper to make a command or give a warning. The believer *in the Spirit* should *walk after that Spirit*. If he doesn't, he comes under temporal condemnation as seen in the next verse.

For if ye live after the flesh ye shall die.... Here is a warning that <u>brethren who *live after the flesh* will die</u>. It is most appropriate that if one should live after that which is dead, he should himself die. This death is the *sin unto death* of the believer whereby his body is killed in order *"that his spirit may be saved in the day of the Lord Jesus (1 Corinthians 5:5)."* A believer is a debtor (duty bound) to walk consistent with his position. The warning is that if a believer does not choose to walk after the spirit, he will be killed by God.

This chastisement unto death will bring him into heaven with loss of reward. *"If any man's work shall be burned, he shall suffer loss: but he himself shall be saved; yet so as by fire (1 Corinthians 3:15)."* See 8:1, under condemnation, for a discussion of *death*. Also see Appendix, under *death*.

For a discussion on *"are after, are in, and walk after"* see comments under 8:5.

...but if ye through the Spirit.... The regenerated man has a capacity not available to the carnal man. The carnal man has the *law of sin* in his members bringing him into captivity to sin, whereas the believer has *the law of the Spirit of life in Christ Jesus* dwelling in him, freeing him from sin's power. Before Adam sinned, the ability to *walk after the Spirit* and not *after the flesh* was not an innate power; it depended on fellowship with God. Likewise, the regenerated believer now has the *Spirit of life*, but the power to overcome the flesh is still not a native force, resident yes, but not constitutional. Fellowship with the Spirit (the saved state) is still essential to overcoming the flesh. The regenerated man cannot depend on the renewal itself to deliver him; he must conquer through active participation with the Spirit.

...do mortify the deeds of the body.... See *mortify* in the Appendix. The believer does not have the responsibility to crucify his flesh. The flesh of every believer is as crucified and as dead as the flesh of Christ. *"Likewise reckon ye also yourselves to be dead indeed unto sin, but alive unto God through Jesus Christ our Lord (Romans 6:11)."* It is the **deeds** of the members of the body, not the body itself that the believer is to mortify through the Spirit. *"Mortify therefore your members which are upon the earth; fornication, uncleanness, inordinate affection, evil concupiscence, and covetousness, which is idolatry (Colossians 3:5)."*

The Spirit of God, that is the presence of God Himself, has a continuing ministry in the crucified, resurrected, and ascended believer. In Christ, the believer's flesh—body of sin—is crucified, dead. Paul says, *"I am crucified with Christ: nevertheless I live; yet not I, but Christ liveth in me: and the life which I now live in the flesh I live by the faith of the Son of God, who loved me, and gave himself for me (Galatians 2:20)."* There is a mystery involved here that must be taken by faith, according to the word of God.

The believer is crucified, his flesh dead, yet it appears quite alive. There are two worlds: the world of the flesh—of the seen, and the world of the Spirit—of the unseen. If we believe our outer experience we will be no better off than the unregenerate of Romans 7. If we believe God, we experience a miracle of sanctification and deliverance from sin's power. *"For though we walk in the flesh, we do not war after the flesh (2 Corinthians 10:2)."*

...deeds of the body.... *"Knowing this, that our old man is crucified with him, that the body of sin might be destroyed, that henceforth we should not serve sin (Romans 6:6)."* Here the **body** is the equivalent of the *flesh*. Before regeneration the believer was *in the flesh*, that is, his entire orientation was toward the flesh. The flesh was the dominant and controlling factor in all moral decisions. Upon believing, the sinner was *planted* into Christ. Christ's crucifixion in the flesh was then accounted to all that are in Him. In Colossians 2:11, Paul calls it the *"circumcision* *made without hands, in putting off the <u>body of the sins of the flesh</u> by the circumcision of Christ."* <u>This is not a question of our experience, but of Christ's experience. We are not told to believe that the body of sin is dead apart from Christ, but in Christ.</u> The death of the flesh is a divine reality. Faith lays hold of that objective truth, and when we experience that freedom from the flesh, it is called *mortifying the deeds of the body.* Mortifying is not creating reality, it is <u>faith appropriating a reality already accomplished in the work of Christ.</u>

...ye shall live. The implication is that if a believer does not mortify the deeds of the body, he will be killed, in the flesh, prematurely.

8:14-18 Sonship

14 For as many as are led by the Spirit of God, they are the sons of God.

15 For ye have not received the spirit of bondage again to fear; but ye have received the Spirit of adoption, whereby we cry, Abba, Father.

16 The Spirit itself beareth witness with our spirit, that we are the children of God:

17 And if children, then heirs; heirs of God, and joint-heirs with Christ; if so be that we suffer with him, that we may be also glorified together.

18 For I reckon that the sufferings of this present time are not worthy to be compared with the glory which shall be revealed in us.

Overview

The theme of 8:14-18 is sonship.

Paul has just laid a heavy burden on the believer in verses 12 and 13. We are *debtors.* We owe it to God to no longer walk after the flesh. As seen in chapter 7, all mankind—though under the Law—was overcome by carnality. The gospel now requires us to do what no one ever did before. The finest of men lived all their lives thwarted in their best religious intentions. We are no longer under the Law, but far more is expected of those in Christ than was ever demanded by the Law. It is overwhelming to those who have lived a life of defeat. "It doesn't seem practical; how can I, a man of flesh, mortify the deeds of my body? It is too much. Surely I will fail and come back under condemnation."

So Paul encourages the believer with assurances of sonship and of God's fatherly care. Reminding us that we are heirs of God, he draws our attention to the future glory. All this with the intention of encouraging us to go forward in faith.

8:14 For as many as are led by the Spirit of God, they are the sons of God.

For links this verse to the former statements. Read it in context. We are debtors to walk after the Spirit. If we don't, we will die, **for** all who are being led by the Spirit are sons. Then the following verses continue the discussion of sonship.

This passage does not say that if you allow yourself to be led by the Spirit you will become a son of God. There is no cause and effect here. One is not the means of the other. It is simply stating that all that are *sons of God* are *led by the Spirit*. Or, to say it another way, all who are led by the Spirit, the same are the sons of God. You can identify the sons of God by the observable fact that they are led by the Spirit and do not walk after the flesh.

You could take this either way and be correct. If you are a son of God, be assured you will be led by the Spirit into walking after the Spirit and not after the flesh. Or you could take it this way: If you are being led by the Spirit and not by the flesh, be assured you are a son of God, and therefore entitled to all the blessings and benefits which that entails. *"Beloved, now are we the sons of God, and it doth not yet appear what we shall be: but we know that, when he shall appear, we shall be like him; for we shall see him as he is (1 John 3:2)."*

8:15 For ye have not received the spirit of bondage again to fear; but ye have received the Spirit of adoption, whereby we cry, Abba, Father.

...spirit of bondage.... The Law, making demands of the flesh, is the *spirit of bondage,* as seen by these and other verses. *"Stand fast therefore in the liberty wherewith Christ hath made us free, and be not entangled again with the yoke of bondage (Galatians 5:1)."* *"Even so we, when we were children, were in bondage under the elements of the world (Galatians 4:3)."*

...fear.... Fear was what the Law engendered. *"And deliver them who through fear of death were all their lifetime subject to bondage (Hebrews 2:15)."*

...Spirit of adoption.... The word *adoption* is used just five times in the Bible. Four of the references clearly refer to glorified bodies. Romans 8:5, 23; Romans 9:4; Galatians 4:5; Ephesians 1:5. *Adoption* occurs at the point when Christ actually glorifies the human bodies and inducts His children into His visible kingdom. That Spirit that prepares the believer for the adoption is now dwelling within. He is the *Spirit of adoption.*

In our Western culture the word *adoption* is reserved for that act wherein one who is not a member of the family is legally taken as a family member. But in the ancient Jewish culture, when one who was already a family member came into his inheritance and was instated in the position of authority, receiving all the rights and privileges of the firstborn heir, it was also called *adoption.*

Believers are already sons of God, but the actual adoption into the visible blessing of the heir is yet future.

...whereby we cry, Abba, Father. The Spirit of adoption has already established an intimate relationship with the children of God. In anticipation of that final act of salvation, the redemption of the body, the believer now cries out to the Father with the most common and personal of names that a child can call his daddy, Abba. *"Beloved, now are we the sons of God, and it doth not yet appear what we shall be: but we know that, when he shall appear, we shall be like him; for we shall see him as he is (1 John 3:2)."*

8:16 The Spirit itself beareth witness with our spirit, that we are the children of God:

Two spirits are present in the believer. The natural human spirit, that all men possess, and the Holy Spirit of God which dwells only in the believer. *"But he that is joined unto the Lord is one spirit (1 Corinthians 6:17)."* See verse 9 for a discussion of the Spirit dwelling in believers. *"But God hath revealed them unto us by his Spirit: for the Spirit searcheth all things, yea, the deep things of God. For what man knoweth the things of a man, save the spirit of man which is in him? even so the things of God knoweth no man, but the Spirit of God. Now we have received, not the spirit of the world, but the spirit which is of God; that we might know the things that are freely given to us of God. Which things also we speak, not in the words which man's wisdom teacheth, but which the Holy Ghost teacheth; comparing spiritual things with spiritual. But the natural man receiveth not the things of the Spirit of God: for they are foolishness unto him: neither can he know them, because they are spiritually discerned (1 Corinthians 2:10-14)."*

The modern approach to assurance of salvation is to encourage the doubter to believe that believing is sufficient to count one's self among the redeemed. This amounts to faith in one's faith—like holding your own hand to keep from falling. But the believer is never left to the resource of his own faith to know that he is in favor with God. The Holy Spirit communicates to the spirit of man, revealing Christ and bringing *much* assurance. *"For our gospel came not unto you in word only, but also in power, and in the Holy Ghost, and in much assurance... (1 Thessalonians 1:5)."*

We are **children of God,** with all the blessings and privileges that entails.

8:17 And if children, then heirs; heirs of God, and joint-heirs with Christ; if so be that we suffer with him, that we may be also glorified together.

...then heirs; heirs of God, and joint-heirs with Christ.... The

salvation of the believer is carried out and completed through his relationship as heir to God. We have the Spirit, therefore we are children; we
call Him Abba Father; and children are *heirs of God* the father and *joint
heirs* with the Son. We can be assured that that which remains of our salvation will be completed because of this intimate relationship we have to
God through the Spirit and the Son.

...**joint-heirs with Christ....** It is conceivable that one could be an
heir, yet inherit very little. He had told us that we were heirs of God, but
he then elevates our position by telling us that we adopted sons have
been instated as *joint* heirs with the natural son. A *joint heir* is one who
shares the inheritance equally with another. Joint ownership ties everything up to the consent of both parties. One cannot inherit without the
other. Jesus cannot inherit heaven without being accompanied by all the
saints of God. The *last will and testament* must be read in the presence of
all, and all must share in its implementation. All that is Christ's is ours.
He partook of all we had to offer—sin and death, that we might share all
He has to offer—righteousness and abundant life.

... **if so be that we suffer with him, that we may be also glorified
together.** Paul now introduces comfort to those believers in Rome who
have suffered persecution for the faith. Christ partook of all that is ours
that we might partake of all that is His. There is now a merging of fates.
As such, Christ bore the suffering for our sins, and we now suffer the reproaches that fell on Christ. His suffering was vicarious—for our sins,
whereas our suffering is not the redemptive suffering of a Savior, but the
suffering of the righteous at the hands of those that despise men of duty
and principle.

Later Paul, quoting from Psalms 69:9, says, *"The reproaches of
them that reproached thee fell on me (Romans 15:1).* That is, when believers suffered persecution for the faith, they were actually receiving the
reproach aimed at Christ. Men hate the light neither will come to the
light lest their deeds should be reproved. The presence of Christians
walking in the light stirs sinners to reproach the light. In Christ's absence, the believer receives all the reproach that is actually provoked by
Him.

Back to our text: *"If we suffer with him, that we may be also glorified together."* Our consolation is found in the understanding that the
suffering we now share with Christ is an indication of our solidarity with
Him. If we now share suffering, we can be sure we will soon be glorified
with Him also.

8:18 For I reckon that the sufferings of this present time are not worthy to be compared with the glory which shall be re- vealed in us.

The magnitude of what he has just told us about being a *joint heir*
gives us a different perspective on the sufferings of this life. The coming

glory far outweighs any present suffering we may incur as a result of our Christian stand. *"For our light affliction, which is but for a moment, worketh for us a far more exceeding and eternal weight of glory; While we look not at the things which are seen, but at the things which are not seen: for the things which are seen are temporal; but the things which are not seen are eternal (2 Corinthians 4:17-18)."*

...the glory which shall be revealed in us.... What glory! That the former sons of Adam should actually become *joint heirs* with Christ! It is incomprehensible that *glory* should radiate from once carnal flesh. The sufferings are so small when compared to the *glory* of sonship. *"But as it is written, Eye hath not seen, nor ear heard, neither have entered into the heart of man, the things which God hath prepared for them that love him. But God hath revealed them unto us by his Spirit... (1 Corinthians 2:9-10)."*

Paul continues in the next section with a description of the coming glory.

8:19-23 Redemption of the body/Lifting of the curse

19 For the earnest expectation of the creature waiteth for the manifestation of the sons of God.
20 For the creature was made subject to vanity, not willingly, but by reason of him who hath subjected the same in hope,
21 Because the creature itself also shall be delivered from the bondage of corruption into the glorious liberty of the children of God.
22 For we know that the whole creation groaneth and travaileth in pain together until now.
23 And not only they, but ourselves also, which have the firstfruits of the Spirit, even we ourselves groan within ourselves, waiting for the adoption, to wit, the redemption of our body.

Verses 19-23 speak of the ultimate triumph of Christ in actually removing the Adamic condition. Verses 19-22 speak of lifting the curse on nature, including the animal kingdom. When the flesh is finally transformed like unto His glorious body, natural creation itself will rejoice at the new liberty.

8:19 For the earnest expectation of the creature waiteth for the manifestation of the sons of God.

The word **creature** is used throughout the New Testament referring to both man and to other created beings, including animals. The context of this passage makes it abundantly clear that the creature referred to here is the animal creation, for verse 23 says, *"not only they* (the creatures) *but ourselves also* (meaning man)...."* Since he has set the creature over against *us,* the creature must be something other than man.

So he has said, the animal kingdom earnestly waits for the completion of human salvation—the glorified state.

The **manifestation of the sons of God** is that time when the sons of God are given glorified bodies. *"Beloved, now are we the sons of God, and it doth not yet appear what we shall be: but we know that, when he shall appear, we shall be like him; for we shall see him as he is (1 John 3:2-3)."*

He has said: The animal kingdom that came under the curse placed on Adam's descendants earnestly looks forward to the time when the sons of God come into their new bodies, for then the curse will be lifted on nature as well.

8:20 For the creature was made subject to vanity, not willingly, but by reason of him who hath subjected the same in hope,

The **creature** (animal kingdom suffering from the curse) was **made subject to** (was caused to partake of) **vanity**. All that is of the flesh is under a death sentence and therefore is vanity—empty futility.

...not willingly.... The creatures had no part in the decision that placed them under the curse. The animals did not sin, but they nonetheless share the consequences of the curse. This is interesting. For if the animals equally share the results of Adam's sin, then we have a clearer understanding of depravity, since the curse that is on man is also on the animals, and we know it to be the same curse occurring at the same time and for the same reason. Likewise, it is lifted at the same time for the same reason. Therefore the curse cannot be more than physical and relational.

...but by reason of him who hath subjected the same in hope.... We are given a most amazing reason for the curse on animal creation. There was a **reason** behind it. The reason was not in nature, but in God who **subjected** nature to the curse. The reason was **hope**. Hope is similar to faith, *without which it is impossible to please God*. We are being told that the curse was part of God's plan in order to create an environment where hope could exist. Hope is that future glory that faith sees and anticipates. See verse 24 for further discussion on hope.

8:21 Because the creature itself also shall be delivered from the bondage of corruption into the glorious liberty of the children of God.

The creature was subjected to the vanity of the curse placed on Adam's race, because it placed the creature in a position to also share in the future, glorious liberty of children of God. Adam fell from ground

182

level and took creation with him. But Adam is destined to be restored, not just to his former level, but to heavenly heights and to a glorified position of sonship. Nature shares the fall that it might also share the exaltation into glory—a glory that is beyond anything Adam could have achieved in the flesh. He will tell us in verse 28 that God *"works all things for good."*

Taking verses 19-21 together, he has told us: The creature is waiting for the sons of God to be glorified, because the creature came under this curse through no fault of its own. Rather, God placed nature under the curse in order to create an environment of hope. Hope holds great possibilities. If nature shares in the curse then it can share also in the great hope to come.

8:22 For we know that the whole creation groaneth and travaileth in pain together until now.

It is known by observation, as well as revelation, that creation is in an unnatural state of decay.

He speaks of creation with terms used for a woman about to deliver a child—**groaneth and travaileth in pain**. He is speaking of nature's anticipation of deliverance, anxious for the coming of new life.

8:23 And not only they, but ourselves also, which have the firstfruits of the Spirit, even we ourselves groan within ourselves, waiting for the adoption, to wit, the redemption of our body.

...not only they.... *They,* the animal kingdom, but also those of us who have the Spirit do *groan* (earnestly desire) as we wait for the completion of the adoption, when the body is glorified.

...which have the firstfruits.... *"But now is Christ risen from the dead, and become the firstfruits of them that slept. For since by man came death, by man came also the resurrection of the dead. For as in Adam all die, even so in Christ shall all be made alive. But every man in his own order: Christ the firstfruits; afterward they that are Christ's at his coming (1 Corinthians 15:20-23)."*

When the time of harvest came, the fruit picked first was called the *firstfruits.* It foreshadowed the harvest to come. It was the first taste and the guarantee of much more to follow. The term is applied to the spiritual experience several ways. As you see in the verse below, Christ is the first of many to rise from the dead. Resurrected saints are all called *firstfruits* because they are the beginning of the resurrection. Tribulation and Millennium saints will be resurrected later.

... firstfruits of the Spirit.... But this passage is not about the resurrected saints as firstfruit; rather the saints are the recipients of the firstfruit. God is the one delivering the firstfruit to the believer. The Spirit given to the believer is assurance of a continuing work, culminating in the redemption of the body. The believer tastes the firstfruit of the Holy Spirit and is satisfied that there is indeed more to come.

...we ourselves groan within ourselves, waiting.... We share nature's longing to enter into that glorified state.

...adoption, to wit, the redemption of our body. See verse 15 for a discussion on *adoption*. When this mortal body is changed to be like Christ's glorious body, it is called an *adoption* or *redemption*.

There is a strong tendency to give one narrow meaning to a word and not allow yourself to think of it in any other context. Many words become cliches or titles, buzz words for certain notable doctrines. This is the case with both *adoption* and *redemption*.

The context is clear; though the soul is saved at the point of faith, the body is not saved until the resurrection. *"Who shall change our vile body, that it may be fashioned like unto his glorious body (Philippians 3:21)."*

To sum up verses 19-23, Paul has said: The creatures of natural creation, who had no part in the sin, yet were subjected to the consequences of corruption and decay, have a powerful desire to see the sons of God come into their own. The saints who have the Spirit also share in this hope of a glorified body and glorified animal kingdom.

8:24-27 Assisting grace

24 For we are saved by hope: but hope that is seen is not hope: for what a man seeth, why doth he yet hope for?

25 But if we hope for that we see not, then do we with patience wait for it.

26 Likewise the Spirit also helpeth our infirmities: for we know not what we should pray for as we ought: but the Spirit itself maketh intercession for us with groanings which cannot be uttered.

27 And he that searcheth the hearts knoweth what is the mind of the Spirit, because he maketh intercession for the saints according to the will of God.

Overview

The key to understanding verses 24-27 is found in the word *waiting*, verse 23. Verses 24-25 are an explanation as to why both the creature and we are left *waiting* for this final stage of redemption—the deliverance of the body from the bondage of corruption. He has already told us that the creature (animal kingdom) was subjected to the curse for a reason (8:20). The soul is saved, why not the body? Why the delay? Because the very nature of salvation is an experience of faith (hope). Waiting in faith is an essential part of spiritual maturity. The time lapse between salvation of the soul and salvation of the body is not a misfortune or an inconvenience; it is a means to a great end. It is God's method of spiritual maturity.

8:24 For we are saved by hope: but hope that is seen is not hope: for what a man seeth, why doth he yet hope for?

For, indicates that an explanation follows as to why we are *waiting* *(v.23)* for the glorified state.

...we are saved.... Here is a word that has fallen out of favor in this present generation. But it remains most prominent in the Holy Bible. See *saved* in the Appendix.

...we are saved by hope: but hope that is seen is not hope: for what a man seeth, why doth he yet hope for?

Biblical Hope

Hope is not an archaic word. It is an irreplaceable English word, not commonly used, but no other word will substitute.

It is suggested by some that all Bible terminology should be reduced to the simplest, most common language of our day. It has never been so, not in the original languages and not in the Authorized Version when it was first produced in 1611. If the Bible were stripped of its specialty terminology it would no longer be a special book. It has some unique things to say. Should we expect it to say so much so well if it resorts to the language of the unlearned, whose vocabulary is capable of saying so little? As always the Bible defines its own terms.

Biblical hope is never a wishful desire, an uncertain longing. Bible *hope* is the certain anticipation of an event yet future. Where there is Bible *hope* there is not doubt, no question, no uncertainty. The end is known as if it were past. *Hope* is both the event itself as well as the state of patiently waiting.

When God promises something, the believer does not doubt that it will come to pass. But God's promises often see far ahead into the future. There is usually a time lapse between the promise and the fulfillment. Those who believe and embrace the promises of God are said to have a *certain hope*. The entire Bible is the drama of hope—God promising, and man waiting. See Hebrews 11, where the entire chapter is a list of men and women who lived by a hope, most of them never seeing the fulfillment in this life.

- *"Looking for that <u>blessed hope</u>, and the glorious appearing of the great God and our Saviour Jesus Christ (Titus 2:13)."* The very nature of hope is *"looking."* The hope is realized only with the return of Christ.

- *"In <u>hope</u> of eternal life, which God, that cannot lie, <u>promised</u> before the world began (Titus 1:2)."* Eternal life is a future hope, and that hope is based on the promise of God.

- *"For the <u>hope</u> which is <u>laid up</u> for you in heaven, whereof ye heard before in the word of the truth of the gospel (Colossians 1:5)."* The object (ultimate salvation) is the hope. It is a future event, not to be realized until the next life.

- *"Who against <u>hope</u> believed in <u>hope</u>, that he might become the father of many nations, <u>according to that which was spoken</u>, So shall thy seed be (Romans 4:18)."* Who against the natural expectation of having a child, yet he believed in the hope promised by God. In other words, against natural hope, he hoped in the word of God.

- *"Blessed be the God and Father of our Lord Jesus Christ, which according to his abundant mercy hath begotten us again unto a <u>lively hope</u> by the resurrection of Jesus Christ from the dead, To <u>an inheritance</u> incorruptible, and undefiled, and that fadeth not away, reserved in heaven for you, Who are kept by the power of God through faith unto salvation ready to be revealed in the last time. Wherein ye greatly rejoice, though now for a season, if need be, ye are in heaviness through manifold temptations: That the <u>trial of your faith</u>, being much more precious than of gold that perisheth, though it be tried with fire, might be found unto praise and honour and glory at the appearing of Jesus Christ (1 Peter 1:3-7)."* Notice that the hope of resurrection is called *lively* because it is based on the assurances we have from the resurrection of Christ.

- *"For if we have been planted together in the likeness of his death, we shall be also in the likeness of his resurrection (Romans 6:5)."* Note also that the hope is of an *inheritance* that does not fade away—yet future, and quite certain. Most significant is the statement that this hope involves a *"trial of faith."* <u>The very nature of hope is a trial of faith</u>, as is seen also in the next passage.

- *"And we desire that every one of you do shew the same diligence to the <u>full assurance of hope</u> unto the end: That ye be not slothful, but followers of them who through <u>faith and patience inherit the promises</u>. For when <u>God made promise</u> to Abraham, because he could swear by no greater, he sware by himself, Saying, Surely blessing I will bless thee, and multiplying I will multiply thee. And so, after he had <u>patiently endured</u>, he obtained the promise. For men verily swear by the greater: and an oath for confirmation is to them an end of all strife. Wherein God, willing more abundantly to shew unto the heirs of promise the immutability of his counsel, confirmed it by an oath: That by two immutable things, in which it was <u>impossible for God to lie</u>, we might <u>have a strong consolation</u>, who have fled for refuge to lay hold upon the hope set before us: Which <u>hope</u> we have as an anchor of the soul, both <u>sure and stedfast</u>, and which entereth into that within the veil (Hebrews 6:11-19)."*

All the elements of hope are expressed in this passage—Hebrews 6:11-19.

- It is a promise from God.
- God does not lie.
- We have full assurance of hope—strong consolation.
- It involves faith and patience.
- The promise will be inherited.
- It is a hope set before us. It is placed there by God. It is our certain expectation based on Him who set it before us.
- The hope is an anchor of the soul.

8:25 But if we hope for that we see not, then do we with patience wait for it.

Again we see from this passage that hope is anticipation of that which is not seen. Yet, while this verse is a restatement of the nature of hope, its purpose is to complete the thought begun in verse 20 and carried to this point. The subject at hand is the vanity of nature and human flesh, which is under the *bondage of corruption* (verse 21). The question raised is why the *creature* (animal kingdom) is made subject to vanity along with man. The answer was that God did this by design in order to make the creature a participant in the future hope (verses 20-21). In the meantime (verses 22-23) there is a *groaning* and a waiting on the part of both the creature and man for this deliverance into the *glorious liberty*. This waiting process is then defined as *hope* (verses 24-25), and that brings us down to this verse, which explains further why God made *hope* an essential element in this ultimate deliverance from the corrupted human body and the curse on the creature. The answer is of tremendous significance. Paul has dedicated several verses to make this point.

...patience.... If we are saved through the process of hope, which involves not seeing, then we develop *patience* while we wait. That may leave you wondering: "So what is the significance of patience?" He is going to tell us in verse 29 that God has designed that we be *conformed to the image of His son*. I am not resorting to cliche when I say, "Patience is a virtue." The ultimate expression of faith is *patience*. Faith necessarily involves the unseen. If the unseen is in doubt, there will be no patience. If one believes the word of God concerning the yet unseen future, then that faith is expressed in patience. Patience is the ultimate crown of faith. God is working all things for our good that He might conform us to the patience of Christ.

- *"And so, after he had patiently endured, he obtained the promise (Hebrews 6:15)."* The fulfillment of the promise to Abraham was delayed for 25 years. The experience God put Abraham through was a deliberate trial of faith to work patience into him. Note the necessity of patience. It was after he *patiently endured* that he *received the promise.*

- *"By faith he forsook Egypt, not fearing the wrath of the king: for he endured, as seeing him who is invisible (Hebrews 11:27)."* Moses' endurance (patience) was due to seeing the invisible.

- *"And not only so, but we glory in tribulations also: knowing that tribulation worketh patience; And patience, experience; and experience, hope: And hope maketh not ashamed; because the love of God is shed abroad in our hearts by the Holy Ghost which is given unto us (Romans 5:3-5)."* Note the order of this process of sanctification.

- When one responds in faith, tribulation produces patience. The experience gained from patiently enduring tribulation produces hope. And that hope, though we have nothing to show for it, does not make us *ashamed*, because in the patient hoping the love of God is shed all over the one who patiently hopes. God pours Himself out on the one who has patience and hope. The one who hopes has nothing to show for it but the love of God. But that is enough to keep hope aflame.

- *"Remembering without ceasing your work of faith, and labour of love, and patience of hope in our Lord Jesus Christ, in the sight of God and our Father (1 Thessalonians 1:3)."* Faith works, love labors, and hope produces patience—in that order.

- *"For ye have need of patience, that, after ye have done the will of God, ye might receive the promise (Hebrews 10:36)."* Biblical patience is more than a naturally relaxed temperament. Patience is that virtue which enables one to endure until the end.

- *"Knowing this, that the trying of your faith worketh patience. But let patience have her perfect work, that ye may be perfect and entire, wanting nothing (James 1:3-4)."* Patience is not born out of tranquility. When faith finds itself standing on one side with nothing but the promise of God, and carnal reality stands in opposition on the other, then faith is *tried*. Faith must be tried if it would produce patience. Patience must be produced if faith would endure. Patience is mature faith. Hope is the eye of faith tempered with patience.

- *"Be patient therefore, brethren, unto the coming of the Lord. Behold, the husbandman waiteth for the precious fruit of the earth, and hath long patience for it, until he receive the early and latter rain. Be ye also patient; stablish your hearts: for the coming of the Lord draweth nigh (James 5:7-8)."* Again patience is called for in anticipation of enduring unto the coming of the Lord.

- *"And beside this, giving all diligence, add to your faith virtue; and to virtue knowledge; And to knowledge temperance; and to temperance patience; and to patience godliness (2 Peter 1:5-6)."* Here is the chronological order of spiritual growth. Note what must precede patience, then note what follows it.

- *"And hast borne, and hast patience, and for my name's sake hast laboured, and hast not fainted (Revelation 2:3)."* There are several passages in the address to churches of Asia where God commends the churches for their patience in the face of persecutions.
- *"In your patience possess ye your souls (Luke 21:19)."* Patience is essential to working out your own salvation (Philippians 2:12). This has nothing to do with being born again.
- *"For whatsoever things were written aforetime were written for our learning, that we through <u>patience</u> and comfort of the scriptures <u>might have hope</u>. Now the <u>God of patience</u> and consolation grant you to be likeminded one toward another according to Christ Jesus (Romans 15:4-5)."* Hope comes through the comfort of Scripture, seeing how others *endured the great fight of affliction.* Here is a promise that the God who requires patience is a God of patience. Doubtlessly, we can *"come boldly unto the throne of grace, that we may obtain mercy, and find grace to help in time of need (Hebrews 4:16)."*

8:26-39 Assurances from God

The Spirit's help 8:26-27

26 Likewise the Spirit also helpeth our infirmities: for we know not what we should pray for as we ought: but the Spirit itself maketh intercession for us with groanings which cannot be uttered.

27 And he that searcheth the hearts knoweth what is the mind of the Spirit, because he maketh intercession for the saints according to the will of God.

Overview 8:26-27

These two verses reflect back on the preceding discussion. In verse 18 he spoke of a believer's sufferings and then went on to explain how God designed that we should experience the walk of faith *(hope)* as a means to maturity. No one likes being told that his father, even if it is the Heavenly Father, has designed for him to go through a period of trial, which may include suffering. Reflecting on the sense of burden this may have caused, Paul goes on to assure his reader that there is divine help through the Spirit.

Not only are we cast upon the unseen hope, prompted by the Spirit to groan within ourselves waiting for the new body, but **(Likewise)** the Spirit helpeth our infirmities, translating those groanings into intelligible prayers that reach heaven and bring Divine help.

The Spirit is the comforter and helper.

...infirmities.... *Infirmities* are weaknesses and sicknesses of the fleshly body. Most commentators ignore the context as well as the meaning of the word and just assume that Paul's doctrine is all in the spiritual realm. The word infirm, in any form, is used 22 times in the Bible, 19 of those are in the New Testament. Without exception it always refers to human flesh. All of the other references are a clear statement of weakness, disease, or sickness. Why impute a different definition in this verse alone?

Observe the context. In verse 18 he speaks of *sufferings*. The nature of the sufferings are such that the saints *groan* for *deliverance from the bondage of corruption (verse 21)*. He again defines the ultimate deliverance as *redemption of our body (verse 23)*. Then in verse 25 he speaks of *waiting* for this manifestation of deliverance, which brings us to this verse in 26. While in this corrupted body of flesh, waiting for deliverance, groaning in the Spirit for the new body, the Spirit will help us in our infirmities (weak bodies from sickness, bodies tired and weary, often too tired to pray).

Because of our infirmities **we know not what we should pray for as we ought,** so the Spirit that dwells within **maketh intercession for us with groanings which cannot be uttered.** When a child of God is so feeble from sickness or weariness of flesh that he cannot focus enough to even know how to pray, the Holy Spirit will take the groanings and translate them into intelligible prayers and deliver them to the throne of God for a speedy answer.

The Holy Spirit of God is the one who **searcheth the hearts** of believers. *"But God hath revealed them unto us by his Spirit: for the Spirit searcheth all things, yea, the deep things of God. For what man knoweth the things of a man, save the spirit of man which is in him? even so the things of God knoweth no man, but the Spirit of God (1 Corinthians 2:10-11)."*

Infirmity prevents us from knowing what we should pray, but the Spirit dwelling in our spirit **knoweth what is the mind of the Spirit.** The Holy Spirit of God mediates our prayers to the throne of God. This is far better than having the best of our prayers reach unto heaven, **because he maketh intercession for the saints according to the will of God.**

8:28-39 Providential care

8:28 And we know that all things work together for good to them that love God, to them who are the called according to his purpose.

We who are in this state of hope, groaning and waiting for deliverance, are given assurance that these trying experiences (the sufferings of v. 18) are not mistakes or inconveniences. We know that our sovereign God has a plan. We are in the center of His program. **We know that all things work together for good**. All things are not good, but God will use the worst of circumstance to enhance the image of Christ in us. *"But as for you, ye thought evil against me; but God meant it unto good (Genesis 50:20)."*

...to them that love God, to them who are the called according to his purpose.... It appears he is adding a qualifier to the promise that all things work for good. Only those *that love God, and are the called according to his purpose* will find profit in infirmities.

He is not dividing Christians into two categories, those that love God and those that don't, those that are responsive to His call and those that are not. Everywhere Scripture assumes that all who have the Spirit of God do love God and are called to His purpose.

One might question, "If all believers love God and are called to fulfill His purpose, then why did he not just say *all believers* instead of describing them?" Paul's entire point is that God has a purpose in subjecting us to the sufferings of this sojourn in the flesh. In the midst of the trials we can be certain that those of us that are called to be a part of God's purpose will never have anything come our way that is not for our good. He tacks on the amendment to remind believers of their relationship to God. We who love God are called according to (in keeping with the purpose) of God. Therefore we can have confidence that this God of purpose will work all things according to our good.

8:29 For whom he did foreknow, he also did predestinate to be conformed to the image of his Son, that he might be the firstborn among many brethren.

For whom.... This is an emphatic statement of how God fulfills His purpose in the believer, working all things for his good. This is strictly God's work on the believer. In it we find great assurance of God's ultimate conquest over the flesh.

...foreknow.... Those philosophers known as "Calvinist" tell us that foreknowledge really means the act of selecting or predestinating. They do not claim to arrive at that interpretation through exegesis of the original languages. They simply break into the plain sense of the text and insert their musings.

Foreknow, **in some form, is used just four times in Scripture.**

- *"Him, being delivered by the determinate counsel and <u>foreknowledge</u> of God, ye have taken, and by wicked hands have crucified and slain (Acts 2:23)."* According to this verse, to determine beforehand is not the same as foreknowledge.

- *"God hath not cast away his people which he <u>foreknew</u> (Romans 11:2)."* This is speaking of Israel. Obviously, in this case, God's foreknowledge of the nation of Israel did not guarantee individual salvation, for many who were objects of God's foreknowledge perished.

- *"Elect according to the <u>foreknowledge</u> of God the Father, through sanctification of the Spirit, unto obedience and sprinkling of the blood of Jesus Christ (1 Peter 1:2)."* Election and foreknowledge are not the same, since one is based on the other. Foreknowledge comes first and is the resource for election.

- *"For whom he did <u>foreknow</u>, he also did predestinate to be conformed to the image of his Son, that he might be the firstborn among many brethren (Ro 8:29)."* Again note that predestination is based on foreknowledge, and therefore cannot be the same.

Foreknow means exactly what it appears on the surface—to have knowledge of beforehand. The Greek, as always, supports the Authorized Version most forcefully. God's designs and purposes began before the foundation of the world. To know all beforehand is the attribute of God alone. God foreknows everything that has been and that will be. *"Remember the former things of old: for I am God, and there is none else; I am God, and there is none like me, Declaring the end from the beginning, and from ancient times the things that are not yet done, saying, My counsel shall stand, and I will do all my pleasure (Isaiah 46:9-10)."*

Knowing the end from the beginning, nothing catches God by surprise. Based on His foreknowledge, He is able to interrupt the normal flow of human events and bring about an influence that controls the destinies of men. *"The king's heart is in the hand of the LORD, as the rivers of water: he turneth it whithersoever he will (Proverbs 21:1)."* *"Blessed be the LORD God of our fathers, which hath put such a thing as this in the king's heart, to beautify the house of the LORD which is in Jerusalem (Ezra 7:27)."* God's foreknowledge is so complete that even before the human race was created, He was able to record in a book the names of those that would believe the gospel and be saved (Revelation 13:8; 17:8).

This is a blessed doctrine and a glorious truth, but the problem arises when carnal men discover how they can employ it as an excuse for irresponsibility. Their thoughts are: "I have an uncontrollable desire to indulge my appetites, so it must be preordained that I should sin. I cannot change what will be, so I might as well just relax and go with the flow. How can I be blamed for doing the inevitable?" Obviously no theologian would ever teach such blasphemy, but Calvinists themselves caution their adherents to use discretion when preaching the TULIP doctrines lest they be misunderstood and misused by the unlearned. Their reticence to preach a supposed Bible truth should be a red flag to us, but the fact is, just as the Calvinists admit, their doctrines are a great source of excuse for the carnally minded.

To know the certainty of all events before they happen does not imply control of events. If science created a time machine, and one were to go into the future and observe the eventual development of all events, upon coming back into the present, full knowledge of all future events would in no way necessarily infringe upon the will of those in the midst of decision.

God's foreknowledge is passive. It is not a determiner. In terms of control, knowledge before the fact is no different from knowledge after the fact. To the omniscient mind, to know that a thing *will* occur is no different from knowing that it *has* occurred. To God all has already occurred, but to us the future is yet to be determined. It is not ours to try to conform to what God already knows, but to conform to what God wills. I know not what God knows. I do know what He wills. God holds every man responsible for every thought and act, because a man determines his destiny by the choices he makes.

Though foreknowledge is the basis of God involving Himself in our lives so as to influence us to the right choice, foreknowledge will never interfere with the choices we make. That God knows what I will do in the future and what will befall me does not relieve me of making responsible choices.

Predestination

For whom he did foreknow, he also did predestinate to be conformed to the image of his Son.... This word **predestinate** is a stone of stumbling to philosophical theologians. The Stoics and fatalists would be at home with much of what is taught in the guise of Bible truth.

If you ask the average man on the street or the average Christian to define biblical predestination, he will tell you something to this effect:

- "Predestination is what God does in deciding the future of everybody."
- "Predestination is the predetermined plan God has for each person's life."
- "Everything happens because God has predestined it to happen."
- "You can't change what God has predestined."

The popular misconceptions surrounding predestination reflect Calvinistic teaching. The theologians would deny that they teach any of the above, and in a strict sense, they don't. But popular opinions are a direct fruit of what is taught. Laymen have a way of cutting through the religious terminology they are hearing and making practical application. The tendency to excuse one's self for sinning finds an ally in Calvinism.

Here are the only four verses in the Bible where the word *predestinate* appears. All of them will be discussed in order.

- *"For whom he did foreknow, he also did predestinate to be conformed to the image of his Son, that he might be the firstborn among many brethren (Ro 8:29)."*
- *"Moreover whom he did predestinate, them he also called: and whom he called, them he also justified: and whom he justified, them*

he also glorified (Ro 8:30)."

- *"Having <u>predestinated</u> us unto the adoption of children by Jesus Christ to himself, according to the good pleasure of his will (Eph 1:5)."*
- *"In whom also we have obtained an inheritance, being <u>predestinated</u> according to the purpose of him who worketh all things after the counsel of his own will (Eph 1:11)."*

There is no question concerning the definition of *predestinate*. It is to determine the destiny before. Only God can have a predetermination concerning our destinies. The questions we must ask Scripture are:

1. When, in the order of events, did predestination take place?
2. What has God predestined?
3. For whom has he predestined it?
4. What means does God use to bring about that which is predestined?

1. When, in the order of events, did predestination take place? *For whom he did foreknow, he also did predestinate to be conformed to the image of his Son.* First notice that foreknowledge comes before predestination. Based on something God knew about the future, He predestined something. Those that would defend the philosophical views of Augustine, Luther, and Calvin, will point out that the foreknowledge, which became the basis of predestination, was in respect only to those that were predestined. They then conclude that the foreknowledge itself was an act of electing certain ones. But human reasoning and speculation fall to Scripture once again. Note Peter says we are *"<u>Elect according to the foreknowledge</u> of God the Father, through sanctification of the Spirit, unto obedience and sprinkling of the blood of Jesus Christ (1 Peter 1:2)."* Foreknowledge is before election, before predestination, before calling, before every work of God in man. Decrees don't exist any more than the Piltdown man. When it becomes necessary to create missing links, somebody is misrepresenting the truth for purposes of their own. Those whom God foreknew, He elected and then predestined. That is the Biblical order.

2. What has God predestined? *...he also did predestinate <u>to be conformed to the image of his Son</u>.* In this verse it is <u>not the person that is predestinated,</u> but something concerning the person.

From before the foundation of the world God knew those that would be his. God had a plan, a desired destiny, for those that would become His children. The entire scenario of Adam, the fall, life on this planet, the nations, the Jews, the Law, Jesus, the Church, the second coming, and the ultimate glorified state is designed for a great and valuable purpose which God foreknew. All this, of which we are a part, is God's studio where He is perfecting a great work of *"bringing many sons into glory*

(Hebrews 2:10)." His goal is not just to restore Adam's race to paradise, but to elevate them to sons of God.

Of only one has God been able to say, *"This is my beloved son in whom I am well pleased."* But God desires to have many sons like the One. The history of Planet Earth is the history of God calling out a family for Himself. He desires that all His children should be like the one Son who pleases Him so well. Therefore God has pre- (before) destined all sons to be like the one son that pleases Him so well. Predestination is not a determination as to who will be God's sons, rather it is a determination as to the final image of those who will become His sons. Look at the text. ...*he also did predestinate <u>to be conformed to the image of his Son.</u>* Those whom God foreknew <u>were predestinated *to be conformed,* not pre-destinated to be saved.</u> This is about ultimate triumph, not justification, about the ultimate image of the saved, not who will be saved.

Paul is not making philosophical speculations, attempting to delve into mysteries known only to God. Looking at the context, it is clear that he was in the midst of delivering a very practical dissertation. He is telling us that we are left in these bodies of flesh to suffer trials and learn patience, because God has a plan to conform all that are His to the image of His son.

3. For whom has he predestined it? *"For whom he did foreknow, he also did predestinate to be conformed to the image of his Son, that he might be the firstborn among many brethren. Moreover whom he did <u>predestinate,</u> them he also called: and whom he called, them he also justified: and whom he justified, them he also glorified (Romans 8:29-30)."* If predestination were a general predetermination by God of who would and who would not be saved, it would of necessity have to include the unsaved as well as the saved. Some would be predestined to life, some predestined to death. But it is clear from the context that the only ones predestined to be conformed to the image of God's son are those whom God foreknew. Therefore it would be ignoring the context to suggest that this is a predestination unto life.

4. What means does God use to bring about that which is predestined? This question is pertinent because the means lends itself to the nature of the predestination. If predestination is the act of choosing certain ones to salvation, then the means would be quite different from pre-destination to be conformed to the image of Christ.

The very word, *conformed,* suggests a process. The predestination of the Calvinists is not a process. It is not even an event. To them it is eternal, as is God. They speak of "eternal decrees." Don't bother trying to find it in a concordance. Ideas like that are invented and entombed in the cold cloistered halls of professional academia. It provides stimulating debate for those too tied up in their minds to minister the gospel to the truly needy. You will never find the soul-winner, evangelist, or missionary talking about such things.

The very statement about predestination is nestled in the midst of the means. Paul introduces the subject as an encouragement to those who are presently experiencing the means to the predestinated end—conformity to the image of God's son. Read the verse in context. We have *received the Spirit of adoption whereby we cry Abba, Father* (v.15). We are heirs and will be glorified together with the Son (v.17). We suffer, but not without reason. Glory will be revealed in us when we shall be delivered from this corrupt body (18-21). God subjected nature and us to this state wherein hope is essential, because He has a reason (20-22). We now have the first installment, the Spirit, but in time the body will be made like unto His glorious body (v.23). There are limitations due to infirmities, but the Spirit makes intercession and helps us (26-27). All these adverse things are working together for our good, because He has determined beforehand that He will conform us to the image of His Son Jesus.

As you can see, this is not the mystery some philosophically minded theorists would have it be.

Now we examine the second of four verses on predestination. We have already covered this somewhat and will go into it with more detail as we come to it in our commentary, but the issue at hand is predestination. *Romans 8:30 "Moreover whom he did predestinate, them he also called: and whom he called, them he also justified: and whom he justified, them he also glorified."*

As we discussed above, the thing predestinated was not the salvation of the individual, but that those who are saved should be conformed to the image of Christ. This list *(called, justified, and glorified)* is the means by which the *predestination to conformity* is brought about. There is the danger of removing this verse from its context and supposing that predestination is the basis of calling, justification, and glorification. Remember in the previous verse we learned that *foreknowledge is the basis of predestination, and predestination is His future plan for the ones whom he calls*. As a means to the predestinated end, they were *called*, then *justified*, and will ultimately be *glorified*. Predestination does not precede the calling; the calling is the means to bring about the predestinated end—conformity to the character and image of Christ.

We will now examine the third of four verses that speak of predestination. *"Having predestinated us unto the adoption of children by Jesus Christ to himself, according to the good pleasure of his will, to the praise of the glory of his grace, wherein he hath made us accepted in the beloved (Ephesians 1:5-6)."* This verse falls in line with the others. The predestination was specific in its aim. It is not the act of God in choosing the individual, but the goal of God for those individuals that are His children. God predestined that the saved would be children of God, accepted into the inner circle of the beloved, a praise and glory to the marvelous grace of God which sustains and delivers the believer. Look at the previous statement: *"...that we should be holy and without blame before him in love."* The predestination involves a <u>process</u> of being conformed, becoming holy and without blame.

We now examine the last of four verses on predestination. *"Having made known unto us the mystery of his will, according to his good pleasure which he hath purposed in himself: That in the dispensation of the fulness of times he might gather together in one all things in Christ, both which are in heaven, and which are on earth; even in him: In whom also we have obtained an inheritance, being <u>predestinated</u> according to the purpose of him who worketh all things after the counsel of his own will (Ephesians 1:9-11)."* A simple reading of this verse in its context should be sufficient to dispel the imaginations of the Stoic Sophists. Note the elements: It has to do with the *will* of God, which *purpose* is fulfilled in *Himself.* It is a future event, *in the fullness of times.* The *purpose* is to *gather together into one* all who have obtained an *inheritance.* Those that will be *gathered together in Christ,* as part of God's family, were *predestinated* to arrive at this inheritance as God *worked all things* after His *own will.*

This predestination is realized, not in salvation, but in the future through the process of God working things according to His will. It has to do with God's goal for the believer not God's selection as to who would be a believer.

...that he might be the firstborn among many brethren. God's ultimate purpose is to exalt and glorify Jesus the son. The destiny (predestination) of the Church is to come into full adoption as sons of God. As co-heirs with Christ, we are to assume the position as worthy sons. Christ is to have the distinction and position of the *firstborn.* The *many brethren* are all saints of all ages as the family of God.

...firstborn.... In the ancient world, and particularly in Israel, the oldest male child held a very high place in the family. Land was family property. It always stayed under the family name and was passed down from one generation to the next. The land was not split up and divided into smaller parcels. It remained one estate under the family name. The firstborn male assumed family leadership when it was passed to him by his old and dying father. The other males born in the family may have received minor inheritance, but they lived on the property of the firstborn and, though they were family, they were always in the shadow of the family head—the firstborn.

So the term *firstborn* came to mean more than first in descent. In fact, when they spoke of the *firstborn,* order of birth or age was not necessarily being considered. It was the position being noted. This is obvious to anyone who reads the many reference in the Old Testament. We will list several to show that *firstborn* was a title often applied to those who were not first in order of birth.

- *"And Joseph called the name of the firstborn Manasseh (Genesis 41:51)."* Joseph had two sons, Manasseh, the *firstborn* (the one born first), and then Ephraim, the younger. But God rejected Manasseh as the family head and chose the younger brother Ephraim to take his office. Later, God called the younger brother, Ephraim, the *firstborn.* *"...for I am a father to Israel, and Ephraim is my firstborn (Jeremiah 31:9)."*

- *"And thou shalt say unto Pharaoh, Thus saith the* LORD, *Israel is my son, even my firstborn (Exodus 4:22)."* God called the entire nations of Israel His *firstborn,* because Israel is given a place of prominence in God's program.

- *"It shall devour the strength of his skin: even the firstborn of death shall devour his strength (Job 18:13)."* Alluding to the overriding power and authority of death, in a figure he calls *death* the *firstborn.*

- *"Also I will make him my firstborn, higher than the kings of the earth (Psalm 89:27)."* David, and Christ whom he typifies, is called *firstborn.* David was the eighth son of Jessie. We are told that David will be raised to sit on the throne of Israel during the Millennium. As supreme king of the earth, ruling over the Kingdom of Heaven, he will be in the position of *firstborn.*

- *"Who is the image of the invisible God, the firstborn of every creature (Colossians 1:15)."* When Jesus took upon himself human flesh and as a man overcame, He became the head of the race, the *last Adam,* the *second man.* He is *bringing many sons into glory,* and as such is the *firstborn* of all whom He gives life.

- *"And he is the head of the body, the church: who is the beginning, the firstborn from the dead; that in all things he might have the preeminence (Colossians 1:18)."* As head of the church, the first one to obey the Law, to overcome, to rise from the dead, he is the beginning of God's work in humanity. He has the position of *firstborn.*

- *"To the general assembly and church of the firstborn, which are written in heaven, and to God the Judge of all, and to the spirits of just men made perfect (Hebrews 12:23)."* The church has a position and is given authority as the *firstborn.*

The verse before us, **that he might be the firstborn among many brethren,** is not a statement about being born. Jesus was indeed born of a woman. He was the first righteous soul to be so born, but, as you can see from the Scripture, this is not a reference to birth. The context of this passage is about how God is working all things for the good of those whom He is bringing into realization of full adoption.

Look at the wording: *"For whom he did foreknow, he also did predestinate to be conformed to the image of his Son, that he might be the firstborn among many brethren."* Jesus Christ becomes the firstborn by having many brethren conformed to His image. The *"that he might be"* defines the relationship of the former to the latter. Those brought into conformity to Christ's image are the basis of Christ becoming the *firstborn*. The emphasis is on the many brethren brought into conformity to Christ, whereby, in that relationship of conformity, Christ is cast into the role of *firstborn*.

8:30 Moreover whom he did predestinate, them he also called: and whom he called, them he also justified: and whom he justified, them he also glorified.

We discussed predestination above. As we have seen, the order is foreknowledge, predestination, election, calling, justification, and then glorification. In its context, Paul is assuring the believer that if he has the firstfruits of the Spirit, then he is in God's program, the purpose being to bring him into full conformity to the image of God's son. To that end God has predestined all whom He foreknew.

...them he also called.... The Augustinian theorists argue that we have before us a proof of limited atonement, for only a certain group are called—those that are saved. It is absolutely true that no one is called except those whom God previously foreknew would be justified. The calling is part of the program that eventually will bring to realization the image of Christ. But the fact remains that the calling is based on predestination to a certain conformity, and the predestination is based on foreknowledge.

That this calling is 100% effectual does not thereby suggest that the provision of salvation was limited to that group only. Salvation was sufficient for all; "many are called, but few are chosen (Mat. 22:14)." That is, many heard a call, but only certain ones whom He foreknew in a particular regard heard the calling that would be effectual and actually result in their conformity. See 1 John 2:2.

"...whom he called, them (the same ones, same number) **he also justified: and whom he justified, them** (the same ones that were called are the same that were justified and will be the same that are glorified) **he also glorified."**

The entire program of conformity began from before the foundation of the world when God determined to have a family of sons like unto his one Holy Son. With this purpose in mind, those whom God foreknew would become His sons, those He did predestinate to be conformed (a process, not just salvation) to that image of His Son. Having predetermined that final image, He called to that conformity all participants. As each one responded to the call of conformity, He justified them. And the justification is only a prelude to the eventual glorification. The process and its outcome is guaranteed from beginning to end because He *is able also to save them to the uttermost that come unto God by him, seeing he ever liveth to make intercession for them (Hebrews 7:25).*

The remainder of this chapter confirms this interpretation, in that it is a discussion of how the trials and sufferings of this life will not prevent that ultimate conformity to the image of God's Son, the prototype for all sons of God. To take such practical teaching and turn it into philosophical speculation, daring to tread where angels would not, is interesting philosophy but poor exegesis.

"...them he also glorified." He speaks of a future event as if it were past. In the foreknowledge of God, all events are past. This just confirms to us the certainty of God's eternal program.

We find great comfort in Paul's assurance that this program is not interruptible. The same number that God foreknew is the same number that were called, and the same number that were justified, and the same number that were glorified. If you are part of the program today, you have every right to believe that you will be part of it until its consummation in the glorified state.

8:31 What shall we then say to these things? If God be for us, who can be against us?

Paul has inquired as to our response to the tremendous truth revealed above. What do we **say** to this program of God that most certainly ends in a glorified body? We say, not as a question, but as an emphatic statement, **"If God be for us, who can be against us?"** The remainder of the chapter is a declaration that nothing can be against us if God is for us.

8:32 He that spared not his own Son, but delivered him up for us all, how shall he not with him also freely give us all things?

Paul presents a great argument to our reason. His logic is based on observations about the consistency of God Himself. His argument follows this line: If a man commences a great project at a tremendous initial cost, the entire price being paid up front, would he then abandon the project when there is so little to be done to bring it to completion? God demonstrated the degree of His commitment to our salvation when He allowed Jesus to become the blood sacrifice. If God failed to carry this project to a satisfactory conclusion, the death of Jesus would be in vain.

After Jesus died, everything else is just an amendment. It is now for God's glory that He causes all that have been made partakers of Christ to persevere. *"According as his divine power hath given unto us all things that pertain unto life and godliness, through the knowledge of him that hath called us to glory and virtue (2 Peter 1:3)."*

"Forasmuch as ye know that ye were not redeemed with corruptible things, as silver and gold, from your vain conversation received by tradition from your fathers; But with the precious blood of Christ, as of a lamb without blemish and without spot (1 Peter 1:18-19)." If the initial price had been silver and gold, God could lose His investment without experiencing personal loss. But with the price of *"the precious blood of Christ"* already paid, would God shy away from providing grace to see us through?

8:33 Who shall lay any thing to the charge of God's elect? It is God that justifieth.

Who shall lay any thing to the charge (go before the court and charge the Christian with being unfit for his position in the family of God) of God's elect?

The elect in this case are all whom God foreknew (1Peter 1:2). There are those that do not see the believer's security in the same light. There is more than one *"accuser of the brethren."* The enemies of God's program are ready to charge God's elect with any apparent inconsistency. What high convictions the unbeliever has when he judges the Christian. But the believer never claimed to be justified by the world. He never asked his accusers for commendation. Is he surprised when evil men charge him with evil?

It is God that justifieth. God is the one that is in charge of Heaven and Hell. He is the Lawgiver and its enforcer. If the Judge grants me a pardon, what difference does it make what the prosecuting attorney thinks?

8:34 Who is he that condemneth? It is Christ that died, yea rather, that is risen again, who is even at the right hand of God, who also maketh intercession for us.

Paul is not seeking the identity of the one condemning. He is challenging his right to condemn—his jurisdiction to condemn. *"Who art thou that judgest another man's servant? to his own master he standeth or falleth. Yea, he shall be holden up: for God is able to make him stand (Romans 14:4)."*

The question is not addressed to the one condemning. It is written to those saints of God who are condemned by others. Its purpose is to remind us not to be slain by the accusers, because their opinions don't count. They are not worthy or qualified to judge in the matter. If Christ thought enough of me to die in my place, rise from the grave, and then sit down beside God to represent me in my continuing infirmities, what difference does it make what a petty accuser thinks? Christ has earned the right to be my Judge or my Savior, as He pleases; no one else has a moral base to do either.

...who also maketh intercession.... This is the third time in this chapter that he has reminded us of Christ's intercession. Intercession is not a past event. It is an ongoing ministry. Intercession is not something Christ does to us, but for us. It is the activity of a mediator standing between two parties. *"For there is one God, and one mediator between God and men, the man Christ Jesus (1Timothy 2:5)."* Remember the context of this latter half of chapter 8; the believer is in the midst of sufferings, waiting for release from this vile flesh. *"Wherefore he is able also to save them to the uttermost that come unto God by him, seeing he ever liveth to make intercession for them (Hebrews 7:25)."*

We have a mediator, an overcoming man who has passed into the heavens to take up office as our personal intercessor. *"Seeing then that we have a great high priest, that is passed into the heavens, Jesus the Son of God, let us hold fast our profession (Hebrews 4:14)."* Such knowledge is great motivation to continue in this sure hope.

8:35 Who shall separate us from the love of Christ? shall tribulation, or distress, or persecution, or famine, or nakedness, or peril, or sword?

The adversities mentioned here are not the ordinary trials of life. They are the result of persecution. The enemies of Christ seek to separate the believer from God through threats and punishments to the body. What fools they are to try to combat a hope in the next life by inflicting sufferings in this one. They only drive the believer to greater hope. All things do *work together for good to those that love God and are called according to his purpose.* Those who see value only in this life cannot understand this. The wedge that our enemy drives between us and our bodily comforts only presses us closer to Christ.

Isn't it profound that so many throughout history have dedicated their lives, their governments, and their resources in an attempt to separate believers from the love of God? Why does it trouble so many? **Tribulation, distress, persecution, famine, nakedness, peril, and sword** have been repeatedly thrown at the believing community. More times than not it is some segment of the professing church that is the persecutor. They mean it for evil, but God uses it for good. The world cannot win, and the believer cannot lose. Every blow they strike drives us closer to Christ. We win one crown by enduring and another for dying. The world slings a curse, but by the time it has landed it is a blessing from God.

If the world were wise, and they wanted to separate us from the love of God, they would bless us, curry us, tolerate us in all things, and then entertain us, marry us, love us, use our speech, go to our churches, sing our praise music to us, adopt most of our ways, profess to be Christian, and then give everything but their hearts to God. The Church can be massaged into apostasy, but it will never be persecuted into apostasy.

8:36 As it is written, For thy sake we are killed all the day long; we are accounted as sheep for the slaughter.

As it is written... in *Psalms 44:22.*

For thy sake can be understood two ways, either of which is true. First, we endure suffering, even unto death, because we love God and count it a privilege to suffer for His name's sake (Acts 5:41). Second, we suffer even unto death because we are associated with His name. It is because we are known as His that we are persecuted unto death.

...we are killed all the day long.... This is not figurative. The killing is real. Jesus warned His disciples, *"They shall put you out of the synagogues: yea, the time cometh, that whosoever <u>killeth you</u> will think that he doeth God service (John 16:2)."*

Paul writes of his daily experience of death: *"And why stand we in jeopardy every hour? I protest by your rejoicing which I have in Christ Jesus our Lord, <u>I die daily</u>. If after the manner of men I have fought with beasts at Ephesus, what advantageth it me, if the dead rise not? (1Corinthians 15:30-32)."* Every day held the eminent possibility of death for those who publicly proclaimed Christ.

"But we have this treasure in earthen vessels, that the excellency of the power may be of God, and not of us. We are troubled on every side, yet not distressed; we are perplexed, but not in despair; Persecuted, but not forsaken; cast down, but not destroyed; Always bearing about in the body the dying of the Lord Jesus, that the life also of Jesus might be made manifest in our body. For we which live are <u>alway delivered unto death</u> for Jesus' sake, that the life also of Jesus might be made manifest in our mortal flesh. So then <u>death worketh in us</u>, but life in you (2 Corinthians 4:7-12)." The frontline minister must risk his life to preach the gospel. He rises in the morning to pick up his cross for another day. At any moment Christ could lead him to the place of crucifixion where he becomes a **sheep for the slaughter** (Romans 12:1).

8:37 Nay, in all these things we are more than conquerors through him that loved us.

As a slaughtered sheep, the martyred Christian is the ultimate conqueror. The world stands over the cold body of a martyred saint and says, "What a waste!" The angels stand over a martyred saint and say, "What an offering!" The martyred saint cries, "What a privilege!" Jesus says, *"Well done, good an faithful servant; I will make thee ruler over many things: enter thou into the joy of thy lord (Matthew 25:23)."* When the world roughs up a Christian it is like kneading bread, it makes them rise higher. When the devil beats a Christian, he beats the world out and makes more room for Jesus.

...in all things.... All things, bar none, no exceptions, **we are more than conquerors**. The Christian is in a battle. God assists by stirring up the enemy. The word *conqueror* is inadequate to describe the outcome. The believer is going to overcome and then some. We are not only going to rise again, we are going to rise far higher than we were before we got knocked down in the Garden of Eden. This is more than paradise restored. In Adam we left paradise; in Christ we gain not paradise, but heaven itself.

We are more than conquerors **through him that loved us** *"and washed us from our sins in his own blood."* It is ever His love that brings all this to pass. If our love purchased heaven, we wouldn't have enough real-estate to insert a flag pole. *"For the love of Christ constraineth us;*

because we thus judge, that if one died for all, then were all dead (2 Corinthians 5:14)."

8:38 For I am persuaded, that neither death, nor life, nor angels, nor principalities, nor powers, nor things present, nor things to come,

39 Nor height, nor depth, nor any other creature, shall be able to separate us from the love of God, which is in Christ Jesus our Lord.

Of all men, Paul had earned the right to make this confident assertion. He recounts some of his experiences in preaching the gospel: *"...in labours more abundant, in stripes above measure, in prisons more frequent, in deaths oft. Of the Jews five times received I forty stripes save one. Thrice was I beaten with rods, once was I stoned, thrice I suffered shipwreck, a night and a day I have been in the deep; In journeyings often, in perils of waters, in perils of robbers, in perils by mine own countrymen, in perils by the heathen, in perils in the city, in perils in the wilderness, in perils in the sea, in perils among false brethren; In weariness and painfulness, in watchings often, in hunger and thirst, in fastings often, in cold and nakedness (2 Corinthians 11:23-27)."*

If Paul was persuaded that nothing could separate him from the love of God, we have reason to hope.

...neither death nor life.... This is an interesting list and bears examination. Sometimes it is easier to die for Christ than it is to live for Him. The threat of violent death, especially when it is well defined as an issue of faithfulness to Christ, often awakens the martyr complex in people. But slow life, lazy life, indulging, comfortable life often has more power to separate from the love of Christ than does all the host of Hell wielding all the implements of torture. Paul was confident to face either *life* or *death*.

....nor angels, nor principalities, nor powers.... Was Paul challenged by **angels** to forsake Christ? Not all angels are righteous. *"For we wrestle not against flesh and blood, but against* principalities, *against* powers, *against the rulers of the darkness of this world, against spiritual wickedness in high places (Ephesians 6:12)."* **Principalities** are organized powers of darkness; and **powers** are forces beyond definition that await us in the spiritual realm. There is no battle with these if you are going their way. It is when you invade their territory that they resist. Paul didn't wait for the powers to come to him. He charged the gates of Hell with the sword of the Spirit. He sought out the *strong man* so he could bind him and steal the souls he unlawfully held.

...nor things present, nor things to come.... Paul had never met a match for the love of God in Christ. Nothing **present** had ever moved him from the love of God. But just in case there is something out there he has not yet confronted, he is confident that **things to come** will not separate him either.

...nor height, nor depth.... Here is one for the mountain climbers and astronauts, for the deep-earth miners and the undersea explorers. Remember that up until this present century, the imaginations of men conceived of threatening races lurking in the subterranean world or in the polar regions. Paul threw this in for those who feared the unknown lurking beyond. This is even more appropriate for our day. Many fear life-forms from outer space. The believer is a life-form from outer space. He just hasn't put on his new body yet.

...nor any other creature, shall be able to separate us from the love of God, which is in Christ Jesus our Lord. That about covers it all and then some. That covers genetic alterations, cloning, mutations, invasions, ghosts, gods, devils, poltergeists, politicians, army officers, new-age spooks, Moslems, Bible critics, and all insects. It can come at us from outer space, they can make it in a laboratory, it can crawl out of a volcano. It can come at us in a suit and tie, a turban, or a torch, but we won't bend or bow, and if we burn we have *"a better city which hath foundations whose builder and maker is God."* When the last curse has been uttered and the last drop of blood shed, when all flesh has gone the way of grass, when the skeptics are silenced in judgment and the marriage supper of the Lamb has come, and all tears are wiped away, no one will say, *"Why did you make me thus?"* For the love of God will be richer, deeper, higher, and broader than all the suffering of all saints. The love of God will be the subject, the song, and the sanctuary of all who once hoped in His promises.

Greece invited the cultured
Rome bid the strong
Judah bid the devout
Christ bids all come.

APPENDIX

Dead, die

"As in Adam all died...." Many take this verse, "in Adam all died," to mean a constitutional change in human nature itself, particularly a change as regards the will—that Adam's descendants are not born with the ability to choose between good and evil, and as a result man is thought to be a helpless slave to sin, not responsible for his own conduct. Or many hold that this death was some kind of a death of the spirit, as if Adam experienced an execution of his spirit within. We hear many sermons based on the assumption that the unregenerate have a dead spirit—as in a spirit that no longer operates or that has actually ceased to exist.

When Adam sinned, his soul did not cease to exist, neither did his body or spirit. Nothing ceased to function. That is, no faculty of the soul became depraved so as to lose some attribute of its nature. God did not reconstitute or downgrade Adam and his descendants after the initial act of disobedience. To view Adam's death as a permanent dysfunction of those attributes of the soul which either enable or motivate one to do good is to view it not as death at all but as a re-creation. If a person were born with an altered will, he could only be held responsible to live according to his abilities. It would be absurd to demand that one live different from his potential. How much more absurd to punish one for the condition of his birth.

Mortality existed prior to Adam's sin.

Upon Adam sinning, sin entered the world, and death by sin, but mortality existed prior to the fall of man. The cherub Lucifer and a great host of heavenly beings had already sinned and suffered the destruction of their bodies, as seen by the fact that right after Adam's creation Lucifer confronted him in a borrowed body. So Satan had already sinned and died before the creation of Adam. But human death owes its origin to the first human sin.

Man was created in a natural body that was corruptible—mortal. According to 1 Corinthians 15:42, *"the first man is earthly, natural,"* which seems to allude to the dissolution of the body as part of nature. Death is the visible proof of the invisible. Man was created capable of dying, but was graciously supplied with a gift of the tree of life, making eternal life conditioned upon continuing in God. Death is a biological phenomenon that must have been part of creation. A seed dies in order to reproduce. A worm dies to become a butterfly. Aging, maturity and decay are part of the cycle of natural creation. This present ecosystem without this cycle is inconceivable. The human body is sustained by cells dying and being replaced. Adam and Eve were given the tree of life as a means to prevent the body from its natural cycle. As long as they continued in fellowship with God they had access to that life sustaining tree. Upon eating they were denied access and death began on that day. Death is the natural consequence of sin, but it is also a divine sentence.

This passage clearly teaches that Adam was created mortal—corruptible.

*1 Corinthians 15:44-54, It is sown a natural body; it is raised a spiritual body. There is a **natural body**, and there is a spiritual body. And so it is written, The first man Adam was made a living soul; the last Adam was made a quickening spirit. Howbeit that was not first which is spiritual, but that which is **natural**; and afterward that which is spiritual. The first man is of the earth, **earthy**: the second man is the Lord from heaven. **As is the earthy, such are they also that are earthy**: and as is the heavenly, such are they also that are heavenly. And as we have borne the image of the earthy, we shall also bear the image of the heavenly. Now this I say, brethren, that **flesh and blood cannot inherit the kingdom of God**; neither doth **corruption** inherit incorruption. Behold, I shew you a mystery; We shall not all sleep, but we shall all be changed, In a moment, in the twinkling of an eye, at the last trump: for the trumpet shall sound, and the dead shall be raised incorruptible, and we shall be changed. For this **corruptible** must put on incorruption, and this **mortal** must put on immortality. So when this corruptible shall have put on incorruption, and this mortal shall have put on immortality, then shall be brought to pass the saying that is written, Death is swallowed up in victory."*

From these verses we conclude that Adam was created in a natural body. He was flesh and blood. Paul says Adam was *"earthy (1 Corinthians 15:47), taken from the earth."* God said to Adam, *"In the sweat of thy face shalt thou eat bread, till thou return unto the ground; for out of it wast thou taken: for **dust thou art**, and unto dust shalt thou return (Genesis 3:19)."*

Adam had a physical constitution of flesh and blood, dependent on the breath of life and the intake of food. Adam was a mortal man with the possibility of immortality. He was potentially corruptible; that is, if Adam had been deprived of food, he would have grown hungry, and eventually his body would have deteriorated. If Adam had lost enough blood, baring sustaining grace and divine intervention, he would have died. The warning God gave Adam that if he ate he would die was an acknowledgment that the body was of such a nature as to be subject to death.

The nature of Adam's flesh is best seen in the nature of Christ's flesh. Jesus was *"made like unto his brethren."* He took on himself a body of flesh just like Adam's before the fall. There was no corruption or depravity in Jesus' body, yet he was mortal, corruptible, as seen by the fact that he did die a natural death by bleeding. He had to eat to sustain his flesh. He aged; which means his cells died and were replaced by new ones. Christ was the second man—man in every sense of the word, the Adam of God before the fall. He was in a mortal body capable of dying, as was Adam.

Adam was created mortal, but placed in an environment that provided for eternal life based on obedience. In addition to the need for natural food, Adam was given access to a special food that would sustain his natural body forever. As long as he ate from the tree of life, he would not die. Adam's eternal life was not within himself, independent of God; it was intimately linked to his continuing relationship to his Creator. The tree and its fruit were natural elements that would sustain the life of any natural person. Even after he sinned, if he had maintained continuing access to the tree, he would have lived forever (Genesis 3:22).

Adam's original state was that of the **natural man**, that is, he was in a state natural to humanity. *"Howbeit that was not first which is spiritual, but that which is **natural**; and afterward that which is spiritual (1 Corinthians 15:46)."*

Adam was not a spiritual man. *"But the natural man receiveth not the things of the Spirit of God: for they are foolishness unto him: neither can he know them, because they are spiritually discerned. But he that is spiritual judgeth all things, yet he himself is judged of no man (1 Corinthians 2:14-15)."*

Before his sin, Adam did not know good and evil. Adam did not have the Spirit of God. In Romans 8:22, Paul says we believers have the *"firstfruits of the Spirit."* It is never said of Adam that he had the Spirit, or that the Spirit departed. He was not created *born again*. Adam's relationship to God was immediate and external.

He was a natural man of flesh, destined to be a spiritual man. He was an *earthy man* with potential to become the *heavenly man*. He was an innocent man with no more knowledge of good and evil than a newborn baby. But with the presence of the temptation, occasioned by the forbidden tree, his environment was conducive to positive growth into a godly knowledge of good and evil. He who knew nothing more of right and wrong than that which he had received in the one prohibition was at the threshold of growth into a mature knowledge of good and evil, beheld from the pinnacle of obedience rather than from the pit of rebellion.

He who was corruptible was given access to a tree that would prevent corruption from ever occurring.

He who was mortal was allowed to converse with the Immortal, living with no fear of death until such time as the fullness of life within should qualify him to be transformed into the immortal, heavenly man.

The weak body of flesh, endowed with passions, was the perfect counterpart to the spirit in man, and by its very weakness provided the best environment for the soul's development and growth.

We become speculative when we say that if Adam had followed the program he would have eventually arrived into moral parity with God. In such a situation, he could have boasted against the angels who had not done so well, but had sinned. Instead, his fall, and subsequently the fall of the race, created a situation whereby all future relationships between God and man would be on the basis of grace and mercy. Love has taken on new meaning. Humility has become possible. Suffering has produced a sweetness otherwise unknown. Death has given way to a life far in advance to any that was possible in the original state. It is now possible to exalt in the statement, *"In Adam all died, even so in Christ shall all be made alive."*

If Adam had not sinned, nor any of the succeeding fathers, today we would be singing, "In Adam the solid rock I stand," or perhaps we would sing, "In obedience I stand, all other ground is sinking sand." Instead of singing of our sinless blood, we now sing of His redeeming blood. The spirit reborn is not just good, it is confirmed in righteousness. The life which grows around the barren soil of Calvary is ever so much richer than that which grew in the garden of innocence.

The word death is found 372 times in the Bible. With but three exceptions, it always refers to physical death. When John wanted to speak of something more than physical death, he said *second death*, referring to Hell.

There are only two verses that one could possibly construe the word *death* to mean "spiritual death."

1. John 5:24 *"...but is passed from **death** unto life."* This passage is commonly used in evangelism to express how Christ gives "spiritual" life to the "spiritually" dead. But even a cursory examination of the context demonstrates that this death is physical, for he goes on to define the cure for this death as physical resurrection of the body. *"The hour is coming, and now is, when the **dead** shall hear the voice of the Son of God: and they that hear shall live."*

2. 1 John 3:14-15 *"We know that we have passed from **death** unto life, because we love the brethren. He that loveth not his brother abideth in death. Whosoever hateth his brother is a murderer: and ye know that no murderer hath eternal life abiding in him."* Again the death is physical as seen by the contrast to eternal life. Eternal life is not "spiritual" life; it is life that never ends, as opposed to life that ends in death. Also, the other times John uses the word (1John 5:16-17), it could only be understood to be physical. Finally, if this is a reference to "spiritual death," it will be the only time out of 372 uses.

The word *dead* occurs 364 times without a single reference to the spirit being dead. We will look at the only verses that could possibly be construed as spiritual death—a dead spirit as opposed to dead flesh.

- Luke 9:60, along with Matthew 8:22. The man says, *"let me go and* bury my father. But Jesus said unto him, Follow me; and let the **dead** bury their dead." He has not defined in what way the ones who bury the *dead* are themselves *dead*. Certainly they were *dead in trespasses and sins*, which has nothing to do with being "spiritually dead." They are also dead in the sense of having the sentence of death upon them. This could be viewed as figurative death, nothing more.

- *Colossians 2:13 "And you, being **dead in your sins** and the uncircumcision of your flesh, hath he quickened together with him, having forgiven you all trespasses."* It is the person who is dead, not the spirit. Notice that the thing dead was also uncircumcised—called flesh. Looking at verse 12, the cure was co-crucifixion with Christ. The thing that was dead was crucified on the cross and raised again with Christ. It couldn't possibly be "spiritual" death.

- *1 Timothy 5:6 "But she that liveth in pleasure is **dead** while she liveth."* Speaking of a sexually unclean woman, he uses a play on words. While living in her sins, she is actually dead in her sins. She herself is under the sentence of death. She is dead in her trespasses. This is not a reference to the functionality of her soulish faculties and spirit, but to her moral and judicial standing before God.

- *Revelation 3:1-2 "And unto the angel of the church in Sardis write; These things saith he that hath the seven Spirits of God, and the seven stars; I know thy works, that thou hast a name that thou livest, and art **dead**. Be watchful, and strengthen the things which remain, that are **ready to die**: for I have not found thy works perfect before God."* Firstly, he is talking to the church corporately, not to individuals. Secondly, they were to strengthen that which remained lest it die also. Since that which was dead was capable of further death, he couldn't possible be talking about a universal, "spiritually dead" condition. If so then Christians who have been made alive can by increments die spiritually—again. Obviously, he is speaking allegorically to the church.

- *Ephesians 2:1-6 And you hath he quickened, who were **dead** in trespasses and sins; Wherein in time past ye walked according to the course of this world, according to the prince of the power of the air, the spirit that now worketh in the children of disobedience: Among whom also we all had our conversation in times past in the lusts of our flesh, fulfilling the desires of the flesh and of the mind; and were by nature the children of wrath, even as others But God, who is rich in mercy, for his great love wherewith he loved us, Even when we were **dead** in sins, hath quickened us together with Christ, (by grace ye are saved;) . And hath raised us up together, and made us sit together in heavenly places in Christ Jesus:"* The cure for this condition of being **dead in sins** was to be crucified and then raised *(quickened)* together with Christ. It was the whole person under the death sentence, who served his sentence in his crucifixion with Christ and was then raised from the dead.

- *"Genesis 2:17 But of the tree of the knowledge of good and evil, thou shalt not eat of it: for in the day that thou eatest thereof thou shalt surely die."* This takes us full circle. *"For since by man came **death**, by man came also the resurrection of the dead. For as in Adam all **die**, even so in Christ shall all be made alive (1 Corinthians 15:21-22)."* It is obvious. <u>The death Adam was threatened with was the death that passed on all men.</u> It is a physical death that anticipates a future resurrection. The cure is yet future as seen by the statement, *"in Christ <u>shall</u> all be made alive."* Believers are alive unto God now. Their spirit has been joined by God's Spirit and the two have become one, but the believer yet anticipates a future when he shall "be made alive." That is physical resurrection of the body and could not possibly be construed to have anything to do with the spirit of man being made alive.

What died in Romans 7

Other commentators say that the husband is the "old nature," the sinful self. Yet those who teach this do not actually follow through and teach that the old sinful self is in fact dead. They teach that the believer is endowed with two realities, the fallen man and the redeemed man, or, as some would say it, the "old nature" and the "new nature." However, they do not believe, as their doctrine would dictate from this passage, that the old nature is actually dead. They teach that Romans 7 is a description of the struggle between the two natures. If that were the case <u>then the woman is married to two men at the same time.</u> According to this popular theology, the old husband did not die and the woman took up with the new man while the first husband liveth. So what is the point of his illustration in 7:1-4? Certainly she would be an adulteress. If they attempt to avoid this charge by saying the old man is "positionally" dead but still exerting an influence, then you have a dead husband who from his grave is competing with the new husband. No wonder they think Paul chose a bad analogy.

Others simply say that the woman is the one who died and was then raised so as to be married to Christ. This in no way fits the analogy, so we can see why the commentators are confused—or why they think Paul was.

Most ultramodern writers see all the confusion of past ages and just skip the passage by saying that Paul intended nothing more than to show that Law has jurisdiction as long as the two shall live, regardless of which one dies.

Did Paul and the Holy Spirit create all this uncertainty, or are the commentators missing something? The thing to do is to read before and after the passage to find something that died. That thing that died should answer to the analogy perfectly. Its death should free the woman (unregenerate sinner, who is a would-be bride of Christ) from some factor that corresponds in kind to the would-be new husband, and whose death is the moment of liberation, permitting a union with Christ. Now if we come across something that died, but our experience, our reason, or our prior doctrine tells us that it didn't die, why don't we just believe it as written and see what happens when we compare it with other Scripture? We might just learn something kept hidden through unbelief.

The previous chapter is overly clear as to what died. *"Knowing this, that our old man is crucified with him, that the body of sin might be destroyed, that henceforth we should not serve sin (Romans 6:6)."* We are clearly told that someone died (was *destroyed*), someone called *the body of sin.* *"Now if we be dead with Christ, we believe that we shall also live with him: For in that he died, he died unto sin once: but in that he liveth, he liveth unto God. Likewise reckon ye also yourselves to be dead indeed unto sin, but alive unto God through Jesus Christ our Lord (Romans 6:8,10-11)."* The woman's *old man* was crucified, leaving the body dead. Marriage is a union of flesh (Genesis 2:23-24; Ephesians 5:31; Hebrews 2:14-18). The death of her husband's flesh freed the woman so she could be married to Christ.

Note the passage says that the *old man* is crucified that the *body of sin* might be destroyed. The basic constitution of the old man is that mortal body full of sin. The object of the old man's crucifixion is the destruction of that body. When Jesus died, we were crucified with Him, planted together, so we share His death. That which died in us must correspond to that which died in Christ. His soul didn't die; His body did.

The passage in question, building on the results of the analogy, says, *"For when we were in the flesh, the motions of sins, which were by the law, did work in our members to bring forth fruit unto death (7:5)."* It assumes that the believer is no longer *in the flesh.* The flesh of the old man is dead. That is what usually happens when someone's husband dies.

As he continues his presentation, he again defines the nature of his former bondage: *"But I see another law in my members, warring against the law of my mind, and bringing me into captivity to the law of sin which is in my members. O wretched man that I am! who shall deliver me from the body of this death (Romans 7:23-24)?* The former captivity was found in the *members* of his body: eyes, ears, nose, tongue, sex organs, feet, hands, etc., all those functions of the body that induce one to sin. His bondage was to a body of death, a body that must die so he could be married to another and bring forth fruit unto God. Romans 6:11-13 bears another look. *"Likewise reckon ye also yourselves to be dead indeed unto sin,* [something died, freeing us from sin] *but alive unto God through Jesus Christ our Lord* [it resulted in a new life in Christ]. *Let not sin therefore reign in your <u>mortal body</u>* [the mortal body was the seat of sin, the thing that must die], *that ye should obey it in the lusts thereof. Neither yield ye your <u>members</u> as instruments of unrighteousness unto sin: but yield yourselves unto God, as those that are alive from the dead* [the believer is on the other side of death], *and <u>your members as instruments of righteousness unto God.</u>"*

Paul further reveals the nature of this former bondage in Romans 7:18: *"For I know that in me (that is, in <u>my flesh</u>,)* [the flesh is the seat of bondage] *dwelleth no good thing: for to will is present with me; but how to perform that which is good I find not."* Though he willed to do right, he was wed to his flesh, which was the seat of all his passions.

He closes the chapter in total defeat, inseparably joined to *the old man, the body of sin, the sinful flesh, the mortal body. "So then with the mind I myself serve the law of God; but with the <u>flesh</u> the law of sin (Romans 7:25)."* The flesh was the point of complete bondage. And in the next chapter we are told, *"they that are <u>in the flesh</u> cannot please God (Romans 8:8)."* In 8:3-4 he says, *"For what the law could not do, in that it was <u>weak through the flesh</u>, God sending his own Son in the likeness of sinful flesh, and for sin, <u>condemned sin in the flesh</u>: That the righteousness of the law might be fulfilled in us, who walk <u>not after the flesh</u>, but after the Spirit."*

Then we are told emphatically, *"But ye are <u>not in the flesh</u>, but in the Spirit, if so be that the Spirit of God dwell in you. Now if any man have not the Spirit of Christ, he is none of his. And if Christ be in you, the <u>body is dead because of sin</u>; but the Spirit is life because of righteousness (Romans 8:9-10)."* This is conclusive. The believer who was formally prevented from righteousness by his association with his flesh is no longer in the flesh. The body is dead. The next verse, v. 11, identifies this body of sin as a *"<u>mortal body</u>."* According to verse 23, the ultimate salvation will be in the redemption of the body.

In Paul's analogy, the old husband is that natural, earthy body which has yielded to the natural passions and appetites to the point of inordinate affections. It is our contact point with the world, a constant opportunity to be sensual, carnal. Of course there is no sin in inanimate matter, but all resources to sin come from the body. Appetites don't have to be evil to be the vehicle of evil.

Sins of the fathers

It is asked, "If it is true that Adam's descendants do not inherit guilt from Adam, why does the Scripture teach that the children inherit the sins of their fathers?" It doesn't teach that at all. It teaches that the sins of the parents will be *visited on the children* to the third and fourth generation. It is the consequences that children inherit, not the guilt or blame.

Furthermore if one appeals to this principle in support of inherent sin, he has proven too much and therefore proven nothing at all. If the "generational sins" theory is an extension of the manner in which Adam's sin affected his descendants, then children must be to blame for all sins of all fathers all the way back to Adam. On the other hand, if the "generational sins" last only to the third or fourth generation, then Adam's sins, now more than four generations removed, could not affect us at all. So it couldn't be said, "In Adam all died." It would be said, "In Great Grandfather, Grandfather, and Father all died." Look at what the Bible actually says about *visiting* sins on the children.

- *"Therefore now go, lead the people unto the place of which I have spoken unto thee: behold, mine Angel shall go before thee: nevertheless in the day when I visit I will <u>visit</u> their sin upon them (Exodus 32:34)."* The visitation of sins does not occur at birth, but at a point in the future when judgment falls.

- *"If his children forsake my law, and walk not in my judgments; If they break my statutes, and keep not my commandments; Then will I <u>visit</u> their transgression with the rod, and their iniquity with stripes (Psalm 89:30-32)."* To visit sins is not to make them sinners, but to punish for sin.

- *"Thus saith the* LORD *unto this people, Thus have they loved to wander, they have not refrained their feet, therefore the* LORD *doth not accept them; he will now remember their iniquity, and <u>visit</u> their sins (Jeremiah 14:10)."* Again, the visitation of sins is judgment, not more sin of the same kind.

- *"Thou shalt not bow down thyself unto them, nor serve them: for I the* LORD *thy God am a jealous God, <u>visiting</u> the iniquity of the fathers upon the children <u>unto the third and fourth generation</u> of them that hate me (Deuteronomy 5:9)."* The sins are visited (judgment falls) on those that hate him.

- *"And they that are left of you shall pine away in their iniquity in your enemies' lands; and also in the iniquities of their fathers shall they pine away with them. If they shall confess their iniquity, and the iniquity of their fathers, with their trespass which they trespassed against me, and that also they have walked contrary unto me (Leviticus 26:39-40)...."* The iniquity of their fathers became their own, and is something from which the children can be free if they repent. The judgment continues only as long as the children are sympathetic to their fathers' sin.

This could not answer to the concept of inherent sinfulness, or it could not be forsaken through repentance. Who teaches that one can repent of Adam's sin and be free from it?

- *"Thou shewest lovingkindness unto thousands, and recompensest the iniquity of the fathers into the bosom of their children after them: the Great, the Mighty God, the* LORD *of hosts, is his name (Jeremiah 32:18)."* A recompense is a judgment on sin, not the transmission of sin itself.

- *"Wherefore, behold, I send unto you prophets, and wise men, and scribes: and some of them ye shall kill and crucify; and some of them shall ye scourge in your synagogues, and persecute them from city to city: That upon you may come all the righteous blood shed upon the earth, from the blood of righteous Abel unto the blood of Zacharias son of Barachias, whom ye slew between the temple and the altar. Verily I say unto you, All these things <u>shall come upon this generation</u> (Matthew 23:34-36)."* They were going to kill prophets in their own generation, and for that the judgment would fall on this one generation, a judgment that had not fallen on previous generations.

Adam's actions affected his descendants in the same way that a man's actions affect his descendants today. Granted, Adam had far more to lose than a man does today. He had further to fall. But the mechanics of offspring inheritance are the same now as they were then.

It is the effects of sin that are inherited, not a sinful disposition. The consequence of original sin is not more sin; it is death. To carry the parallel through, when the Scripture says that in Christ we are made righteous, it is referring to our being treated in a way that we are in fact not. That is the point, that from Adam to Moses death was universally experienced by those who had not in fact personally sinned as did Adam. It is the consequences that are passed on, both in Adam and in Christ. If in Adam one is made actually sinful, then in Christ one must be made actually righteous. Absurdity abounds.

Flesh

What is the flesh? The unschooled and untutored could answer this accurately. There is nothing mystical about it. *"That which is born of the flesh is flesh (John 3:6)."* One simple and most common Greek work, **sarx**, is used 143 times, and is always translated **flesh** in the King James Bible

The weakness of the flesh is found in its inability to deny pleasure. The flesh of a human, like the flesh of an animal, has but one end—self-gratification. The flesh does not come with a built-in governor that says "enough." It has no discrimination. It does not matter to the flesh whether the pleasure is legitimate or selfish.

Flesh is amoral, neither righteous nor evil. There is nothing evil in appetite itself—Christ hungered. Adam and Eve were created in bodies of flesh. Even before they sinned, their flesh craved indulgence. They had eyes for things lovely, an appetite for things pleasant to the taste, and a desire to have knowledge like the gods. Eve could be tempted to disobey God because of the innate desires of her flesh.

The original sin of Lucifer sprang from pride over his beauty (Ezekiel 28:17). He lusted after the promotion of his beautiful self to a place of prominence. Many thousands of years later he still regarded that drive so highly that when he had an opportunity to tempt the Son of God he offered Him the kingdoms of the world if he would just fall down and worship.

The flesh is sinful or righteous only in its application, that is, as it is used by a moral agent. The flesh does not have a mind or a will of its own. It has no responsibility. The flesh should be the agent of the mind. The flesh answers to the natural world, the mind answers to God. The mind should rule as the spirit directs. When knowledge of duty—of that which is good and just—is set aside for the desires of the flesh, the mind becomes servant to the appetite. When the mind becomes the agent of the flesh, answering to the desires of the flesh, then the state of the mind is altogether one of sinfulness. The selfish habits formed in the flesh are called sinful. But the sin is with the moral agent who has allowed his mind and will to be taken captive by the desires of the flesh.

Sinful flesh is flesh that has been allowed to selfishly indulge. It is nonsensical to speak of the flesh as evil in nature. It can be neither good nor evil since it has no intentions and no responsibility. Flesh is the creation of God. When it is allowed to run out of control, used to do evil, even when it is conditioned to evil lusts, it remains natural flesh as originally created. Preference for evil would involve moral values and choice. The flesh cannot choose. The person living in the flesh chooses. The fleshly desire for pleasure is the same in saint and sinner.

All of the verses below have the word flesh in them. This list represents the 144 times the word flesh appears in the King James Bible.

Every time the word *flesh* appears in these verses it is translated from the one Greek word *"sarx."*

Matthew 26:41 *"Watch and pray, that ye enter not into temptation: the spirit indeed is willing, but the <u>flesh is weak</u>."* The disciples were yet unregenerate, still they experienced a struggle between the flesh and spirit.

John 1:14 *"And the Word was <u>made flesh</u>, and dwelt among us, (and we beheld his glory, the glory as of the only begotten of the Father,) full of grace and truth."* Jesus was made flesh, the same flesh (sarx) that is weak in man and leads to sin.

John 6:51 *"I am the living bread which came down from heaven: if any man eat of this bread, he shall live for ever: and the bread that I will give is my <u>flesh</u>, which I will give for the life of the world."* Jesus gave his "sarx" to save the world. This is the same "sarx" of man that is called *sinful flesh.*

Romans 13:14 *"But put ye on the Lord Jesus Christ, and make not provision for the <u>flesh</u>, to fulfil the lusts thereof."* The Christian is to not provide occasion to fulfill the lust of the flesh. Lust is in the "sarx."

1 Corinthians 15:50 *"Now this I say, brethren, that <u>flesh</u> and blood cannot inherit the kingdom of God; neither doth corruption inherit incorruption."* Flesh is corruption, it has the ability to decay.

2 Corinthians 4:11 *"For we which live are alway delivered unto death for Jesus' sake, that the life also of Jesus might be made manifest in our <u>mortal flesh</u>."*

2 Corinthians 7:1 *"Having therefore these promises, dearly beloved, let us cleanse ourselves from all filthiness of the <u>flesh</u> and spirit, perfecting holiness in the fear of God."* It is clear from this verse that the word flesh cannot apply to any part or function of the spirit, for flesh and spirit are sharply distinguished.

2 Corinthians 10:2-3 *"But I beseech you, that I may not be bold when I am present with that confidence, wherewith I think to be bold against some, which think of us as if we walked according to the <u>flesh</u>. For though we walk in the <u>flesh</u>, we do not war after the <u>flesh</u>:"* The same Greek word, "sarx," is used these three times. To *walk according to the flesh* would be to walk in accord with the desires of the flesh. To *walk in the flesh* is nothing more than having the flesh as the earthly tabernacle of the soul. To *war after the flesh* would be to enter spiritual battle in the power of and with the resources of the flesh. No Christian walks *according to the flesh*. All Christians *walk in the flesh* until they get their glorified bodies. Though a Christian could attempt to *war after the flesh*, and be a total failure, he should war after the Spirit only. The first is never true, the second is always true, and the third should not, but could be, true of the believer.

Galatians 5:13 *"For, brethren, ye have been called unto liberty; only*

use not liberty for an occasion to the *flesh,* but by love serve one another."

Galatians 5:16-17 *"This I say then, Walk in the Spirit, and ye shall not
fulfil the lust of the flesh. For the flesh lusteth against the Spirit, and the
Spirit against the flesh: and these are contrary the one to the other: so
that ye cannot do the things that ye would."*

Galatians 5:24-25 *"And they that are Christ's have* <u>*crucified the flesh*</u>
*with the affections and lusts. If we live in the Spirit, let us also walk in
the Spirit."* No one is ever told to crucify the flesh. All that are in Christ
have crucified the flesh when buried into His death.

Galatians 6:12-13 *"As many as desire to make a fair shew in the* <u>*flesh,*</u>
*they constrain you to be circumcised; only lest they should suffer perse-
cution for the cross of Christ. For neither they themselves who are circumcised keep the law; but desire to have you circumcised, that they
may glory in your* <u>*flesh.*</u>*"* Flesh can be circumcised. That rather limits
the possibilities in seeking to identify the flesh.

Ephesians 2:3,15 *"Among whom also we all had our conversation in
times past in the lusts of our flesh, fulfilling* <u>*the desires of the flesh*</u> *and
of the mind; and were by nature the children of wrath, even as others.
Having abolished in* <u>*his flesh*</u> *the enmity, even the law of commandments
contained in ordinances; for to make in himself of twain one new man,
so making peace;"* The mind, even a sinful mind, is not the flesh. Christ
terminated sin in His flesh.

Ephesians 5:29 *"For no man ever yet hated his own* <u>*flesh;*</u> *but nour-
isheth and cherisheth it, even as the Lord the church."*

Philippians 3:3 *"For we are the circumcision, which worship God in the
spirit, and rejoice in Christ Jesus, and have no confidence in the* <u>*flesh.*</u>*"*

Colossians 1:22 *"In the* <u>*body of his flesh*</u> *through death, to present you
holy and unblameable and unreproveable in his sight:"*

Colossians 2:11 *"In whom also ye are circumcised with the circumcision made without hands, in putting off the* <u>*body of the sins of the flesh*</u>
by the circumcision of Christ:" Christ's death and our entrance into it
was a circumcision of the flesh. In circumcision the flesh is discarded.

Colossians 2:18-23 *"Let no man beguile you of your reward in a voluntary humility and worshipping of angels, intruding into those things
which he hath not seen, vainly puffed up by his* <u>*fleshly mind,*</u> *And not
holding the Head, from which all the body by joints and bands having
nourishment ministered, and knit together, increaseth with the increase
of God. Wherefore if ye be dead with Christ from the rudiments of the
world, why, as though living in the world, are ye subject to ordinances,
(Touch not; taste not; handle not; Which all are to perish with the using;) after the commandments and doctrines of men? Which things have
indeed a shew of wisdom in will worship, and humility, and neglecting of
the body; not in any honour to the satisfying of the* <u>*flesh.*</u>*"* A fleshly

218

mind is a mind set on fulfilling the desires of the flesh. The believer does not have two minds, a fleshly mind and spiritual mind.

Hebrews 2:14-15 *"By a new and living way, which he hath consecrated for us, through the veil, that is to say, his flesh; Forasmuch then as the children are partakers of flesh and blood, he also himself likewise took part of the same; that through death he might destroy him that had the power of death, that is, the devil; And deliver them who through fear of death were all their lifetime subject to bondage."*

1 Peter 2:11 *"Dearly beloved, I beseech you as strangers and pilgrims, abstain from fleshly lusts, which war against the soul."* The flesh is distinct from the soul or it could not war against it.

1 Peter 3:18 *"For Christ also hath once suffered for sins, the just for the unjust, that he might bring us to God, being put to death in the flesh, but quickened by the Spirit:"*

1 Peter 4:1, 2 *"Forasmuch then as Christ hath suffered for us in the flesh, arm yourselves likewise with the same mind: for he that hath suffered in the flesh hath ceased from sin; That he no longer should live the rest of his time in the flesh to the lusts of men, but to the will of God."*

2 Peter 2:10 *"But chiefly them that walk after the flesh in the lust of uncleanness, and despise government. Presumptuous are they, selfwilled, they are not afraid to speak evil of dignities."*

2 Peter 2:18 *"For when they speak great swelling words of vanity, they allure through the lusts of the flesh, through much wantonness, those that were clean escaped from them who live in error."*

1 John 2:15-17 *"Love not the world, neither the things that are in the world. If any man love the world, the love of the Father is not in him. For all that is in the world, the lust of the flesh, and the lust of the eyes, and the pride of life, is not of the Father, but is of the world. And the world passeth away, and the lust thereof: but he that doeth the will of God abideth for ever."*

Summary of flesh

The flesh is endowed with certain needs. When those needs are met, it gives a sensation of bodily pleasure. The meeting of legitimate needs gives pleasure—to eat when hungry, to be made warm when cold, etc. Legitimate needs give way to wants, and pleasure becomes an addiction. To be stroked, curried and comforted, to be fed to the full, and to feel till it tingles becomes an end. The line between needs and wants grows indistinct, even nonexistent, where the mind loses control—a constant occasion to the mind and will that inhabit it

The nature of man is not altered, but the nature of his relationship is. Man is called flesh because the flesh is now his primary orientation. The regenerate man is called spiritual, the unregenerate is called natural.

Man was created to be in community with God. The faculties of man as created, and remaining such after the fall, are sufficient for self-direction. But without the fellowship of God, the attention is easily captivated by the ever-present desires of the flesh.

The crucifixion of the flesh and the introduction of the Spirit of life restores fellowship and completes the original relationship. Regenerate man is now circumcised out of the body of flesh but is still in such close proximity to it so as to be drawn away of its lusts. The battle continues between the flesh and spirit but this time it is with a spiritual orientation.

Mortify

- *"For if ye live after the flesh, ye shall die: but if ye through the Spirit <u>do mortify</u> the deeds of the body, ye shall live (Romans 8:13)."* Note: in this passage, *ye shall die* is the common term for die, whereas *do mortify* is the exception. Both Greek words are used in the same passage, demonstrating that they are not synonymous.

- *"<u>Mortify</u> therefore your members which are upon the earth; fornication, uncleanness, inordinate affection, evil concupiscence, and covetousness, which is idolatry (Colossians 3:5)."* The Greek word translated as mortify is most often translated *put to death*, though it is not the common word for *put to death*. <u>It is employed when we would commonly use the word *killed* but intend to imply something other than the act of taking a life.</u> The difference is subtle, hard to define in the English language. To mortify a person would be to terminate the witness, presence, influence, strength, or power of the individual, most probably by killing, but not necessarily in the normal sense of the violence of physical death.

- *"As it is written, For thy sake we <u>are killed</u> all the day long; we are accounted as sheep for the slaughter (Romans 8:36)."* The word *killed* here is the same Greek word that is translated *mortify* in Romans 8:13 and Col. 3:5. When Paul says, *"we are killed all the day long,"* obviously he was not dead, but he suffered the constant threat of being physically killed, his witness terminated.

- *"Wherefore, my brethren, ye also <u>are become dead</u> to the law by the body of Christ; that ye should be married to another, even to him who is raised from the dead, that we should bring forth fruit unto God (Romans 7:4)."* Obviously the Law is not dead and the brethren who are dead to the Law are also still breathing, but in Christ the Law's power and authority was mortified.

- *"For Christ also hath once suffered for sins, the just for the unjust, that he might bring us to God, <u>being put to death</u> in the flesh, but quickened by the Spirit (1 Peter 3:18):"*

- *"As unknown, and yet well known; as dying, and, behold, we live; as chastened, and not <u>killed</u> (2 Corinthians 6:9)."* Obviously they were not yet killed—dead in the physical sense. Paul is not discussing termination of physical life. He is discussing his ongoing ministry, which despite the physical threats, they were not mortified (not stopped in their ministry or witness). They were still active preaching the gospel.

- *"When the morning was come, all the chief priests and elders of the people took counsel against Jesus <u>to put him to death</u> (Matthew 27:1)."* Obviously they were taking counsel to terminate his life, but the emphasis is on the termination of His influence among them.

Saved

- *"For the Son of man is come to <u>save</u> that which was lost (Matthew 18:11)."*

- *"For God sent not his Son into the world to condemn the world; but that the world through him might be <u>saved</u> (John 3:17)."*

- *"But I receive not testimony from man: but these things I say, that ye might be <u>saved</u> (John 5:34)."*

- *"I am the door: by me if any man enter in, he shall be <u>saved</u>, and shall go in and out, and find pasture (John 10:9)."*

- *"And if any man hear my words, and believe not, I judge him not: for I came not to judge the world, but to <u>save</u> the world (John 12:47)."*

- *"And it shall come to pass, that whosoever shall call on the name of the Lord shall be <u>saved</u> (Acts 2:21)."*

- *"Neither is there salvation in any other: for there is none other name under heaven given among men, whereby we must be <u>saved</u> (Acts 4:12)."*

- *"And brought them out, and said, Sirs, what must I do to be <u>saved</u>? And they said, Believe on the Lord Jesus Christ, and thou shalt be <u>saved</u>, and thy house (Acts 16:30-31)."*

- *"Much more then, being now justified by his blood, we shall be <u>saved</u> from wrath through him (Romans 5:9)."*

- *"This is a faithful saying, and worthy of all acceptation, that Christ Jesus came into the world to <u>save</u> sinners; of whom I am chief (1 Timothy 1:15)."*

- *"Who hath <u>saved</u> us, and called us with an holy calling, not according to our works, but according to his own purpose and grace, which was given us in Christ Jesus before the world began (2 Timothy 1:9)."*

- *"Not by works of righteousness which we have done, but according to his mercy he <u>saved</u> us, by the washing of regeneration, and renewing of the Holy Ghost (Titus 3:5)."*

- *"Wherefore he is able also to <u>save</u> them to the uttermost that come unto God by him, seeing he ever liveth to make intercession for them (Hebrews 7:25)."*